Repetition, Difference, and Knowledge in the Work of Samuel Beckett, Jacques Derrida, and Gilles Deleuze

STUDIES IN
LITERARY
CRITICISM
& THEORY

Hans H. Rudnick
General Editor

Vol. 19

PETER LANG
New York • Washington, D.C./Baltimore • Bern
Frankfurt am Main • Berlin • Brussels • Vienna • Oxford

Sarah Gendron

Repetition, Difference, and Knowledge in the Work of Samuel Beckett, Jacques Derrida, and Gilles Deleuze

PETER LANG
New York • Washington, D.C./Baltimore • Bern
Frankfurt am Main • Berlin • Brussels • Vienna • Oxford

Library of Congress Cataloging-in-Publication Data

Gendron, Sarah.
Repetition, difference, and knowledge in the work of
Samuel Beckett, Jacques Derrida, and Gilles Deleuze / Sarah Gendron.
p. cm. — (Studies in literary criticism and theory; v. 19)
Includes bibliographical references and index.
1. Repetition (Philosophy). 2. Difference (Philosophy). 3. Knowledge, Theory of.
4. Beckett, Samuel, 1906–1989. 5. Derrida, Jacques.
6. Deleuze, Gilles, 1925–1995. I. Title.
B105.R37G46   194—dc22   2008031564
ISBN 978-1-4331-0375-9
ISSN 1073-2004

Bibliographic information published by **Die Deutsche Bibliothek**.
Die Deutsche Bibliothek lists this publication in the "Deutsche
Nationalbibliografie"; detailed bibliographic data is available
on the Internet at http://dnb.ddb.de/.

© 2008 Peter Lang Publishing, Inc., New York
29 Broadway, 18th floor, New York, NY 10006
www.peterlang.com

With love for H.B, and in memory of Mary

‡ Table of Contents

Acknowledgments xi

Introduction.. xiii
Beginnings... xiii
The Circulation of Beckett's Work in Twentieth Century Philosophy:
    The Modern/Postmodern Debate... xv
Poststructuralism and the Modern/Postmodern Debate.............................. xvii
On the Line: Beckett's Engagement with Modernism
    and Postmodernism xviii
Poststructuralism and Contemporary Beckett Scholarship xix
Repetition and Difference in *Repetition, Difference, and Knowledge* xxi

I. The Unthinkable: A History and Evolution of Repetition
    in Western Thought.. 1
Repetition in the Humanities 1
Cyclical Representations of Time: Primitive Man
    and Early Religious Societies 3
"Nothing New Under the Sun": The Eternal Return
    in Ancient Greek Philosophy 4
Linear Conceptualizations of Duration: Christianity and Judaism................ 5
Søren Kierkegaard's Repetitions 6
Friedrich Nietzsche's Eternal Return(s) 8
Gilles Deleuze's *Difference and Repetition*... 11
Beginning Again: Theories of Mimesis and the Question of Doubles............ 13
Plato and the Irresistible Longing for an Origin 14
Aristotle and Mimesis... 16
Walter Benjamin's Theories of Mimesis.. 17
The Double World of Derrida: Mimesis and *Différance*.............................. 18
Entre eux: Beckett and Philosophy.. 26

II. A Critical Reader: Repetition, Difference, and Genre............................ 31
"Crossing the Line": Beckett's Beginnings and Endings.............................. 31

"What Stink of Artifice": The Case for the Fortification
    of the Boundaries of Genre 35
Derrida and the Institution of "The Law of Genre" 37
"When Genre is on the Line": Interpreting Genre 39
"*Fort/da*": The Give and Take of Beckett's Genres 43
"Ill Said, Ill Read": Beckett's Poetry, Beckett's Prose 48
"Poetic Prose": Reading *Ill Seen, Ill Said* with Marjorie Perloff 50
"What a Broadening of the Mind": Philosophical Interpretations
    of Beckett 53
"No Happiness": The Failure of Philosophical Interpretations of Beckett 55
"Pigsty Latin and Perjury": Beckett's Perversion of Philosophy 56
"Enlighten Me": The Nature of Reading and Interpretation 58
"Come and Go, Come and Go": Weaving the Beckettian Tapestry 60
Reading on the Edge of Literature 62

III. **"The Text Which is Not One": The Multiplicity of Writing
    and the Singularity of Translation** **65**
In the Beginning: The End of the Book 65
Writing on the Edge of Knowledge: The Beginning of the Text 67
"Seeing Double": Creation and Repetition 74
"Hearing Double": The Many Voices of a Text 78
"The Tower of Babel": The "Origin" of the Multiplicity of Language 83
Traduttore, Traditore: Derrida on the Impossibility of Translation 86
"That's it, Babble": Translation and Difference in Beckett's Work 87
"What Truth is There in All This Babble?": The Search for the Origin 92

IV. **"The Ether of Metaphysics": Repetition and Presence
    on Stage and Page** **95**
"Je ne peux pas continuer, je vais continuer": Beckett After
    The Unnamable 95
"Being There": Presence and the Body 96
"Being? Where?": The Absence of Presence in Beckett's Theatre 98
"Writing is Dirty, Speech is Clean": The Moralization
    of Speech and Presence 102
"Speaking is Dirty, Writing is Clean": Revisiting the
    Speech/Writing Polarity 106

"Play It Again, Sam": Presence, Speech, and Repetition
  in Beckett's Theatrical Productions 109
"The Aborted Cogito": Writing, Presence, and the Subject 113
"Let's Just Say You're Not Quite There": Self Presence
  and the Beckettian Subject 115
"Virtual Subjects": Beckett's Subjects and Deleuze's Virtual Objects 116
"Any Old Pronoun Will Do": Attempts to Stabilize the Subject 120
"A Man of Letters": Language and the Self in *Malone Dies* and
  The Unnamable 124

Conclusion 129
Hegel and the End of the Narrative... 129
Arthur Danto's Age(s) of Representation 131
Jean Baudrillard's Age of Simulation... 134

Notes... 139
Bibliography.. 167
Index... 177

‡ Acknowledgments

I would like to express my gratitude to everyone who generously contributed their time and support to me while writing this book. I would first like to thank Drs. Mary Lydon, Elaine Marks, Peter Schofer, Anne Vila, Keith Cohen, and William Berg for their guidance and advice. Sadly, Drs. Mary Lydon and Elaine Marks have since passed away. They were both exceptional teachers and mentors who never simply gave anyone anything they knew the person could find—with some effort—on their own. To Mary in particular, I am thankful for making me aware of the beauty of simplicity when writing about complicated ideas. I learned that this was something that she applied to life as well. I was fortunate to have been able to spend time with her before her death. She often spoke of the details of her illness as well what she was learning from being ill. She specifically mentioned having gained a rare appreciation of the beauty to be found in the small moments of the day-to-day and in the simplest of language.

I thank my dear friends for their support and humor. In particular, Bill Castagnozzi, Eileen Ketchum McEwan, Christopher Bolander, Kennedy Schultz, Christian Flaugh, Nelly Halzen, Sage Hirby, Sarah Davies-Cordova, Jean-Pierre Lafouge, Omega Burckhardt, Janet Banhidi, Dorothée Mertz-Weigel and Jennifer Vanderheyden, and Colleen Coffey.

My greatest debt of gratitude goes to my family—my father Bernard Gendron, my mother Margaret Thornton, and my brother Timothy Gendron—to whom I owe my love of reading and reflection as well as my tenacity. To my husband Bill Bristoll and to our little ones, Jim, Max and Maizie, I thank you for your belief in me, your infectious love of life, and your patience.

I would like to thank Dr. Hans Rudnick, Caitlin Lavelle and Jackie Pavlovic at Peter Lang Publishing for their invaluable suggestions throughout the publishing process. In addition, I am grateful to my research assistants Christopher Swiderski and Christine Beck for their help preparing the manuscript for publication. I owe a debt of gratitude to Dr. Belén Castaneda, The Helen Way Klingler College of Arts and Sciences, the Graduate School, the Gettel Foundation, and the Office of Research and Sponsored Programs of Marquette University for awarding the grants which enabled me to finish this project.

Grateful acknowledgment is hereby made to copyright holders for permission to use the following copyrighted material:

Samuel Beckett, *The Complete Dramatic Works*, 1964. Used by permission of Faber and Faber LTD.

Samuel Beckett, *The Collected Shorter Plays* ("Krapp's Last Tape" Copyright © 1958 Samuel Beckett; "Not I" Copyright © 1973 by Samuel Beckett; and "Footfalls" Copyright © 1976 by Samuel Beckett). Copyright © 1984 by Samuel Beckett. Used by permission of Grove/Atlantic, Inc.

Samuel Beckett, *"Endgame" and "Act without Words."* Copyright © 1958 by Grove Press, Inc. Used by permission of Grove/Atlantic, Inc.

Samuel Beckett, *Happy Days*. Copyright © 1961 by Grove Press, inc. Used by permission of Grove/Atlantic, Inc.

Samuel Beckett, *Waiting for Godot*. Copyright © 1954 by Grove Press, Inc. Copyright © renewed by 1982 by Samuel Beckett. Used by permission of Grove/Atlantic, Inc.

Sarah Gendron, "A Cogito for the Dissolved Self," *Journal of Modern Literature*, 28:2 (2005). Reprinted by permission of Indiana University Press.

Sarah Gendron, "Death of a Dynasty: Presence in Drama and Theory: Samuel Beckett and Jacques Derrida," *Journal of Dramatic Theory and Criticism*, 18:2 (2004). Reprinted by permission of The University of Kansas Press.

‡ Introduction

> One cannot (therefore) have begun, for one will always only have begun again, redoubling what will always already have commenced.
>
> —Hegel, Enzyklopädie Zusatz

Beginnings

[handwritten: ✓ this is a nice idea for the beginning of my thesis]

The problematic of beginning—of where or how to begin, of what it means to begin—is one that has greatly impacted Western thought, for once one agrees to the idea that there can be such a thing as *a beginning*, one must also accept the proliferation of notions that generate from this premise; the presumption, for example, that one can identify with precision limits that demarcate one thing or being from another, or that it is possible to distinguish some "original" and "authentic" entity from that which follows it; the lower priority second, its inferior copy. In short, accepting the existence of *a beginning* allows us to establish a surplus of other notions which, in turn, permit us to see clearly, identify, and classify. The possibility of beginning *once and for all* enables us to come to what we think of as meaning.

If however, as Hegel's words propose, the concept of *a beginning* is illusory—if, in other words, every beginning has already happened, if every beginning is really just *beginning again*—what happens to the notions that were derived from this now potentially incorrect assumption? How can one differentiate definitively between one thing and another without reference to where each object begins? What becomes of authenticity and authority—concepts that are based on the idea of *a first time*—if the first time has no more claim to legitimacy or originality than the second? What if the original is no more original than the copy? How do we determine truth? Clearly, there can be knowledge that is not rigidly defined by borders: knowledge that is, for example, provisional or partial. But in the strictest sense of these words, "true" meaning or knowledge cannot exist without boundaries distinguishing them from what is outside, or from what is considered "false." In other words, they must begin and end at some specific point and time. *Repetition, Difference, and Knowledge* is a meditation on just such limits and on what repetition in its various manifestations can show us about how limits have come to determine our way of thinking and knowing.

[handwritten: → What is the place of those in your research?]

Repetition, Difference, and Knowledge

whole chapter about endings?

Samuel Beckett's readers would surely acknowledge an apparent preoccupation on his part with beginnings and endings in his work. The compulsively persistent attempts to begin in *Molloy* and to end in texts like *Endgame* and *Embers* read like an illustration of Hegel's words, where the appearance of beginning or ending decisively is exposed by repetition to be simply cloaking the hidden reality that one is really beginning and ending again, and again. Significantly, the convulsive openings and closings of *Molloy*, *Endgame*, and *Embers* are not exceptions in his œuvre—they are the rule. Regardless of the particular text or genre, there is often the suggestion that nothing ever simply begins or ends, but is always instead *in the process* of beginning or ending, and differently each time. Likewise, it is difficult to remain oblivious to Beckett's proclivity for repeating objects (sticks, hats, greycoats), characters (his many "M" named characters—the Murphys, Malones, Molloys, Maloses, and Mollys), and words or phrases ("On," "come and go"). This has the unfortunate result of leading readers to believe that they are seeing double, triple, or even quadruple, as in readings that conflate the nameless narrator of *The Unnamable*, with Molloy, Murphy, and Malone, as if they were all versions of the same archetypal character draped in new skin.[1] Caught up in waves of what appear to be textual "memories" within individual texts, but sometimes also flowing from text to text, what reader could help but find himself bound in a perpetual cycle of *déjà vu*, or more precisely, *déjà lu.* *repetition as memory vs presence*

However, like the struggles to begin and end that generate further attempts to start or end anew, rarely are these objects, individuals, or phrases ever simply "re-presented." While many of the same things, proper names, and words reappear from work to work, sometimes even crossing genres, they are often changed dramatically as a result of their reemergence. Though elements may indeed be "re-presented," it is each time, as the narrator of *Malone meurt* repeatedly states, "sous un certain angle."[2] *question of representation needs to be addressed + answered*

Those familiar with twentieth century literary theory and philosophy will certainly need no prompting to appreciate the resemblance between Beckett's use of repetition and the type of repetition often associated with poststructuralist theory.[3] Simply dubbed "repetition and difference," this variety of repetition maintains that there can be no identity without difference. As such, it presents a direct challenge to the classical form of repetition, or the return of the self Same. This last form of repetition—often mislabeled "platonic"[4]—with its emphasis on a beginning, an origin, and an original, sustains Western metaphysical conceptualizations of formal or knowable knowledge. Placing its value instead on the disruption of supposed inaugural moments, repetition with difference triggers a disturbance at the foundations of Western thought. Notions such as those of origins and ends, arche and telos, fixed coordinates and stable identities, indeed the idea that there can be such a thing as meaning or truth, are all rendered suspect by this contemporary formulation of repetition. It is this particular strain of repetition that Beckett features in his work without ever making overt reference to poststructuralism or to specific poststructuralist theorists.

Thinkers who have stressed the crucial role of repetition in unveiling what we find meaningful and what we believe to be "true" is vast. Philosophers as distinct in thought and style as Plato, Descartes, and Hegel, and fiction writers from Cervantes to Diderot to Duras all recognize and comment upon repetition's potential to unveil the specificity of Western thought. This book examines repetition in the work of Samuel Beckett, Jacques Derrida, and Gilles Deleuze because they theorize a type of repetition that corresponds to a pivotal moment in the history of repetition theory. Moreover, they did so in a similar way, yielding, not surprisingly, similar, though certainly not identical, results. Far from employing repetition as a simple stylistic devise in the service of accentuating particular elements or moments or in order to establish rhythm, repetition in their work becomes the agent of an unmasking. Thus, although Beckett never directly refers to poststructuralism in his work, Derrida has never written about Beckett, and Deleuze has only done so on rare occasions and mostly parenthetically, their common practice of repetition and difference makes them, nonetheless, strong theoretical allies at a time when repetition theory was in the process of radical change.

→ performerly
→ insistence, presence
→ climax, fulfillment, syncope
→ pleasure - familiarity
→ return

The Circulation of Beckett's Work in Twentieth Century Philosophy: The Modern/Postmodern Debate

The coupling of Beckett and philosophy is, of course, not uncommon. Given the frequent crossover between philosophy and literary, linguistic, and aesthetic theory—particularly since the end of the nineteenth century—it is not difficult to see why reading any contemporary writer alongside philosophy would be a principal orientation of literary scholarship.[5] Nor is the pairing of Beckett with philosophy gratuitous. Beckett's œuvre's compulsive preoccupation with itself—with the nature of the textual object, the exigencies particular to writing and to performance, and the relationship between language and

what does it mean: repetition as an epistemological concept?

Repetition, Difference, and Knowledge

meaning–lends itself easily, perhaps *too easily*, to such analyses. Offering itself up to many interpretations at once, Beckett's corpus goads its readers into floundering around in what Thomas Trezise refers to as the "breech," and thus into producing what often seems like an unending mass of messily divergent theoretical readings, where his texts can be said to represent, simultaneously, platonism, nihilism, existentialism, humanism in general, structuralism and poststructuralism.

Arguably, the most contested critical or philosophical terrain in Beckett scholarship–and one that is pertinent in the context of this study because of the potential tie to poststructural theory–is that concerned with determining whether Beckett's writing aspires to a modernist or a postmodernist aesthetic. The divergent opinions regarding this determination are due in part to the timing of the supposed fracturing off of postmodernism from modernism, for it was not long after the publication of Beckett's "trilogy" and *Waiting for Godot* in the mid to late 1950's that the term "postmodernism" first emerged in literary criticism.[6] From that point on, Beckett's status as a modernist *or* postmodernist writer has been hotly contested in critical circles, with the field pretty evenly split.[7]

However, the lack of concordance with respect to how to characterize Beckett's aesthetic or philosophical leaning could also be attributed to the fact that the distinction between such terms is not often clear even to those attempting to employ them. According to Andreas Huyssen, this is particularly true for the words "modern" and "postmodern," which have become overburdened in part by their application to such a great variety of disciplines.[8] As a reaction to the apparent broadening of the postmodern space, critics began theorizing an ever increasing chasm thought to divide postmodernism from modernism. The result is that definitions of both terms vary enormously depending on the source from which they emanate. As Huyssen notes, the French conceive of modernism as an essentially aesthetic notion "relating to the energies released by the deliberate destruction of language and other forms of representation," whereas for the Germans in general and Habermas in particular, modernism's roots can be traced back to the tenants of 18th century Enlightenment, and thus necessarily engage with the political and the social.[9] Postmodernism too has been defined in such a great variety of ways that it has attained the status of a Derridian floating signifier. For Jean-François Lyotard,[10] it is an epistemological concept. For Huyssen, it represents, instead, a cultural transformation in society.

Huyssen argues that the major aesthetic divide of the 20th century was not in fact the modernism/postmodernism discord per se, but rather the distinction between high and low culture which occurred within both modernist and postmodernist twentieth century discourses.[11] But this second distinction can inform us about the first. If modernism, as theorized by Adorno and Greenberg, cultivates and perpetuates the idea of "division" with its insistence on art for art's sake, its rejection of the culture of the everyday, and its hostile "anxiety of contamination by its other" (vii), postmodernism—which "devotes itself to an active engagement of obsessive negotiation with the terms of the modern [...]" (x)—must then play with and reimagine "the theories and practices of the Great Divide" (viii). This is not to imply that postmodernism represents an all out rejection of modernist tendencies. After all, as Vattimo has noted, the word "postmodern" does contain within itself its imagined Other.[12] Rather than shedding itself of its Other then abandoning it, postmodernism literally embraces its Other. By attempting to heal the rift of the high/low culture dichotomy, postmodernism allows for the emergence of formerly marginalized discourses.

Given the variance in the above definitions, it is difficult to identify with precision where Beckett's work fits within the modernist/postmodernist paradigms. If we accept the so-called French reading of modernism, most scholars would probably feel at ease categorizing Beckett—known for his "deliberate destruction of language and other forms of representation,"—as a modernist. However, his cultivation of fragmentation and hybridization might place him neatly within the domain of the postmodern. Richard Begam has argued for the latter, based in part on a mutual concern for the "unnamable" held by Hassan, Lyotard, Kristeva, Derrida, and Beckett.[13] Then again, if we rely instead on Huyssen's interpretation of the high/low culture division as indicative of modernism and the destabilizing of this split as representative of postmodernism, we might take another view as to whether Beckett is modern or postmodern.[14]

Poststructuralism and the Modern / Postmodern Debate

The ubiquitous critical engagement of Beckett with aesthetic theory and philosophy, and specifically as they relate to the modern/postmodern dispute about his work, also stems from the fact that Beckett's name and œuvre circulated in some of the major philosophical discourses of his time. Georg

Lukács,[15] Julia Kristeva,[16] Jean-François Lyotard,[17] Philippe Sollers,[18] Michel Foucault,[19] Roland Barthes,[20] and Theodor Adorno [21] have all written about his work. Which leads to yet another potential reason for the lack of agreement on the part of critics *vis a vis* Beckett's aesthetic; the discord regarding the relationship between postmodernism and poststructuralism. While poststructuralism is often regarded as the theoretical counterpart to postmodernism, Huyssen argues convincingly that it is instead "primarily a discourse of and about modernism."[22] Hence the engagement of so many so-called poststructural critics with the demands of the modernist aesthetic. When Beckett's work began to exceed the sphere of literary and dramatic criticism and started circulating in European philosophical and theoretical discourses in the late 1950s and early 1960s, it was taken up primarily by poststructural theorists, as evidenced by the list of names above. Moreover, the majority of these essays, although varying in length and enthusiasm for his work,[23] almost invariably position Beckett neatly within the modernist domain.[24]

On the Line: Beckett's Engagement with Modernism and Postmodernism

Some theorists have argued that because Beckett's writing represents such a radical break from what had preceded it, it belongs instead somewhere in the no-mans-land between what had long since past and what was still to come. Barthes, Foucault, and Lyotard are three philosophers who describe his work as teetering on the edge of modernism and postmodernism. The reason for this indefinite designation is different for each of these scholars, but they all evoke the idea of Beckett's writing as the embodiment of the *as yet unknown.* For example, Barthes credits Beckett with liberating language of many of its former obligations, including that of bearing the responsibility of meaning. Describing his language as free of some of the more fundamental restrictions imposed by linguistic systems, Barthes argues that this language consequently eludes reading and thus analysis, or at least the type of reading and analyzing employed prior to this species of writing. As he expresses it, a text like *Godot* demands new norms of reading and analyzing, not simply because *Godot* does not resemble the texts that came before it, but rather because *Godot* resembles nothing at all.

Foucault likewise attributes to Beckett the birth of a new, formerly unknown, intellectual mindset. Admittedly, the time was right for such a transformation. For a generation of students "enclosed," as Foucault describes them and even "suffocated" within a horizon dominated by Marxism, phenomenology, and existentialism, change in the form of "an altogether different cultural, esthetic, scientific, and artistic planet" was inevitable. Although he also recognizes Robbe-Grillet, Butor, Barthes, and Lévi-Strauss for their part in the creation of this "new world," Foucault credits Beckett's *Godot* with the actual "rupture" that initiated the split with past ideologies and knowledge. And despite his understated way of expressing it, the change for Foucault was radical: "when things change," he says, "they change."

In a conversation with Gary A. Olson, Lyotard too names Beckett as partially responsible for carving out this new—as yet unknown—terrain. For Lyotard, this tenacious engagement with the unknown is precisely what qualifies Beckett as a "true writer." As he explains, it is only by consciously "progressing in a space [...] in which they don't know what they have to write" that authors confront the unknown—which is to say "language itself"—and thus transform themselves into "writers." In questioning the authority of the author/narrator, in confronting the limits of beginnings and endings and the boundaries of meaning, Beckett's words and works exemplified the writer and the writerly during a critical time when modernism was unfolding into postmodernism. His work was emblematic of crossing over; of change, as Foucault suggests, as it was in the process of changing.

Poststructuralism and Contemporary Beckett Scholarship

This moment in time and in consciousness, when one aesthetic was slowly giving way to the dawn of another, could also be said to have been governed by an aesthetic of its own; one largely determined by its "*in between*" position. This *in between* status is precisely what makes Beckett attractive for poststructuralist readers[25] who are predisposed to seek the destabilization of hierarchies, centers, boundaries, and all claims to authority, authenticity, and nomination.

Although this present text also concentrates on such so-called poststructuralist concerns, I am well aware of the fact that the coupling of any kind of philosophy or theory with literature is not without its problems, the most basic of which is the question of which mode of writing should take priority. In traditional literary criticism, although it is generally guided by theoretical questions, the literature is usually given more space on the page. This can be read in two ways. On one hand, one could say that such critiques allow the literary texts to dominate over the theory. In traditional literary criticism, the scholar examines one literary work at a time, from beginning to end, often one genre at a time. In contrast, he only permits the theoretical works accessory status, by excerpting quotes from texts in a seemingly arbitrary manner and employing them here and there in the critique when useful to the analysis of the literature. The theory becomes secondary to the fiction as if it were written for just this purpose—to faithfully explicate a literary text. The textuality of the theoretical text is disregarded for its "message."

On the other hand, the act of bringing theory into a literary critique at all can suggest that it is the theory that somehow shapes the literary work. If the theoretical questions are permitted to determine the direction of the criticism—to circulate around and restrain the literature as if pressed to do so by some natural gravitational force—it implies that the theoretical text has some natural priority over the literary text; that it is somehow responsible for what is at work in the fiction. The underlying assumption is that the literary text is a simple secondary illustration or a copy of the primary, original theoretical text. In the case of the pairing up of Beckett with philosophers like Derrida and Deleuze the implication that the theory occurred before the example is simply incorrect. Many of Beckett's "illustrations" of repetition and difference actually preceded Deleuze and Derrida's theorizations of the same. Sometimes, as with his poetry, Beckett's "examples" heralded Derrida and Deleuze's "explanations" by some twenty years. This situation exemplifies the central problem associated with repetition. If an "original" thing or entity follows chronologically its "illustration," "imitation," or "copy," then it can hardly be called "original."

Regardless of which perspective one takes, this type of traditional literary criticism, dominated as it is by the weight and presence of the literary work, but guided by the message of the theory, reduces both the literature and the philosophy to a single dimension where one of the two inevitably takes precedence over the other. While *Repetition, Difference, and Knowledge* does begin and end with an exploration of repetition theory itself—where it has come from and where it might be going—the body of the text was structured around the idea of a conversation where the notion of priority becomes less important than the idea of exchange. Here, texts intermingle and cross over into each others' margins, genres, and intellectual domains, not in an effort to level the differences between them, but in order to show how much they are already implicated within one another. To this same end, this text examines the fiction and the theory not simply as producers of "meaning" but also as textual objects, meant to be looked at in their material reality as much as analyzed for their ostensible "message." This type of dialogue-style and doubly stratified reading enables us to better experience the intimate and, in the words of Deleuze, "mobile," relationship not simply between works of the same author, or between different authors, but also between literature and philosophy. It allows us to see how philosophy and fiction inform each other, and perhaps always have.

Repetition and Difference in *Repetition, Difference, and Knowledge*

While indebted to the existing critical scholarship on Beckett and on post-structuralism, as already stated, this present text is not *about* Beckett, Derrida and/or Deleuze *per se*. It is first and foremost about repetition. This is not to suggest that the text as a whole is a sweeping, far-reaching, survey of repetition in the manner of Erich Auerbach's seminal study of Western representation *Mimesis*. That text has been written, written well, and has no need for duplication or revision. *Repetition, Difference, and Knowledge*'s aspirations are comparatively modest. It begins with a brief exploration of the evolution of the concept of repetition in Western philosophy simply as means of contextualizing a particular species of repetition—repetition and difference—within history. The major focus of this book thereafter is the way in which three particular thinkers exploit this type of repetition for its capacity to reveal, if not produce, diversity, and in so doing to expose how we view our world.

Cursory though it may be, Chapter One's outline of the history of repetition in Western thought addresses what seems to be a void in scholarship on repetition and literature: that of research on repetition as an epistemological ? concept that has evolved over time. More often than not, the literary critique focuses exclusively on contemporary versions of repetition. When a traditional model is evoked, it is invariably that of Plato alone. In an attempt to speak to this absence, this text begins with a presentation that traces the impact that repetition has had on Western conceptualizations of duration and mimesis in the work of Plato, Aristotle, St. Augustine, Benjamin, Kierkegaard, Nietzsche, Derrida, and Deleuze, among others. However, I should note that this preliminary chapter is intended only as a means of situating repetition and difference within certain parts of the history of philosophy—which is already a large undertaking—and is not meant to be an exhaustive exploration of the impact that repetition that has had on every discipline, culture, or mode of thought.

The chapter closes by introducing the problematic of the "unthinkable," or that which lies beyond our current means of representation. While I argue that one can certainly identify elements of the pairing of this concept with repetition in the writings of Kierkegaard and Nietzsche, it is my contention that this particular coupling was not fully exploited in repetition theory until the writing of Deleuze and Derrida.

In addition, in an effort to open up the playing field to a wider audience, this text periodically gives an overview of the major arguments of several key theoretical texts. Obviously, readers who are familiar with Derrida's work will need no introduction to such canonical texts as *Of Grammatology* or *Margins of Philosophy*, for example. Nor will readers who are accustomed to reading Deleuze need a summary of such a well-known text as *Difference and Repetition*. However, since a clear understanding of these works will be essential to appreciate the relationship between repetition and notions like presence and time as they manifest themselves in Beckett's texts, the elucidation of aspects of these texts will prove of use to those readers for whom their work is not as well known.

The chapters that follow the introduction focus on the relationship between repetition, knowledge, and language. In Chapter Two, I examine the link between repetition and the boundaries involved in reading. In particular, I explore what Beckett's own treatment of repetition can unveil about the mechanics of the reading process and the role of the reader in the creation of meaning. To this end, the chapter opens with a reflection on beginnings and endings in Beckett's trilogy, then continues with an investigation of several interpretations—those of Habermas, Derrida, Genette, and Sartre—of the concept of genre as a classificatory term. But this chapter is not simply a meditation on *reading*—reading, for example, Beckett. It is also a study on *reading reading*—reading other scholar's work on how one reads Beckett. By examining the work of several prominent Beckett scholars—who are arguably some of his best readers and most skilled scholars on the dynamics of reading[26]—we witness how Beckett's texts actively solicit interpretations that cannot hope to be maintained; above all, those highlighting genre or discursive form.

Chapter Three explores the link between repetition and writing. The first half of this chapter focuses on how repetition in Beckett, Derrida, and Deleuze's work reveals the problematic of originality. No text can be "original" because no text can ever truly be "singular" or self-sufficient. In this sense, all texts are already multiple. In the second half of this chapter, I examine the

repetition + boundaries of reading
     ↳ perhaps I could address the non-boundaries

relationship between repetition with difference and translation. I argue that repetition and difference demonstrates how translation as an exact transposition of signification from one language to another cannot exist. As such, while every text is multiple, every translation is as singular and "original" as the "original" text itself.

Chapter Four probes the bond between repetition, writing, and speech. The first part of this chapter is primarily concerned with the question of how repetition in Beckett's theatre allows him to collapse the speech/writing hierarchy and expose the illusion of "full presence" much in the same way as Derrida both theorized and illustrated this in his lectures and texts. I conclude this chapter by exploring how repetition in both Beckett and Deleuze's work renders ambiguous the traditional conceptualization of the subject as the embodiment of presence. Far from being a unified, independent, and authoritative being, the subject in Beckett's work is revealed to be fragmented, indefinable, only partially present at best, and ultimately the product of language.

It is in this gap in existing criticism—where repetition is not explored theoretically or treated as an epistemological concept, where it is not credited with producing identity through difference, but is instead reduced to the production of the "self-same"—that I situate this present work. Examining repetition in conjunction with literary texts such as those by Beckett and with poststructuralist theories, like those of Derrida and Deleuze, allows us to become aware of the vital role that repetition plays in exposing the functions of representation and, by extension, also those of the human mind. For in studying the dialogue between repetition and difference in the context of the acts of reading, writing, and speaking, we also necessarily learn something about how we conceive of some of the most basic notions that form the foundation of the human experience: among them knowledge, truth, and being.

problematic

to also reading reading reading.

Chapter 1

‡ The Unthinkable: A History and Evolution of Repetition in Western Thought

Au commencement, la re-présentation.

—Jacques Derrida

Repetition in the Humanities

> Here's my beginning [...]. I took a lot of trouble with it. Here it is. It gave me a lot of trouble. It was the beginning, do you understand? Whereas now it's nearly the end. Is what I do now any better? I don't know. That's beside the point. Here's my beginning. It must mean something [...]. Here it is.[1] *Molloy*

Where to begin? Is there "a" beginning from which to start? These are the questions the narrator indirectly raises in the opening pages of Samuel Beckett's *Molloy*. Yet while the narrator voices his concern about where to begin before he tells his "story," it is significant that this discussion of beginnings—while appearing within the opening pages of this text—does not appear at the actual "beginning" of the text. The result is that, by speaking of what supposedly will be the "beginning" of his narration after he has already narrated a page of text, the narrator calls attention to the problematic nature of origins. By *repeating* his beginning numerous times and slightly *differently* each time (oscillating between the present and the past tense)—by *beginning again*—the narrator suggests the possibility that there is no "one" origin: that any "beginning" has always already taken place.

This instance of *Molloy*'s convulsive beginnings is not an anomaly in Beckett's work. Repetition and difference play a principal role in his aesthetic. Like a character featured in more than one text, it is woven throughout his entire œuvre. In his poetry, short stories, novels, plays, teleplays, and film, *Kapp* things rarely begin once and for all, but rather begin multiple times, and each time in a slightly different manner. Likewise, while there is a significant amount of repeating of objects, characters, and language from work to work and even from genre to genre, these things, words, and individuals seldom reappear unchanged. For readers acquainted with twentieth century theorizations of repetition, this notion of belated beginnings that constitutes the approximate "beginning" of Beckett's *Molloy* will bear an uncanny resemblance to the types of repetition that are articulated in the work of philosophers such as Friedrich Nietzsche, Søren Kierkegaard, Jacques Derrida, and Gilles Deleuze. For a fiction writer who is known for his constant philosophical references, it is surprising that Beckett never refers directly to these particular philosophers or to their work.

Of course Beckett is not the sole author to offer repetition a privileged space in his creative process. Repetition is a recurrent motif in literary texts from the Middle Ages to the present and has been exploited by a vast variety of writers, among them Cervantes, Joyce, Borges, Camus, Duras, Kundera, and the Russian mystics Gurdjieff and P.D. Ouspensky. By the same token, Nietzsche, Kierkegaard, Derrida, and Deleuze are evidently not the only philosophers to explicitly theorize repetition. Highly slippery in nature and function, repetition in its diverse manifestations has a rich history in philosophy, just as it does in disciplines as varied as religious studies, economics, political science, and history.

Perhaps one reason for the apparent widespread interest in repetition is its dominant presence in nature. Nature functions by and generates iterative cycles. Our cosmos is populated by black holes, spiral universes, and revolving astral bodies. The hydrosphere recycles continual rounds of water, oxygen, and carbon dioxide. The human body is maintained by cycles of all kinds: vital, reproductive, menstrual, hormonal, sleep, respiratory, spiral strands of DNA, and the cyclical regeneration of cells. On a molecular level, repetition manifests itself in the continual exchange of matter and energy that represents the lifespan of all things organic and inorganic.

In the 19th and 20th centuries, repetition becomes a critical component of a variety of fields, among them psychoanalysis, cultural anthropology, linguistics, and computer science. For Freud, repetition forms the basis for habit, memory, the Repetition Compulsion, and the Death Drive. For Lévi-Strauss, repetition is necessary for revealing the structure of myths. In the work of Saussure, repetition with difference becomes the model for the linguistic Sign. In computer science, it represents both the binary one/zero, yes/no logic that is the foundation of computer systems, and, coincidentally, the DNS Change Pending Loops that signal the breakdown of that binary logic.

As one might expect, repetition has also played and continues to play an important role in the domains of religious and philosophical thought. However, the apparent universality of repetition should not lead one to believe that it evokes identical questions and contexts in each discipline. On the contrary, far from unifying and thus leveling the differences between diverse discourses, contemporary understandings of repetition serve to highlight divergence. The result is a thorough unsettling of notions that have served as the foundation for Western thought, among them the concepts of subjects and objects, beginnings and endings, originals and copies. However, repetition has not always been theorized as a producer of difference. Over the centuries, repetition has undergone fundamental shifts in meaning and function depending on when it was conceived and on the particular conceiver. The radical impact that theorizations of repetition and difference such as those made manifest in the fiction of Samuel Beckett and the theory of Jacques Derrida and Gilles Deleuze have had on Western thought might be best appreciated by first contextualizing these theories within history. The following is a brief sketch of a few decisive moments in the evolution of repetition theory, particularly as they relate to the key concepts of duration and mimesis.

Cyclical Representations of Time: Primitive Man and Early Religious Societies

It is not difficult to imagine how repetition came to play a significant role in our conception of duration. Primitive man was undoubtedly influenced by cyclical patterns related to life sustaining activities. His days were punctuated, just as they are today, by rituals of all kinds; the rising and setting of the sun, eating, working, sleeping, and rising again. The need for knowledge about the migration of animals, the sowing and harvesting of crops, the construction of appropriate shelter, all precipitated an understanding of the annual passing of the seasons. This dependence upon such knowledge gave rise to the need for time keeping devices such as calendars. Needless to say, many of the earliest known calendars were based on such cycles.[2]

Repetition was also a vital part of some of the earliest religious societies. In Western religious communities, curative or purification rituals allowed both the individual and the social unit to cleanse themselves of sins or inappropriate behaviors and to return to a purer state. Analogous cyclical concepts can be found in the commonly held belief among pantheistic societies in *me-tempsychosis*,[3] or the rebirth of the spirit through reincarnation. Similar to the Hindu concept of time as made up of ever spiraling units (*Kalpas*), this *Punar-janma*, or rebirth of the spirit, represented a continuous progression towards a more evolved state of being. In 500 BC, the notions of both reincarnation and self-rebirth continued in both Buddhist thought and in early Pythagorianism.

"Nothing New Under the Sun":[4] The Eternal Return in Ancient Greek Philosophy

The sun shone having no alternative on the nothing new

The cyclical concepts that dominated the daily lives and religious practices of primitive man were later expressed in early Greek philosophical thought, particularly with regard to the belief in the circular nature of time and history. In the sixth century BC, the Ionian philosopher and astronomer Anaximander (611-547 BC) proposed that everything in the universe perpetually derived from and reverted back to the same, limitless matter, the *apeiron*. Pythagoras offered a theory of history in which time would be infinite, but within this infinite time only a limited amount of actions could ever occur. In these conceptualizations of the Eternal Return, after a series of unfolding and apparently transformative cosmic cycles, the Same returns to its initial, undifferentiated state, only to begin again. In short, the origin returns unto itself and thus the past comes back infinitely.

In *The Myth of the Eternal Return*, Mircea Eliade argues that the idea of a continual renewal of the Same through the periodic playing out of cosmic cycles became the basis for the various versions of the doctrine of the Great Year. For Heraclitus (540-460 BC), as well as for Empedocles (490-430 BC) and Archytas of Tarentum (428-350 BC), the Great Year marked the recurrent annihilation and regeneration of the universe. For Plato (428-347 BC),[5] the Great Year represented the time needed for the planets, the moon, and the sun to regain the same location in space as they had held at some point in the past.[6] These two variations of the Great Year were later combined in Stoic philosophy. Zenon and his disciple Posidonius postulated that when the celestial bodies eventually regained the positions they once held in space, the universe and everything in it would be exactly as it once had been. The cycle would then begin again, and again.

Regardless of the differences in the variations of the Great Year, each of the various conceptualizations retains the common symbol of the circle turning back upon itself. This cycle keeps the universe bound up for all perpetuity, not simply in "auroral [...] beginnings"[7] as Eliade claims, but rather, I would argue, in "*the* beginning" where the Same is forever re-produced.

Linear Conceptualizations of Duration: Christianity and Judaism

The Greco-Roman cyclical conceptualization of time was eclipsed by linear theories of duration in the texts of the ancient Hebrew, Iranian, and Islamic theologians. History was no longer theorized as an endlessly repetitive cycle, but rather as a progressively advancing line, delineating a precise past, present, and future. In this future oriented progression, one was always in the process of moving towards some definitive end result, the most important of which was the coming of a Messiah. ending point

Early Christian theologians later embraced and adapted the linear interpretation of history. Nonetheless, cyclical time was not rigorously debated in Christian doctrines until the fourth century with St. Augustine, who presented history as a straight path from Genesis to Judgment day. Along the way, one encountered the major events of the bible: the creation *ex nihilo* and the fall of man (*Genesis*) the passion, the birth of Christ, the Crucifixion, and resurrection (the Johannine and synoptic gospels) and judgment (*Revelations*).[8]

Throughout the four centuries that followed, linear ways of understanding time dominated philosophical and religious thought. However, little by little cyclical conceptualizations regained importance and came to coexist with their linear counterparts.[9] While these new cyclical interpretations represented a departure from the Greco-Roman model of repetition as that which produced "nothing new under the sun," they still conceived of duration and history as folding back upon themselves in a perpetual attempt to reproduce the Same. The consequence was a privileging of the past—of the return to some original, primordial condition—with little regard for the state of *becoming*.

It was not until the work of Kierkegaard, and later Nietzsche, Deleuze, and Derrida that repetition was subject to its own doubling. This happened on several levels. Firstly, each philosopher theorized multiple, competing forms of repetition, thus complicating repetition's capacity to be responsible for producing *a* conclusive truth. Secondly, for each of the above thinkers, one of the two versions of repetition combined linear and cyclical models of duration allowing them to converge as they once had in Eastern philosophy.[10] The result was the conception of repetition as a force that simultaneously *reproduced* one thing and *produced* another thing *anew*. No longer privileging a past by honoring the return of the Self same or the return to an origin or *a beginning*, repetition looked forward to the future and to the production of difference.

Søren Kierkegaard's Repetitions

Undoubtedly one of the most influential texts on modern repetition was and is still Søren Kierkegaard's *Repetition*. As a text about doubling, *Repetition* is composed of a variety of pairs, not the least of which is the melding together of philosophy and fiction, recalling the philosophically inspired Enlightenment literature of the eighteenth century and anticipating the work of writers like Beckett and Derrida. Apart from this pairing, the most obvious doubling of this text is the fact that it is divided into two parts. Part One is an untitled report by a narrator, tellingly referred to as *Constantin Constantius*. Part Two, which is comprised of letters and observations from both an anonymous young man and the narrator, repeats the name of the text itself, calling itself simply "repetition." In line with the book's subtitle, "A Venture in Experimenting Psychology," the ostensible subject of the text is the relationship between Constantius and his psychological experiment, the fictive and anonymous lovelorn man with whom he corresponds. As both the text's title and that of Part Two imply, the actual subject is repetition.

Constantius begins his narrative with a comparison of two ways of understanding movement: one put forth by the pre-socratic Eleatics and the other by the cynic Diogenes of Sinope:

> When the Eleatics denied motion, Diogenes, as everyone knows, came forward as an opponent. He literally did come forward, because he did not say a word, but merely paced back and forth a few times, thereby assuming that he had sufficiently refuted them.[11]

The Eleatics conceived of being as unchanging. Everything that truly could be said to "be" would therefore have to be static in nature. Likewise, anything susceptible to change could not be said to "be." In an attempt to illustrate his objection to privileging invariability, Diogenes, as Kierkegaard writes, "literally came forward." This anecdote highlights an important distinction not only between the particular players involved in that specific exchange, but also more generally between ancient and modern ways of conceiving of repetition: one that is cyclical and self-contained and another that continuously changes and evolves. To these two types of repetition, Kierkegaard gives the titles "recollection" and "repetition." "Recollection" refers to Plato's theory of *anamnesis*[12] which states that knowledge is formed through a process of recognition. Simply put, we know something because we have had some prior experience with it; we have known it before.[13] In comparison to recollection which favors the past—"for what is recollected has been, is repeated backward [...]"—what the narrator calls "genuine repetition" privileges the future. As a movement of "forward recollection," repetition allows the repeater not simply to re-view a past long since gone, but rather to reappropriate that past; to *take it* again, as is suggested in the Danish word for repetition, *Gjentagelse*. Despite the evident dependence of repetition on recollection—that in order to recognize something as repetition, one must first be able to recollect that it has already taken place—Constantius not only maintains a strict division between the two, he even deepens it by assigning to each an affective quality. Recollection, which allows one to simply re-cognize a lost thing or moment, is characterized as an "unhappy" movement, while repetition, which allows for the retrieval of a past, is considered "happy" in nature.

Of course, even though it allows for the possibility of *taking* the past *back again*, the paradox of repetition, even of "genuine repetition," remains: "the dialectic of repetition is easy, for that which is repeated has been—otherwise it could not be repeated—but the very fact that it has been makes the repetition into something new."[14] In repetition, the only real certainty is the impossibility of *exact* repetition. Constantius, both through his own actions and through those of his advisee, continues to be made aware of this fact. In an attempt to recreate an earlier visit to Berlin, he returns to the city only to find that regardless of how hard he tries to perceive things as they once were, they have already undergone much change. It is now winter, his hotel room is slightly different, and although the landlord of his hotel remains on site, he has married since Constantius' last visit. Constantius then decides to return to the Königstädter Theatre when he hears that a farce he had once seen played there—*Der Talismann*—will be playing there again. But this experience is also very different from the last. He finds that he cannot sit where he once sat, is not amused by the actor Beckmann as he had been before, and the girl in the audience who had once so captured his attention is nowhere to be seen. When he returns from this trip—expecting at the least to experience a repetition of what he had seen in his house when last home—he finds the house has been cleaned and the furniture rearranged. He learns that "the only repetition is the impossibility of a repetition" (170). The impossibility is, in other words, the impossibility of a repetition that does not—at once—produce resemblance and difference. Samuel Weber has argued that this multidirectional movement at the heart of repetition is also embodied by the actor Beckmann of the Königstädter Theatre, whose real "genius" is not acting *per se*, but rather his ability to "come walking," (63) or—as Weber signals is implied in the Danish *komme gaaende*—to simultaneously "come" and "go." Later, in Samuel Beckett's work, this "coming" and "going" will not only be a favorite expression of several of his narrators, it will even become a survival mechanism, for as we will see the only way to avoid ending anything—a life, a discourse, etc.—is to "come and go, come and go."

Friedrich Nietzsche's Eternal Return(s)

Although Nietzsche wrote only parenthetically about repetition, his aphoristic writings which reference multiple varieties of the Eternal Return represent a major contribution to modern repetition theory. Though first formulated by Anaximander in the sixth century BC, it is thought that Nietzsche came across the idea of the Eternal Return in the writings of the German poets Heinrich Heine and Friedrich Hölderlin. Both Heine and Hölderlin, like Anaximander, hinted to a belief that all things in life were caught up in an "eternal play of repetition," whereby everything would one day, and continuously, return to its former state. In Heine, we read:

> Now, however long a time may pass, according to the eternal laws governing the combinations of this eternal play of repetition, all configurations that have previously existed on this earth must yet meet, attract, repulse, kiss, and corrupt each other again...And thus it will happen one day that a man will be born again, just like me, and a woman will be born, just like Mary.[15]

In Hölderlin's unfinished *The Death of Empedocles* (1798), this conceptualization of the Eternal Return reappears in the words of the title character when he urges "Go, and fear nothing. Everything recurs. And what's to come already is complete."

Although now informed by the principles of Newtonian physics, Nietzsche's cosmological version of the Eternal Return does share some similarities with the ancient Greek versions, where despite their differences there is a privileging of the Self same. With Nietzsche's formulation, the basic assumption is that, because time is infinite, space finite, and because there is a finite quantum of force in the universe, all events will eventually be exhausted and will thus be obliged to repeat themselves *ad infinitum*. One of Nietzsche's earliest references to this type of Eternal Return can be found in *Thus Spoke Zarathustra*[16] uttered by his notional "Superman" who ponders the effect that the Eternal Return will have upon himself:

> The plexus of causes returneth in which I am intertwined,—it will again create me! I myself pertain to the causes of the Eternal Return. I will come again with this sun, with this earth, with this eagle, with this serpent—not to a new life, or a better life, or a similar life: I come again eternally to this *identical* and *selfsame* life, in its greatest and its smallest, to teach again the Eternal Return of all things,—to speak again the word of the great noontide of earth and man, to announce again to man the Superman.[17]

[margin note: Zarathustra]

This conception of the Eternal Return is analogous to a chess game taking place in a universe in which time would stretch on indefinitely. Given that there are a finite number of moves that could take place within any given game and since there are consequently a finite number of games that could be played, eventually all moves and games will have been played once. If time is infinite, these moves and games will thus be played again and again. In the *Will to Power*,[18] Nietzsche also compares the Eternal Return to a game, but here it is a game of chance that, paradoxically, ends up leaving little to chance:

> If the world may be thought of as a certain definite quantity of force and as a certain definite number of centers of force—and every other representation remains indefinite and therefore useless—it follows that, in the great dice game of existence, it must pass through a calculable number of combinations. In infinite time, every possible combination would at some time or another be realized; more, it would be realized an infinite number of times.[19]

While the examples of both the dice game and the chess game illustrate the considerable play at work in the Eternal Return, it is play in which the outcomes are determined well before the games begin. The Eternal Return, as Nietzsche describes it, is a "Dionysian world of the eternally self-creating, the eternally self-destroying" (WP 1067), characterized by a "circular movement of absolutely *identical* series" in which the world must "play its game in infinitum" (WP 1066). In this cosmological formulation of the Eternal Return, there is no difference produced within each turning over of the events of the universe. As such, it represents both "the greatest weight"[20] (*das schwerste Gewicht*) and "the most paralyzing idea"[21] of the endlessly unchanging. It is this psychological crisis—originating from an awareness of the continual return to prior events and states—that eventually gives birth to Nietzsche's second—this time morally and psychologically inspired—expression of the Eternal Return:

> What, if some day or night a demon were to steal after you into your loneliest loneliness and say to you: 'This life as you now live it and have lived it, you will have to live once more and innumerable times more; and there will be nothing new in it, but every pain and every joy and every thought and sigh and everything unutterably small or great in your life will have to return to you, all in the same succession and sequence [....]. The eternal hourglass of existence is turned upside down again and again, and you with it, speck of dust! Would you not throw yourself down and gnash your teeth and curse the demon who spoke thus? (*The Gay Science*, 341)

If everything is destined to be forever repeated—as in the cosmological version—this must include our lives, our actions, and our choices, hence the resultant moral/psychological dilemma. We must then learn to act according to this possibility; to behave in such a way so as to best tolerate the infinite repetition of our actions.

Despite the evident similarities between the above expressions of the Eternal Return and those of the ancient Greeks, there are several important differences. The first divergence between the two is Nietzsche's bifurcation of the Eternal Return along astrophysical and moral lines. The second way in which Nietzsche's theory of the Eternal Return deviates from the various Greek interpretations is more dramatic, for he also developed a competing form of the Eternal Return. In this version, the Eternal Return is no longer something that simply *revolves*, but actually *evolves*. It is here that one can identify a direct link between Nietzsche's theorizations of repetition and those of Beckett, Deleuze, and Derrida, among others. In other words, while in some writings Nietzsche characterizes the Eternal Return as the return of the identical and the Self same, in other writings produced around the same time period, he bestows upon it the power to produce difference. For example, in the *Posthumous Fragments* of Spring-Fall 1884—written around the same time as *Thus Spoke Zarathustra*—Nietzsche suggests a connection between Darwinian natural selection and the Eternal Return. Yet while natural selection allows the return of the species that are best able to adapt to their environment and to master their environment—even if it is only by sheer numbers, and thus by their *sameness*—the Eternal Return permits the return of the most *divergent*. Here, it is only those who are less adapted to their exterior environment and to their neighbors, and more attuned to their internal, individual force—which is, according to Nietzsche, "infinitely superior" to that of exterior influences[22]—who survive. As a form of selection that favors difference, it is the uncommon rather than the common, the few in place of the numerous, that manages to begin again, even in the face of extinction: "An incalculable number of individuals are now in the process of dying: but he who escapes is as strong as the devil himself."[23]

Gilles Deleuze's *Difference and Repetition*

Inspired by both Kierkegaard's and Nietzsche's theories on repetition, Gilles Deleuze set out to write the definitive book on the subject. With its three prefaces, an invitation to the reader to read the conclusion before the introduction, and its highly repetitive style of writing, Deleuze's *Différence et Répétition* could be characterized as something *between* an explanation and an illustration of the concept of repetition with difference.

The explicit aim of *Difference and Repetition* is to pose a challenge to a variety of metaphysical "fictions," among them the idea that philosophy is a closed system, and that there is such a thing as truth, origins, and knowledge. According to Deleuze, these fictions have managed to persist in Western thought because difference has always been subordinated to identity. Deleuze's strategy is to substitute what he refers to as "nomadic thought" for traditional ways of thinking in an attempt to transcend or "pervert" institutional norms and thus eventually to expose the general failure of Western representation.

Although Deleuze targets Aristotle, Hegel, and Leibniz as particularly responsible for subordinating difference to identity by "confusing the concept of difference with merely a conceptual difference,"[24] he suggests that these philosophers alone are not to blame. The same critique can be leveled against all thinkers who present centered, cyclical forms of thought that equate the Same with wholeness and affirmation, and difference solely with lack and negation. For Deleuze, difference cannot be described as negative because difference—as something that is "neither a name nor concept"—is indeterminate. To say that one thing "is not" another is a determination. Deleuze argues that if anything could be referred to as negative, it is in fact all thought which permits "the infinite circulation of the identical" by way of a denial of difference.[25] For the practitioners of negativity, Deleuze has but one, biblically inspired, word of caution: "those who bear the negative know not what they do [...]." The penalty for philosophers, writers, and critics who bear such "false witness," is to fall victim to their proper fictions: "they take the shadow for the reality, they encourage phantoms, they uncouple consequences from premises and they give epiphenomena the value of phenomena and essences."[26]

Deleuze conceives of repetition with difference as having a dual character situated somewhere between the affirmative and the negative. Elaborating and expanding upon Nietzsche's second conceptualization of the Eternal Return, Deleuze describes repetition as a "differential centrifuge," selectively eliminating the "reactive and the weak"—those who deny difference—and permitting only the "active and the strong"—or those who "affirm their difference" (71-72)—to return. Thus, there is within repetition simultaneously an "auto-destruction" of the negative (79) and a production of difference. But not all difference survives. Deleuze observes that there is some "practical selection" that takes place according to the strength of their capacity to produce difference. Only those forms characterized as extreme return to "pass the test of the Eternal Return" (60). In Darwinian terms, what is at stake in repetition is therefore the "differentiation of difference: the survival of the most divergent" (148).

As theorizations of repetition have evolved over time, so too has the shape one imagines them to embody. As previously stated, in Hindu philosophy, time is understood to be comprised of repetitive spirals. In Greco-roman thought, the dominant symbol of duration was that of the circle falling back upon itself in a self-seeking, self-absorbed way. Judeo-Christian belief systems flattened and straightened out the circle by theorizing linear interpretations of history. The 19th and 20th century thought of Kierkegaard, Nietzsche, and Deleuze, combined both ways of conceiving of duration, thereby bestowing on repetition the possibility of producing difference. Rather than closing back upon itself, the Eternal Return, by the addition of an "imperceptible difference," is thrown off center and propelled in another direction.[27] While it may be propelled onward, upward, backward, even Beckett's preferred "worstward," what remains constant is that it is always propelled *away* from itself. The insistence on repetition with difference by Kierkegaard, Nietzsche, and Deleuze—again, despite the differences in how they choose to articulate the Eternal Return—represents, therefore, a departure from both Occidental cyclical and linear theorizations of duration and a *return* to ancient Oriental celebrations of cyclical growth, flow, movement, and deviation. The prevailing symbol is now—and again—that of the spiral.[28]

Beginning Again: Theories of Mimesis and the Question of Doubles

The second fundamental way that repetition has been theorized throughout the centuries is with respect to the notion of mimesis, or imitation. Historically, ancient societies practiced a variety of forms of *imitatio dei*, whereby the faithful were permitted closer access to their Gods through imitative acts. In many religions, divine imitation occurred additionally at the level of the community or even the world. In these cases, the universe was thought to be cleaved into two distinct but related parts; the celestial world and its terrestrial counterpart.[29] As Eliade has suggested, such mirroring not only allowed societies to regulate the conduct of their followers, it also enabled them to legitimize certain behaviors as "real." It follows that if an act is only "real" when "it imitates or repeats an archetype," then reality can be "acquired solely through repetition."[30]

However, while the practice of mimesis can be traced to primitive man and while the terms generally associated with it—imitation, repetition, and representation—were in common use in the fourth and fifth centuries BC,[31] the most frequent point of departure for scholars seeking an origin of these ideas is Plato. Of course, given the ambiguous nature of "origins," to suggest that Plato is the father of repetition or mimesis[32] is clearly problematic. Firstly, because it would be historically inaccurate to do so, given that the terms were employed long before Plato's time.[33] An additional problem with crediting Plato with "the" exemplary and original model of mimesis is that there is no "one" platonic model. In *Cratylus* and *The Republic* alone, Plato conceives of at least two types of mimesis.[34] Admittedly, both theorizations have a common foundation in the sense that they are both based on the distinction between an "original," privileged, term and its copy. According to this idea, where the ideal form of mimesis is regarded as the return of the Same, what is repeated is dependent upon and subject to what it repeats; the "original," preexisting, thing or idea. These two ways of considering repetition therefore seem to be very similar. Yet, as Socrates observes, "we are all in the habit [...] of positing a single idea or form in the case of the various multiplicities to which we give the same name..." (596A), and while there are certain parallels between the two varieties of mimesis in these texts, there are also marked differences.

Plato and the Irresistible Longing for an Origin

The main subject of Plato's *Cratylus*[35] is the nature of the linguistic sign. The objective of this dialogue between Socrates and Cratylus is to affect a natural, or "essential" relation between what is now referred to as the signifier and the signified. They begin by describing the ideal "name-maker." As expected, this being would be someone capable of "imitate[ing] the essential nature of each thing by means of letters and syllables" (423E). Thus, in order to create as close a relationship as possible between the idea and its graphic or vocal representation, the name itself must be the vocal "imitation"[36] (423B) of that which is imitated. The accurateness of any give name then depends on how well it is able to imitate the object named. If the name is not a close vocal imitation of the phenomenon signified, it is considered to be less true and is therefore of poorer quality. However, the real danger associated with this type of mimetic relation does not result from the signifier being too distant from the signified, but from its being too close. If the name is to best perform its function, it must evoke some of the "essential" qualities of the object, but if it shares too many of these qualities it ceases to be a simple "likeness" and risks becoming instead a duplicate. In other words, it comes dangerously close to becoming what Derrida will later refer to as a "dangerous supplement," which simultaneously adds on to and threatens to replace what it was thought simply to designate. If a name is to remain a name and not transform itself into the object of nomination, it must not reproduce all of the qualities of that which it imitates (432B, D).

While it is the mimetic nature of language that is investigated in *Cratylus*, *The Republic*[37] takes for its subject mimetic art. One step removed from the type of mimesis examined in *Cratylus* where it is the "essential nature" of the phenomenon that is imitated, the discussion of mimetic art in *The Republic* focuses on the representation of the physical appearance of the object or idea in question. One can understand the discussion between Socrates and Glaucon in the tenth book of *The Republic* as an extension of the conversation between Socrates and Cratylus. In both cases, a hierarchy is established that enables one to distinguish between an "original" entity and its "copy." However, the dialogue in *The Republic* seems to advance the conversation by also distinguishing between varying degrees of mimesis. According to this text, the first—and thus most perfect—state of an object is that of its "idea," which Socrates also refers to as the object's "truth." But this idea is the property of the divine alone (597A). One stage removed from the creation of the "truth" of the object is its physical imitation. To illustrate his argument, Socrates takes the case of the couch. The idea of the couch, derived from its "truth," is the product of a God. Below the God, there is the cabinet maker who produces the physical manifestation of this "idea-couch." The final element of Socrates' mimetic hierarchy is the painter with his reproduction of the "object-couch." Although they might not initially seem to be so different, the distinction between the furniture maker and the painter is as great as that between a man and a God. While the end product of his work is only a simple mock-up of the object's "truth," the cabinet maker is required to have some knowledge about its "idea" (its function) in order to reproduce it in physical form. The painter, however, is obliged to only seize of the couch what his senses can perceive. Instead of imitating the couch "as it is," the painter only reproduces the couch "as it appears" (598A). "At the third generation from nature" (597E), the painting itself "lays hold of a certain small part of each thing, and that part is itself only a phantom" (598B).

This initial description of mimetic activity as inadequate later intensifies to the point of becoming potentially hazardous. In books two and three of *The Republic*, poetry—like painting—is described as duplicitous and inherently false. This is true firstly in the sense that the poet tends to fictionalize what his poem represents: the lives and characters of men and gods. Infinitely worse, however, is that in employing direct discourse to craft his verse—as in the case of true mimesis—the poet actually takes the place of and thus assumes the identity of the persons and gods represented in his work. In the tenth book Plato focuses his critique on drama for similar reasons. By presenting fictions as if they were realities, the poet inflames the passions of his audience, thus allowing the passions to "rule, although they ought to be controlled."[38] The characterization of both linguistic and artistic mimetic activity as dangerous stems from the threat that they appear to pose to philosophy for entitlement to the production of "truth" claims. However, because art, according to Plato, has little more than a trivial relationship with knowledge, in the sense that neither the art itself nor the spectator requires any real knowledge of the original Idea in order to imitate and appreciate it, it cannot hope to be more than a childish rival.

Although mimesis in both *Cratylus* and *The Republic* privileges some "essential nature" or "Idea" over all imitations—material or immaterial—the two descriptions of mimesis differ not only with respect to the particular objects under investigation but also regarding the way in which each could potentially pose a risk to the original object or idea. In *Cratylus*, the danger occurs when the copy bears too great a resemblance to the "original," thus threatening the originality of the original element. In *The Republic* the threat increases the further the "copy" strays from the model. Thrice removed from the "truth" of the object, the image produced by the painter is a deceptive "form of play [paidian]" (602B). Taking both forms of mimesis into consideration, one can then conclude that if the imitation approaches too close to the "original" it could consume it: if it strays too far, it distorts the original and is "deceptive." In order for the imitation to both retain its own truth (that it is an "imitation") and eschew moral judgment (that it is "deceptive"), it must therefore neither imitate too well nor too poorly. Instead, the imitation must hover somewhere between these two extremes.

Aristotle and Mimesis

In his *Poetics*, Aristotle approaches mimesis from a different perspective than Plato, for here mimesis clearly loses its pejorative association. Imitation is no longer conceived of as a deceptive and inferior art, Plato's "inferior who marries an inferior, and has inferior offspring."[39] In the *Poetics*, mimesis takes on an anthropological association that has a decidedly positive connotation. No longer described as unnatural, here it is characterized as a biological attribute, "implanted in man from childhood,"[40] that distinguishes him from all other creatures. Far from being detrimental to the well being of the spectator, mimesis is imbued with healing properties. Rather than arousing and troubling the passions, the imitation or acting out of "pitiable and fearful incidents" (11) stimulates a cathartic response in its spectator. In addition, viewing mimesis affords the spectator cognitive satisfaction as well, for when he recognizes that mimesis is taking place, he appreciates not simply the sight of it, but also the vision of himself as he is in the process of coming to a realization: "Thus the reason why men enjoy seeing a likeness is, that in contemplating it they find themselves learning or inferring, and saying perhaps, (Ah, that is he."[41]

An additional distinguishing factor between Plato's mimesis and that of Aristotle is that for Aristotle poetry or art is not restricted to representing a fictionalized version of reality or reality at a distant, second-level. Art is not limited to imitating things as they were or as they are. Mimesis allows for the representation of an as yet unactualized, and perhaps idealized, reality. Thus, in addition to being capable of reproducing things as they were or are, the poet can also represent things "as they are *said* or *thought* to be," and even "as they *ought* to be."[42] As something capable of re-presenting events that have perhaps not yet happened, the so-called imitation now begins to assume a sense of autonomy from the represented events. Simply put, Aristotle's copies begin to threaten the originality of the original.

Walter Benjamin's Theories of Mimesis

Both Plato's and Aristotle's conceptualizations of mimesis continue to inform repetition theory well into the 19th and 20th centuries. Walter Benjamin's well known essay "The Work of Art in the Age of Mechanical Reproduction" testifies to their enduring influence. In this essay, Benjamin explores the relationship between originality and mimesis by investigating the impact of mechanical reproduction on objects of art. Benjamin argues that there is and has always been a strong, symbiotic bond between "original" art and replication. The reproductions clearly depend on the existence of the original for their own existence. However, as Benjamin asserts, art also necessitates reproduction. Students perfect their art by imitating the masters, the masters replicate their work in hopes of finding a wider audience, and dealers have the works of the masters reproduced for financial gain.[43]

Prior to the age of mechanical production—in other words, before the advent of woodcut graphic art—the original retained its "original" or "authentic" status in relation to the copy. Regardless of how well the object was imitated, the original work, Benjamin argues, always managed to preserve its "aura": "its presence in time and space, its unique existence at the place were it happens to be."[44] In the age of mechanical reproduction, this changes. Mechanical reproductions become capable of attaining a degree of authenticity unknown to the copies made by manual reproduction. In part, this is because these new means of reproduction are often able—as in the case of photography—to gain access to a part of the object that was formerly inaccessible because invisible to the naked eye. The product of the reproduction thus challenges the "aura" of the original object, becoming itself as original as the original.[45] Moreover, the mechanical reproduction is able to establish its own original status because its reproducibility allows the object to circulate in places or situations unknown to the original. From the age of mechanical reproduction on, reproducibility becomes more than just the product of art, it becomes its goal. Now, more than ever, "[...] the work of art reproduced becomes the work of art designed for reproducibility" (67).

In his initial discussion of reproduction, it is significant that Benjamin never describes the repetition of the original term as exact duplication. Yet, this does not mean that mechanical reproduction does not allow for this possibility. When mechanical reproduction produces a copy which can be taken as another original upon which the other mechanical copies will be based, everything changes. In this instance, we find ourselves—as Plato feared—in the age of (virtual) identical reproduction, where every copy has the potential to become simultaneously both a copy and an original.

The Double World of Derrida: Mimesis and *Différance*

In *Le même et l'autre*, Vincent Descombes characterizes modern philosophy in particular as consumed by the idea of doubles.[46] Clearly positioning himself as a player in this domain, he doubles modern philosophy by cleaving it into two distinct parts. From the 1930's until the 1960's, Descombes identifies the reign of the "generation of the three H's" (Hegel, Husserl, Heidegger). In the 1960's this generation gives way to those influenced by the "masters of suspicion"; Marx, Nietzsche, and Freud.[47] For Descombes, these two generations are severed irreparably from one another by a fundamentally different way of theorizing doubles. Whereas the principal gesture of the first generation, which he also places under the general umbrella term of "metaphysics," is, as it was in classical philosophy, to double the world ("dédoubler le monde")—to distinguish, for example, between the sensible and the intelligible, the body and the mind, the Same and the Other, and even two compatible ways of understanding repetition—contemporary philosophy (which he attributes in large part to the "double science of Derrida,") doubles the western metaphysical text itself ("dédouble le texte métaphysique lui-même").

As we have seen, Kierkegaard, Nietzsche, and Benjamin's respective dual and *mutually incompatible* theories of repetition—where two conceptualizations of repetition compete for plausibility[48]—could be appreciated as precursors to this second generation. At the forefront of twentieth century French poststructuralist theories of repetition that may also be said to belong to this generation are Gilles Deleuze and Jacques Derrida. Here, the concept of mimesis as a form of repetition that is bound up in the return of the identical not only becomes suspect, it becomes a theoretical impossibility. For according to Deleuze and Derrida, for the "Same" to return, it has to be already different.

Combining both psychoanalytic and post-structuralist thought, Deleuze—much like his predecessors—examines repetition's double nature by distinguishing between two types of repetition: "naked" or "mechanical" repetition that faithfully reproduces its original and "clothed" repetition—the Darwinian inspired variety introduced earlier in this chapter—that distorts or adds to its original, creating difference from within. The difference between Deleuze's dual conceptualization of repetition and those who came before him is that the first form—"naked/mechanical"—is theorized as necessary for the sake of argument, in the sense that it sets up a relationship between an original or authentic element and a copy that seeks to duplicate it exactly. This form is nonetheless described as ultimately unattainable. The only possible repetition is therefore the "clothed" version which seeks to expose the difference that is inevitable.

No more than Deleuze, Derrida does not deny that repetition, by definition, is obliged to repeat something deemed "original," yet he likewise insists that there would be no conception of an "original" entity or an "origin" if there were no potential for its repetition. Because repetition hesitates somewhere between "re-presentation" (the so-called platonic model) and pre-presentation (a notion that is already implied in the French definition of the word, since "répétition" also signifies "rehearsal"), it calls into question all so-called "absolute" and "primary" notions of an "original" entity or "origin." For Derrida, this is particularly important because, as he argues, much of Western thought is the result of a "metaphysical hankering"[49] or "nostalgia"[50] for transcendental signifiers, the supposed guarantees of meaning. The privileging of origins—which also translates into to a favoring of such notions as clarity, singularity, presence, a center, and truth—breeds hierarchical pairs where one element of the pair becomes privileged and the other marginalized. Derrida calls his reimagining of this hierarchy "the enigmatic quality of the first time," or the "retard originaire."[51] The argument is that in order for there to be a "first time" there must also be a "second time," for if this "first time" is the "only time," it is the "first" of nothing at all. Likewise, if there were not, from the "first time," a différance (a differing and deferring) between that "first time" and what follows it—designating it as a "second"—there would, again, be no "first time" of which to speak. In an attempt to elucidate this concept, Vincent

Descombes presents a syllogism that ends, appropriately enough, by refusing to conclude, preferring to resolve itself indefinitely:

> ...it must be said that the first is not the first if there is not a second to follow it. Consequently, the second is not that which merely arrives, like a latecomer, *after* the first, but that which permits the first to be the first [...]. The "second time" thus has priority of a kind over the "first time": it is present from the first time onwards as the prerequisite of the first's priority [...]. The origin must therefore be conceived as a dress rehearsal (*la répétition d'une première*), in the theatrical sense of these words: the reproduction of the first public performance, yet prior to this performance.[52]

> ... il faut dire que le premier n'est pas le premier s'il n'y a pas, après lui, un second. Par conséquent, le second n'est pas ce qui vient seulement, tel un retardataire, *après* le premier, mais il est ce qui permet au premier d'être le premier. [...] La "seconde fois" a donc une sorte de priorité sur la "première fois": elle est présente, dès la première fois, comme la condition préalable de la priorité de la première fois. [...] Il faut alors concevoir l'origine comme la répétition d'une première, au sens théâtral de ces mots : reproduction de la première représentation en public, préalable à cette représentation.[53]

In the end, what we find is the beginning, and in the beginning, the end. In the words of Derrida, it is indeed the non-origin(al) that is original.[54] At the origin, there is no "origin."

The question remains as to how one should deal with the realization that there is perhaps no one "origin"—of repetition, for example—and even no "single" conceptualization of a particular type of repetition, such as so-called platonic repetition. Problematic though it may be, one can always conceal such discoveries in order to create some semblance of continuity and clarity. On the other hand, one could choose, as Derrida attempts to do, to *reveal* the discovery that there is perhaps no clear response to the question of when and where something begins and ends; that such notions are artificial constructs, the product of our will to knowledge and our compulsion to master our ultimately indeterminable environment. Derrida suggests that in the final analysis, this is perhaps the best (if not the safest) decision to make, as in this "game" where "whoever loses, wins" ("où qui perd gagne"), difference will always rear its head.

Although Descombes' classification of the second generation as one that doubles metaphysics itself is compelling, in attributing the latter principally to Derrida he confers upon him an authorship that the theorist would surely deny. His reticence to accept such credit would not be the result of modesty, but rather of his conviction that for deconstruction, as for *différance*, "there is no subject who is agent, author and master [...]."[55] Deconstruction is not an action to be performed; it designates what is always already happening within a "text." If it appears that Derrida is able to "double" the metaphysical text, it is only because its logic and language was always already duplicitous, was always already as intrinsically doubled as the human body itself:

> Two texts, two hands, two visions, two ways of listening. Together, simultaneously and separately.[56]

> Deux textes deux mains, deux regards, deux écoutes. Ensemble à la fois et séparément.[57]

Derrida unveiled the inherent duplicity of the metaphysical text in his controversial 1966 lecture at Johns Hopkins University entitled "La structure, le signe et le jeu dans le discours des sciences humaines." In this piece, which doubles as a conference speech and a written essay, Derrida's main concern is to expose what he considers to be the intrinsic weakness of humanistic philosophy: its desire to "master the anguish"[58] of the intangible and the void—the "reality" of our world—by encasing them in flesh. In other words, the fatal flaw of philosophy in general and structuralism in particular is their dependence upon an artificially constructed "center"—a god, a truth, an origin—for their stability.

Derrida states that the subject of this lecture/text is a groundbreaking event that occurred in the 1950's with the birth of structuralism. This "event," which resulted in a "rupture" of the fundamental structure of western philosophy, was the moment when the structuralists revealed that all systems (philosophy, language, etc.) were indeed structures. This opened up the possibility for philosophers to examine more than just a particular system in and of itself. Now, the investigation could focus on the structure of that system: the inherent "structurality of the structure." According to Derrida, this rather simplistic sounding revelation deserved the title "event" because it allowed philosophers to see their own systems and the centers that were once imagined to hold them in place as constructs rather than as representatives of some absolute truth.

For Derrida, this moment is decisive in the history of philosophy because it was the moment when it became difficult for philosophers to continue to see themselves as structural "engineers," whose primary gesture was the heavy-handed one of creating centers in order to neutralize or arrest the free-play ("le jeu," 410) that all systems are. They could no longer claim to design stable structures that explain everything. Instead, they must consider themselves "*bricoleurs*"; theorists who acknowledge that the system they use is unstable, but who use part of it anyway in order to complete a task.

The term "*bricoleur*" is one that Derrida borrows from the structural anthropologist Claude Lévi-Strauss. Derrida argues that, while Lévi-Strauss does conceive of myth (and culture in general) as primarily structural, (based upon binary oppositions where each term gives the other meaning), he nonetheless manages to escape the false title of "engineer." In *The Raw and the Cooked*, Lévi-Strauss initially sees the nature/culture dichotomy as clearly demarcated and therefore as structurally stable. What is "natural" is defined as "universal." "Cultural" is that which is dictated by the norms of a particular society. In spite of what seems to be a clear break separating the two, Lévi-Strauss eventually discovers what he refers to as a "scandal": an element that belongs to not one category or the other, but rather to both. That scandal is the interdiction of incest, which is both universal—in that it is a common, genetically generated tendency—and culturally specific in the way that each culture deals with it. If the stability of the structure is dependent upon binary oppositions, and these pairs do not remain distinct, then the whole system risks coming to pieces. Again, we find a situation where an agent is faced with two choices. He can either conceal this exception to the rule that destabilizes his system and continue to pass himself off as an "engineer," or, as Derrida observes that Lévi-Strauss does, he can keep using the structure, recognizing however that it is flawed, and proudly bear the title of "*bricoleur*." Again, the "safest" choice, Derrida seems to suggest, is the latter. Just as difference is unavoidable, so too is the free-play that renders the notion of a centered-structure "contradictorily coherent." Without such stabilizers as centers, also referred to indiscriminately as "origins" or "ends," structures, concepts, and all guarantees of meaning become unhinged. They become, in the words of Derrida, the now "unthinkable" (410).

In "La double séance," a lecture given in two sessions for the *Groupe d'Etudes théoriques* (February 26 and March 5, 1969), Derrida demonstrates this internal decay as it manifests itself in the notion of mimesis. By placing two texts side-by-side—one by Plato and the other by Mallarmé—he exposes not only the process of deconstruction at work in the binary opposition between literature and philosophy, fiction and "truth," but he also unveils what happens when mimesis itself loses its foundation. When the idea of an "original" and its "copy" starts to come apart, the notion of mimesis is forced to surrender its fundamental stability, revealing what Derrida refers to as an origin that has always been in "play."

Participants of these two sessions were given a sheet on which two texts were printed side-by-side. On the top, left-hand side of the page was an excerpt from Plato's "Philebus" (38e-39e). Dwarfed by this text, and tucked into the wing of its upside-down "L" shape, was a shorter text taken from Mallarmé's "Mimique." Each of the texts illustrates a different definition of mimesis. In Plato's "Philebus," mimesis is divided along moral lines. "Good" mimesis is described as (faithful) re-presentation or duplication of the idea. "Bad" mimesis occurs when the imitation depicts a "false" rendering of the idea. What is therefore identified and sustained in this type of repetition—which Derrida states represents the history of Western philosophy in general—is the ontological: "the presumed possibility of a discourse about what is [...]." The thing or idea that is imitated stands for the "being-present." The imitation simply doubles this initial thing or idea, and in presenting it again the copy inaugurates an order which itself establishes a hierarchy of levels of the real: "there is thus the 1 and the 2, the simple and the double."[59]

Mallarmé's model, on the other hand, presents a very different conceptualization of mimesis. While mimesis in the *Philebus* is based upon a pair of terms—the "being-present" or the "1" and its copy or the "2"—mimesis in *Mimique*[60] has no original term. Here, *no thing* is re-presented or imitated—*nothing* but the idea of imitation itself. The principal subject of Mallarmé's text is a certain monsieur Pierrot who we first encounter after he has already murdered his unfaithful wife, Columbine. The drama presented by Pierrot is his own re-staging of the events leading up to the murder. Pierrot first demonstrates the various ways of killing his wife that he had considered. The last of these possibilities is to tickle her into a frenzied "supreme spasm" (201) or "orgasm" so as to leave behind no evidence that a murder took place. However, because Pierrot is a mime, he is obliged to play both his role and that of Columbine. The result is that while he is victorious in the murder of his wife, he too must succumb to the tickling, which now becomes a "masturbatory suicide" (201), and dies.

While one might assume that minimally the mime playing the role of Pierrot participates in a conventional understanding of re-presentation by simply performing and thus repeating a script, this is not the case. For there was actually no script preceding this enactment. "Composed and set down by himself" (175), the mime re-presents "nothing that in anyway preexists his operation" (198). Reproducing no action and no word, the mime "must *himself* inscribe *himself* through gestures and plays of facial expressions." "At once page and quill," he inscribes himself "on the white page he is" (198).[61]

What is true for the mime is also true for the character Pierrot. Although Pierrot is supposedly reenacting a crime that was already committed in the past, thus bringing a lived, real, or actual past into the present-time of the re-enactment, this is not really what happens. For as Derrida argues, because the first crime never occurs on stage, and in fact "has never been perceived by anyone," this reenactment mimes no original act. Furthermore, since the initial crime was never even enacted in any of the booklets written about the drama, no initial crime can be said to have ever really taken place. Not even in the "theatrical fiction."[62] The crime that is performed on stage by the character Pierrot is then a copy for which there is no original, just as the mimo-or mono-drama performed by the mime is a representation based on no original presentation.

Finally, the story itself—represented numerous times before it ever reaches Derrida's pages—is also a demonstration of the failure of mimesis. Derrida was introduced to the drama by way of Mallarmé's text. Mallarmé, for his part, notes in the first version of *Mimique* (*La revue indépendante*, Nov. 1886) that he first read about the play in a pantomime booklet entitled "Pierrot's Murderer of his Wife." But, as Derrida argues, this booklet is itself just a *second* edition of the original booklet published four years earlier. The original booklet was published one year *after* the first performance, which again, was a mimo-drama miming nothing. Thus, each of the representations represents nothing original, but rather further representations.

This opportunity to witness mimesis coming apart is possible because the center on which this notion relies for its stability, its "structurability," is an artificial construct—the result of an attempt to freeze what cannot be arrested. However, knowledge, thought, logic, the "text" of metaphysics itself, is not just composed of concepts or structures, but rather of words. It is language and particularly the duplicity of words that ultimately reveals the inherent lack of stability in all claims to meaning. To paraphrase Derrida, language carries within itself the necessity of its proper critique.[63]

Derrida's description of metaphysics' creation of artificial meaning appears in several essays and indeed seems to be a *fil conducteur* throughout his œuvre. Nevertheless, it is principally in "La structure, le signe et le jeu dans le discours des sciences humaines," and "La différance"[64] that Derrida reveals the foundations for such a critique. Derrida begins his exploration of metaphysical language by examining Ferdinand de Saussure's premise that all concrete manifestations of language are based upon an abstract structure. Within this structure there are no terms that are entirely self-determined or self-contained. To be within language is to roam about in a system constituted by difference, where every linguistic element exists only because it contains a trace of what it purports to negate. Thus, Derrida asserts, the same is only the same in designating itself as other ("le même n'est le même qu'en s'affectant de l'autre"[65]). Because of this inherent undecidability of language, one cannot make a claim that would not also be simultaneously undermined. For Derrida, it is just this inevitable stalemate generated by language that is responsible for rendering impossible any attempt to level a definitive critique against anyone. The moment one speaks against someone, one confirms that person; one would have "already confirmed [him]."[66] On the other hand, it is also this paradoxical nature of language that makes it possible to speak at precisely that moment when, as Descombes points out, "all is said and done."[67]

Derrida argues that the duplicity—or deceitfulness—of metaphysics lies in its constant attempts to conceal the duplicity—or duality—intrinsic to all language. Yet for Derrida it is not merely that any word signifies both what it appears to signify and what it seems to deny, but rather that its meaning is always located somewhere in the space between assertion and denial. The neologism différance, which Derrida describes as neither a word nor a concept—and thus, significantly for a study of Beckett, representative of the "unnamable"[68]—graphically illustrates this idea by setting up a disturbance at the level of the signifier. Through a play on the French verb différer, signifying both "to defer" and "to differ," Derrida demonstrates how no one meaning can ever be fully present at any one time. No single signification can therefore ever fully capture the meaning of any word. Since it is in a constant process of folding over, meaning never quite arrives and instead remains suspended between two seemingly contradictory ideas. Derrida's différance, Plato's pharmakon, and Mallarmé's hymen all demonstrate the inevitability of this perpetual slippage of meaning. Oscillating between two meanings—between "differing" and "deferring," "poison" and "antidote," "outer" and "inner,"—such couples are destined to forever stage only their very undecidability. The only certainty that they can hope to guarantee is that if there is "meaning" to be found within a term or a text its precise location cannot be charted. Instead, it is roaming back and forth along the linguistic chain, like one of Beckett's wandering protagonists, disappearing from sight in the fold of the inter-space, the *entre*, of that word or text. Far from obediently offering itself up for immediate cognitive grasp, the signification of a term can only be glimpsed if one is willing to enter the vast darkness of the cave or lair of the term, the *antre*, where nothing is truly clear. As Derrida signals at the beginning of "La double séance," if one is looking for the meaning of the Mallarménian text, one should not seek it in the extreme points of the text: at the beginning or the end. As Derrida might say, the signification of his text, like the signification of all texts and all words, lies in the ambiguous space of the "in between": the "entre de Mallarmé," the "entre-deux Mallarmés"; in the dark passages of the "antre de Mallarmé."

Entre eux: Beckett and Philosophy

As noted in the introduction, when Beckett began producing what became his most well-known works in the late 1950's and early 1960's they were immediately taken up not only by a wide range of academics, but also by scholars who also happened to be arguably some of the most influential aestheticians and philosophers of the era. At one time or another, Georg Lukács, Julia Kristeva, Jean-François Lyotard, Philippe Sollers, Michel Foucault, Roland Barthes, and Theodor Adorno all wrote about his aesthetic. For many, Beckett's œuvre became emblematic of an explosion of the parameters of one frame of reference and the inauguration of another.

Conspicuously absent amongst these scholars was Jacques Derrida who made direct reference to Beckett's work only once and not in writing. Moreover, it was only after being prodded to do so by interviewer Derek Attridge[69] who believed he saw between the two men (*entre eux*) some common ground. Although Attridge uses the term "deconstruction," I would suggest that what Derrida and Beckett seem to share is a mutual appreciation of the *in between*— the between space of literature and philosophy, writing and speech, subject and object, beginnings and ends. It is by examining this inter-space that one learns that the real signification of a word cannot simply be found in what it claims to mean but also in what it denies. There can be no life that is not tainted by death, and no death that is not implicated already in life. The truth of all existence, if there is indeed a "truth" of which to speak, lies somewhere in between. Indeed, to quote Pozzo in *Waiting for Godot*, "one day we were born, one day we'll die, the same day [...]. They give birth astride of a grave."[70] Ironically, Derrida cites this very proximity as the reason he has intentionally avoided addressing Beckett's work in the past. As texts that are at once *too familiar* theoretically and *too foreign* linguistically,[71] Derrida claims that writing about Beckett would simply be too easy or too hard—"too easy *and* too hard."

Unlike Derrida, Gilles Deleuze made relatively frequent—although mostly parenthetical—references to Beckett's work.[72] More curious than Derrida's silence with regard to an author to whom he claims to feel so "close," is the fact that both Derrida and Deleuze respond to Beckett in strikingly similar ways. In fact, they both employ the very same word to describe the motivating force of his textual practice, perhaps because it is also one of the principal gestures performed in their own work. That word is "exhaustion."

In his interview with Attridge, Derrida states that what he finds intriguing about Beckett's writing, and what constitutes his very "signature," is not his treatment of character or plot—not the quintessential "monuments" of traditional narrative. Instead, it is the "ruins" of such monuments—the "remainder which remains" only after their destruction—that, for Derrida, characterize Beckett's texts. In his own words, what is interesting to him in Beckett's work is what remains once the thematics are "exhausted." *exhaustion*

While Derrida's explanation of "exhaustion" seems uncharacteristically cut and dried, Deleuze's description of this "exhaustion," as outlined in "L'épuisé," is for its part, characteristically cryptic. This text directly exploits its very ambiguity, as it raises the question as to who or what is the agent of the exhaustion and who or what is exhausted. Is it Beckett himself, one of his narrators, or one of his texts? Never settling these concerns in a definitive manner, the essay instead seems to promise that the response to such questions is an equally enigmatic "all of the above." Beckett—his texts, his narrators, his characters, his thematics, his textual practice, his words—are all, at once, some combination of the "exhausters," the "exhaustive," and the "exhausted."

Deleuze's primary concern in this piece is the way in which Beckett manages to "exhaust" what he refers to as "the possible." Although he does not define just what is meant by "the possible," his description of it is consistent with the standard *Robert* definition. What is "possible" is manageable, believable, even "permissible." In other words, "the possible" is that which "constitutes a limit, a maximum or a minimum," ("ce qui constitue une limite, un maximum ou un minimum"). It is the privileged seat of centered structures, fixed limits, transcendental signifiers, and origins and copies. It is all that we

exhaust the possible

know: the namable and the conceivable—the conceivable precisely because namable. In literary terms, "the possible" translates to teleological story telling, singular beginnings, conclusive ends, and clearly defined subjects, perhaps best represented by the nineteenth century novel. It is what has come to be known as traditional "representation" or "mimetic story telling": the mirroring or representation of the physical world.

In "Tympan," the introductory essay in *Marges de la philosophie*, Derrida theorizes "the possible" as it manifests itself in contemporary philosophy. In order to illustrate this, he characterizes the whole of Western metaphysics as a rigorously self-contained "text." As the philosophy of "the possible," and thus by definition concerned with boundaries and limits, this text's primary objective is to "know and master" its very margins: "to define the line, align the page, enveloping it in its volume" (xxiv). One must clarify though that these margins are not continuously drawn and redrawn simply in order to isolate this "text" from another text outside of it. The margins are not maintained so as to distinguish *something* from *something else*. Entirely convinced of its singularity and validity, the text of Western metaphysics lays down its margins in order to distinguish *something*—Western metaphysics itself—from *nothing*. There is nothing outside of the metaphysical text, save the impossible, inconceivable, the unnamable beyond.

Critics of Western metaphysics would argue that this is of course its great illusion: that it alone exists. It is just such a fiction that Derrida interrogates by asserting that beyond the philosophical text there is no "blank, virgin, empty margin." Beyond the metaphysical text there is no void, but rather "another text" comprised of "a weave of differences of forces without any present center of reference [...]" (xxiii). Knowing that there is a "beyond metaphysics," "beyond representation," is not enough to launch a successful critique against metaphysics. For, while there may well be, as Derrida claims, a place of "exteriority or alterity," from which one might "treat of philosophy" (xii), it is still an *impossible*, *inconceivable* place. Though there may be a place outside of metaphysics, it is inhabited by difference and for this reason cannot be accessed or expressed by traditional ways of thinking and articulating. The critique of metaphysics and the expression of what lies beyond, must therefore come not from the limitless space outside of this text, but from somewhere between its beginning and end, within its very margins.

Derrida critiques metaphysics from within by making use of Heidegger's textual practice of putting particularly questionable terms "under erasure" (*sous rature).* Barring or crossing out words that he considers either to be suspect or inadequate allows Derrida to register his skepticism about fundamental metaphysical principles such as "being" or "presence," while simultaneously conceding his inability to express such skepticism without them. Beckett's work, like that of other so-called modern writers, also displays graphically its suspicion of traditional narrative space. For Beckett, this skepticism is inscribed through his frequent manipulation of conventional typographical form; for example, excessive paragraph length, a lack or inappropriate use of punctuation, and the exploitation of blank space on the page. Like Derrida's erasure, this critical wariness is visually evident when scanning the pages of Beckett's texts.

Deleuze has argued that Beckett's real subversion was to question representation within language itself. He contends that it is Beckett's exploitation of various levels of language—or that which "names the possible"[73]— that allows him to ultimately undermine or exhaust the possible. In "L'épuisé," Deleuze describes Beckett's use of language to unsettle the foundations of representation as a process involving three different types of language. The first language, referred to as simply "Language One" (the language of the novels), is characterized as a "jerky," "disjunctive," "atomic" language[74]—that of the "minimally less. No more" sort, whose aim it is to strip words of their weight. "Language Two"—found in Beckett's later novels, his theatre, and especially his radio plays—is expressed by Deleuze as the language of "the exhaustive series" (68). The purpose of this language is to "dry up the flow":[75] to weaken the current of the voices and of their stories. *Molloy's* fourteen-page narrative of the sucking stones is one among many such series. The last language, "Language Three"—that "finds its secret in television"[76]—is, paradoxically, the language intended to dispense with language altogether. Here, speech becomes image, movement, and music: all of which are then subjected to their own dismantling. It is with this last language that Deleuze claims that Beckett attempts to extenuate the potentialities of space and dissipate the power of the image, challenging one final aspect of traditional representation.

Deleuze explains Beckett's transition from literature to television, from "Language One" to "Language Three," as the result of a growing frustration with language and the "terrible materiality of the word surface."[77] Just as the metaphysical "text" appears to be encased within the impenetrable barricades of beginnings and endings, words—overburdened with "signification, intentions"[78] and personal memories—seem to be enclosed in infinite layers of regenerating protective armor. Try as one might to chip away at the layers so that "what lurks behind [metaphysics, language] might appear at last,"[79] the surface barely broken simply "heal[s] over again."[80] At least, that is how it appears. Certainly this is the case for theories or practices governed by notions of Identity and the Same—cyclical versions of duration, for example, where the Same is repeated *ad infinitum*, or conceptualizations of mimesis as the duplication of the self-same—that only feign a desire to move beyond traditional representation. Far from puncturing the "margins" or "membrane" *between* the interior and the exterior of philosophy to offer a glimpse of the beyond, these ideas do little more than press against the tissue, producing only microscopic, circular impressions that, if undisturbed, eventually close back upon themselves.

In order to puncture through the protective film in hopes of articulating or at least pointing to what "lurks" beyond, what are needed are practices that do more than trace and retrace their circumferences, unable to resist the impulse to fall back upon themselves. What are needed, in other words, are theories and practices that produce difference, and as a result continuously forge, as is Beckett's wont—"on." Derrida's self-denying erasure and Beckett's "three languages" are two such practices, but the tool that is employed most effectively by Beckett, Derrida—and perhaps to a lesser extent Deleuze—to this end, is repetition and difference. Like the spiraling Tower of Babel piercing through the heavens, repetition and difference in its various manifestations allows them to auger or, as Beckett expresses it, to "bore," through the surface of language in order to begin to move in the direction of the "unthinkable unspeakable"[81] that lies beyond the margins of representation.

The unnamable.

Chapter 2

‡ A Critical Reader: Repetition, Difference, and Genre

"Crossing the Line": Beckett's Beginnings and Endings

Beginnings and endings are the mainstays of teleological storytelling. Whether they are as directly established as the formulaic "once upon a time," or "and they lived happily ever after" of fairy tales, or whether they simply set the affective stage for the text to come, as in "They were the best of times, they were the worst of times," beginnings and endings act to bookend a text, and as a consequence, they effectively determine the limits of reading.

Clearly, the significance of beginnings and endings is not limited to textual material. These notions have long occupied a singular position in Western thought. Forming the lines of demarcation delineating where every being, every thing, and every idea begins and ends and thus permitting us to distinguish one entity from another, beginnings and endings allow us to read our world. They help us to classify, organize, and consequently immobilize everything we know. It follows that if, as Derrida observed, all the world is a text, beginnings and endings are its margins.

Beginnings and endings also figure prominently in the Beckettian œuvre. As is evidenced in the KWIC Concordance to Samuel Beckett's Trilogy,[1] Beckett's narrators refer directly and often to these notions. This text identifies approximately two hundred and fifty references to the word "beginning" (or one of its derivatives) and two hundred and nine to the word "end" in what Beckett has referred to as his "entire œuvre"; Molloy, Malone Dies, The Unnamable and Waiting for Godot. Fittingly perhaps, there are at least twice as many references to the word "end" in the last text of the "trilogy" than in the first.[2] This emphasis on "ends" at the end of the trilogy might lead one to believe that the trilogy, in its own compulsive way, is attempting to faithfully mimic teleological story telling. However, apart from these numerous allusions to ending there is little evidence for such a claim. While there are indeed a significant number of references to beginnings in the first book Molloy (ninety-two), the majority—one hundred and two to be exact[3]—are in *The Unnamable*. Furthermore, although *The Unnamable* is the text that most often calls out, in a direct fashion, to beginnings and ends, its narrator does not hesitate at every turn to undermine the utility of such conventions. "All idea of beginning and end" is for him a simple matter of dogma, the equivalent of "orthodox damnation."[4]

If the trilogy as a whole does not conform to the traditional literary convention of having distinct starting and ending points, this is no less true of the individual works that make up the trilogy. As illustrated at the beginning of Chapter One, the incessant attempts to begin that are laced throughout the beginning of *Molloy* prevent the reader from designating any one "true" beginning. Although this narrator takes great pains to come to a clear beginning, in his effort he actually makes this task impossible by exposing that there were always already far too many. Worse yet, he learns that his beginnings were tainted from the start by endings. By narrating the story of his failed quest for his mother after the quest had already taken place, Molloy begins at his end, a fact of which even he is aware: "It was the beginning, do you understand? Whereas now it's nearly the end." This qualifier "nearly" reveals that even the "end" lacks the ability to achieve its standard function. In a text where "to decompose is to live too" (25), it is not surprising that there would also be no firm conclusion. Instead, one finds a "finality without end" (111).[5] With no definitive beginning or end, Beckett's second narrator of *Molloy*—Moran—also muddles the distinction between the two terms: "For I had no illusions, I knew that all was about to end, or to begin again, it little mattered which [...]" (161). As Derrida observed about the narrator of Blanchot's *La Folie du jour*, Beckett's *Molloy* "begins again to begin," that is to say, "to begin with an end that precedes the beginning."[6]

Aborted beginnings and inconclusive ends are just as apparent in the second and third books of the trilogy. The title of the second of these texts, *Malone Dies*, suggests before the binding is ever cracked that ending is the subject of the book, insofar as the title character will, one imagines, die. This is reinforced in the opening pages when the narrator states directly, "I shall soon be quite dead at last, in spite of it all."[7] Nonetheless, this never happens. This too is hinted to from the very start of the text, for although Malone announces his death on the opening page, he does not speak of it as if it were looming in the present:

What is your second chapter's argument? Stein —

emotion + time
temporality
of affect
repetition
presence

A Critical Reader

I *shall* be neutral [...]I *shall* be natural at last, I *shall* suffer more [...] I *shall* pay less heed
to myself, I *shall* be neither hot nor cold any more, I *shall* be tepid, I *shall* die tepid
[...] I *shall* not watch myself die [...].

Imminent though it may seem, all talk of Malone's death is shrouded in the
future; the "shall" of the English version, and the simple future tense in the
French. It follows that while Malone—as the present tense in the title *Malone
Dies* indicates—is in the process of dying throughout the book, and thus, as
one of the narrators of *The Unnamable* often says, "begins to end" from the
first page of the text, he never actually ceases to be. Just as in *Molloy*, here there
are no "true ends": not even for the text which mimics Malone's impending
yet unfulfilled closure. Admittedly, the words on the page do stop. They even
diminish to the point of becoming literally "plus rien" (190). Despite this, the
lack of a period, which would serve to close the text, leaves open the possibility
for a continuation of the narrative discourse. The narrator's "final" sentence,
made up of over one hundred words, could, it seems, go on indefinitely.

In contrast to *Malone Dies*, *The Unnamable* does close with a definitive
ending, at least in a grammatical sense, as a period follows the final word. The
resolution suggested by the punctuation is all the more palpable for the reader,
as by this point he would have just finished reading six pages of text on which
there was no punctuation whatsoever. Yet, while the period would seem to
end the text in a definitive manner, the last words of the book—"I will go on"—
call such closure into question. In fact, this statement, when combined with
the one that precedes it—"I can't go on"—and the period that follows it, takes
part in a movement that neither precisely confirms nor denies the possibility
of ending, but rather does both simultaneously. It presents not an end but just
one example among many of an "ending end" (408). In the off chance that the
reader is seduced into reading any of the ends as conclusive, the narrator
explains in no uncertain terms that this would be a misreading: "I never
stopped. Halts don't count. Their purpose is to enable me to go on" (320). By
continuously denying the likelihood of going on, then denying that denial by
proclaiming that he will go on—a statement that is itself then denied at the end
of the text by the addition of a period preventing the narrator from going on—
this text reveals something that the narrator of *Molloy* hinted to long before
The Unnamable ever came to be: that "in spite of appearances, its end brought
[its beginning] forth." "Ending, it began," he adds. "Is it clear enough?" (40)

Of course Beckett is not the only author to question the precision of
beginnings and ends. Nor is he alone in choosing to illustrate rather than

"I never stopped. Halts don't count".

simply articulate the inadequacy of such notions. This type of willful dissolution of boundaries is something of an everyday occurrence in twentieth century philosophy, post-structural theory, and modernist literature, as is evidenced by the work of de Man, Joyce, and Robbe-Grillet among many others. Gilles Deleuze, for his part, advises readers of *Difference and Repetition* to participate in the questioning of these terms by asserting that "prefaces should be read only at the end" and "conclusions should be read at the outset."[8]

In *Modern French Philosophy*, Vincent Descombes both addresses and demonstrates the incapacity of these terms to fully signify. As mentioned in the first chapter, Descombes, like Beckett, creates a proliferation of beginnings by doubling his title page. In a similar way, he suggests the possibility of a "finality without end" by continuously hinting to an end which either comes too early or never arrives at all. One glance at the table of contents (found at the end of French texts and the beginning of English texts) justifies this seemingly contradictory claim. There are five references to a "fin" in the table of contents. Interestingly, the first of the five is found at the beginning of the book in the first chapter, "La *fin* de l'histoire." The four other allusions to an end are located within the final chapter. This last chapter ("La *fin* des temps") is followed by the subchapters "Le mal de la *fin* du siècle," "Le récit de la *fin* de l'histoire," and, finally, "Remarque *finale*." Appropriate though this may seem, the abundant endings at the end of the text do not solidify any idea of conclusiveness. They demonstrate the inability of the text to actually finish once and for all. Descombes also verbalizes the lack of determination by asserting that the final words of the "Remarque finale" include in fact "aucune conclusion."[9] Indeed, this final subchapter does not close with any decisive claim, but rather reopens the subject for further discussion, proposing that the moment will soon come when it will be necessary to reconsider the initial hypothesis entirely (221). In this way, Descombes' book, like Beckett's trilogy, seems to concur with Lyotard's contention that even if humanity were to leave the historic and enter once again into the realm of the myth—even if history were to finally "end"—there would still be no real end, for there would always be "récits" about this end, and "récits" about those "récits." Even if history were to come to a close, the proliferation of "récits" would never itself stop. As both Beckett and Descombes illustrate, there would always be at least one more "récit (de la fin du récit) de la fin de l'histoire" (210).

"What Stink of Artifice"[10]: The Case for the Fortification of the Boundaries of Genre

The repercussions of allowing for beginnings that are not definitive and endings that never truly end are evident. Lines that were once thought to differentiate objects, subjects, and ideas from other objects, subjects, and ideas dissolve. Contamination from without is not far behind. In *Excursus on Leveling the Genre-distinction Between Philosophy and Literature*,[11] Jürgen Habermas launches his celebrated condemnation of such contamination when it comes to genre. Although the target of his interrogation is Jacques Derrida and not Samuel Beckett, there are many similarities between Habermas' reading of genre in the work of Derrida and those of many Beckett scholars. In question is the commingling of various types of textual forms and discourses within one text. Specifically, the bringing together of "literary language," or language governed by the poetic function, with philosophic language, or language devoted to problem-solving; a distinction that recalls that of poetry and prose.

Undoubtedly, there are other philosophers besides Derrida who deliberately invite the corruption of philosophy by other genres. Gilles Deleuze writes, for example, that philosophy should, at least in part, be "a very particular species of detective novel," and, again at least in part, "a kind of science fiction."[12] Habermas' choice of Derrida as the object of his critique is reasonable nonetheless, especially given his propensity to create hybrid texts. This is often the result of a doubling of the narrative voice. "Tympan," an essay in which Derrida places his own writing alongside that of Michel Leiris, is but one example of such a composite. "The Double Session," as illustrated in chapter one, goes one step further by inserting on the same page and side-by-side not only writings from two different pens, but also texts that belong to two different genres; a philosophical text of Plato and a literary text of Mallarmé. Since many of Derrida's most well-known pieces are actually lectures that have been published, one could even say that the majority of his work does double duty, as they are spoken and written, meant to be heard and read. However, the text that Habermas takes particular issue with is not one that was voiced (orally) before it was voiced (textually), nor is it one in which Derrida places two different voices beside each other on the same page. It is instead a text entitled "La carte postale,"[13] in which Derrida blends his own voice with the memory of Plato's in his re-vision of one of the Socratic dialogues.

According to Habermas, it is Derrida's manipulation of form that makes "La carte postale" threatening. Here, he is referring to the heavy-handed gesture of reversing the roles of Socrates and Plato and then re-imagining his dialogue in epistolary form. In Habermas' view, this type of intentional "holistic leveling,"[14] produces a dangerous combination of philosophy and fiction that threatens the very identity of both types of discourse. And while he argues that this blurring of the genre distinction would pose an equally great risk for both disciplines, his ultimate concern is for the fate of philosophical discourse. In particular, he fears that this intentional blending of literary language and fictive elements with philosophy will eventually lead to the merging of both types of discourse into an indistinguishable mass. Mixed with literary language, philosophy becomes a simple rhetorical construct, and thus, as Richard Rorty has described it, just one "kind of writing,"[15] on a par with novels, letters, and here, even postcards.

This is not to say that Habermas was unaware of the fact that every discourse—whether it is literary, the language of "every day," or language that is oriented to problem solving—is always already contaminated by elements of other types of language. He is evidently aware that everyday language and philosophical discourse both employ rhetorical elements associated with literary language such as repetition, metaphor, and so on, just as literary language often contains elements of philosophical and everyday language. What is in question is the role that each type of language should play when inhabiting the margins of the other language. Although rhetorical devices and metaphorical tropes can be found in the "specialized languages" of philosophy, science, economics, and political science, they are "tamed, as it were" and "enlisted for special purposes of problem-solving."[16] He is not, therefore, making a claim for a "return" to some idyllic and natural origin of genre where categories were once pure and thus entirely distinct from one another. On the contrary, what Habermas advocates is a greater maintenance of such constructs in an appeal that resembles a plea to protect an endangered species, a dying breed. He is petitioning for a cleansing within each genre in order to sanitize one from the contamination of another. This sanitization would then be followed by a fortification of the boundaries that would differentiate one genre from another in order to prevent further corruption from without.

Derrida, for his part, clearly understands that the desire for pure genre is reasonable. We have a need for "readability": we need to be able to see things clearly, in an orderly and organized manner, in order to reach a consensus or, minimally, to understand the thoughts of others. If terms commingle, they lose the ability to signify individually. As "order's principle," genre attempts to prevent this from happening. Its goal is to allow for—even to engender—"resemblance, analogy, identity, taxonomic classification, organization and genealogical tree, order of reason, order of reasons' sense of sense, truth of truth, natural light, and sense of history."[17]

Yet, while the buttressing of the genre-distinction allows us to understand each other more plainly by affording various discourses the "liberty" to perform the task they were meant to perform, for Derrida this understanding offers little in the way of emancipation. There is a price to pay, and that price is, paradoxically, "freedom." While it may appear necessary for the sake of readability, for Derrida, the establishment of "pure" genres represents nothing less than the initial step of the willful founding of a (textual) police state, for in adhering to genre, one supports a restriction. In mixing genre, one breaks a law.

Derrida and the Institution of "The Law of Genre"

In "The Law of Genre," Derrida explains just how genre distinctions, such as those desired by Habermas, ultimately lead to the loss of the very thing these distinctions were supposed to ensure:

> As soon as the word "genre" is sounded, as soon as it is heard, as soon as one attempts to conceive it, a limit is drawn. And when a limit is established norms and interdictions are not far behind: "Do," "Do not" says "genre," the word "genre," the figure, the voice, or the law of genre. (203)

From the moment genre is announced, "must" and "must not" are sure to follow. One must, for example, "respect a norm." One must not "cross a line of demarcation," or "risk impurity, anomaly or monstrosity" (203-204). It makes sense then to assume that if one wants genre to adequately perform its task, as Derrida puts it, "one should not mix genres." One even "owes it to oneself," he asserts, "to not get mixed up in mixing genres." "Or more rigorously," as if he had not already made his point, "genres should not intermix" (204). But in reformulating these statements in different tones, he, ironically, does just that.

Derrida begins his lecture/text, "The Law of Genre," by appearing to vow rather emphatically to serve and uphold this law. He starts by stating that

"Genres are not to be mixed." This is followed by "I will not mix genres." Then finally, "I repeat: genres are not to be mixed. I will not mix them." But while each phrase, in and of itself, seems to reinforce Derrida's allegiance to the "law of genre," taken together they do the very opposite, for each phrase could belong to any one of several different genres. This is something Derrida does not hesitate to make immediately apparent to the listener/reader, by drawing his attention to the various possibilities. Depending on the context, each statement could be considered "descriptive, constative, and neutral" (202). But this opening is more than just a clever way to illustrate how one can, at once, both appear to support and yet undermine the law. What it reveals is a fact about this law; that it is already inherently and necessarily flawed. It is "affected straight away by an essential disruption," an "internal division," that Derrida refuses to name. Instead, he provides us with several options: "impurity, corruption, contamination, decomposition, inversion, deformation, even cancerization, generous proliferation or degenerescence." Within the law, even as its reason for being, is the *a priori* of a counter law, "an axiom of impossibility that would confound its sense, order and reason" (204). This law "is threatened immediately and in advance by a counter-law that [...] renders it possible." But this is done only to then condemn it "and thereby render it impossible," and so on *ad infinitum*. "The law and the counter-law" it follows, necessarily "serve" and, I would add, disserve each other (205).

Derrida argues, perhaps a bit too quickly, that the anomalies and thus the counter-law are engendered by repetition, "one might even say by citation or re-citation" (204). Admittedly, if not for the repetition of the opening lines—all, of course, repeated with a difference that Derrida does not allow his listener/reader to miss, directly stating that "from one repetition to the next a change had insinuated itself"—it would be impossible to recognize that he was both supporting and undermining the notion of genre. However, by suggesting that repetition would be or even could be responsible for *engendering* anything, Derrida associates it with a notion to which it is directly antithetical; that of origins. Repetition, like deconstruction, is the agent of nothing, and therefore does not produce anything as such. Instead, repetition, again like deconstruction, reveals the existence of contamination, of an anti-law, that had formerly been concealed but that was always there as the condition for the law's possibility.

The existence of an inherent counter-law within a law is certainly not peculiar to the "law of genre" but is rather a characteristic of all laws, whether they are literary, scientific, or mathematical in nature. Bertrand Russell's paradox of set theory is a case in point. Although set theory was developed within the domain of mathematics, and therefore may seem irrelevant to Derrida's concerns, as the theory that deals with defining collections, higher concepts, and reasoning, it is quite appropriate to this discussion of genre. The paradox, one of many in set theory, is the following: if "S" is the set of all sets that do not belong to themselves, then one could not say "S" is equal to, or identical to, itself, for in that case S would fail to meet its own, and only, prerequisite. Thus, paradoxically, in order for S to be the same as S, it must not be S (S ϵ S then S $\neq$ S, and vice verse). In order for something to be the same, it must also be different.

This paradox, in which belonging requires that one not belong, describes the principle mechanism driving what Derrida calls not simply the "law of genre," but rather the "law of the law" of genre. As Derek Attridge expresses it in his introduction to "The Law of Genre," in order for a text to participate in genre, it must implicitly or explicitly signal this belonging. The complication is that this mark itself cannot belong to the genre it points to. Genre therefore always "potentially exceeds the boundaries that bring it into being."[18] Any attempt to fortify the margins of genre will only result in its weakening and subsequent contamination, for genre is always already "on the line." Focusing on genre will itself only *engender* "the now or never" of the "most necessary mediation on the fold."[19] The end result of Derrida's reflection on the law(s) of genre is the exposition of a necessary relationship between "what has now happened"—the simultaneous engendering and putting to death of genre—and the origin of literature, "as well as its aborigine or its abortion."[20] At the moment either a genre or literature is named, "at that very moment, degenerescence has begun." "The end begins" (213). Molloy might respond, "Is that clear enough?"

"When Genre is on the Line"[21]: Interpreting Genre

The term "genre" is, from the beginning, a problematic one at best. As we have seen, for Derrida genre cannot name anything in a definitive fashion because as soon as it attempts to do so, it is subject to the "counter-law" that both threatens it and is its very condition of possibility. The minute genre tries to name something as such—the moment a text marks itself as a "novel" or a "play"—it begins to un-name it. But one need not look to the work of Derrida to find the conceptualization of genre imbued with ambiguity. According to the French *Robert*, the word genre is derived from the Latin *genus, generic*, denoting *"origine, naissance."* Thus, from the outset, it begins to trace a boundary. However paradoxically, this word *genre*—a word that is classificatory in nature and function, that seeks to draw a line around things—resists any single and clear classification. The *Robert* defines genre as that which designates a type, kind, or sort of thing, a way of looking or behaving, or even appreciating something (aesthetic taste). It is not uncommon in French for someone to express their indifference, for example, by stating that some thing or person "n'est pas mon genre," does not, in other words, belong to the category of things or people that is pleasing to the speaker. Genre also designates characteristics that are common to beings or things, and thus, it also represents that which is *generic* or the Same. In a similar vein, *Webster's Dictionary* offers the additional definition of genre as a painting that portrays everyday life, and does so "usually realistically," or mimetically.

Undoubtedly, the most common English definition of the word "genre" is that which characterizes a type of art, whether it is written, filmed, voiced, or expressed physically on stage, to name a few possible arenas. But even this definition fails to truly give shape to the term and instead remains ultimately too vague to be of much service. This is evidenced by the following two dictionary entries. The *Oxford English Dictionary* defines genre as denoting "a particular style or category of works of art; esp. a type of literary work characterized by a particular form, style, or purpose." Similarly, the *Robert* describes it as designating a category of written work "according to the subject, the tone and the style" (d'après le sujet, le ton, le style"). Both definitions describe genre as a means of labeling a work according to a combination of its content (history, suspense, etc.), the type of discourse used (poetic, didactic, lyric, etc.), and its basic textual form (a play, a novel, an essay).

These definitions are vast, no doubt. Yet any definition that is too limiting in the sense that it would privilege one of the three categories over the others would result in restricting this word's very ability to perform its most fundamental task: to classify accurately. In "The Law of Genre," Derrida argues that Gérard Genette's definition of genre does just that; it fails to accommodate the entirety of genres' possibilities. In an attempt to clarify and solidify *genre*, Genette divides off its functions. The word "genre" becomes associated solely with content. Against genre, he positions the term *mode* which would speak to the formal elements of the text. Derrida explains it in the following way:

> Genette's definition of mode contains this singular and interesting characteristic: it remains, in contradistinction to genre, purely formal. Reference to a content has no pertinence. This is not the case with genre. The generic criterion and the modal criterion, Genette says, are absolutely heterogeneous: "each genre defined itself essentially by a specification of content which was not prescribed by the definition of mode" (209).

Simply put, "genre" represents a literary or aesthetic category for Genette, whereas "mode" refers to categories that deal with linguistics. But in distinguishing genre from *mode*, Genette risks stripping it of much of its power to classify, for it no longer has the capacity to speak of the formal elements of a text. If genre is to retain its ability to classify a text in its entirety in a conclusive fashion, it must have at its disposal a full range of possibilities for categorizing, which would account for both content and form. In order for genre to classify a text in the most definitive way, its own definition must therefore remain ambiguous.

The idea that genre carries within itself the paradox that it must simultaneously do and undo itself—classify and yet struggle to remain open enough to account for everything, including that which escapes classification; the idea, in other words, of Derrida's so-called "law of the law of genre"— manifests itself in yet one more dictionary definition of the word. In French, genre also describes linguistic gender; that of nouns, adjectives, and articles. For Derrida, this signifies that genre therefore acts as a "hymen," both dividing and bringing together the masculine and the feminine. As a hymen, and thus a membrane whose intact presence signifies virginity, it physiologically prohibits a union. On the other hand, as a hymen, and so a wedding or marriage, the term legally encourages such coupling.

The *Princeton Encyclopedia of Poetry and Poetics*, for its part, attributes the inherent vagueness of genre not to any one definition per se, but more precisely to the magnitude of the task with which it is entrusted. Any one definition of genre cannot help but fail to perform its task of classifying textual representations because "the advance of modern writing is so vast and multifarious that all classifications crumble in front of it." The inability of one definition of genre to compensate for all writing gives rise to a surplus of definitions of the word—Genette's, Habermas', and Derrida's, among others—resulting in a literary field that is literally strewn with "the ruins of past definitions," which, it cautions, "have convinced no one [of their validity] save the author."

All too aware of the hopelessness of the endeavor, J.E. Dearlove, circumvents the mire of trying to define what genre is and instead focuses on its point of origin. For Dearlove, what we think of genre is really nothing more specific than the "collection of expectations a reader holds about a work."[22] Clearly, texts themselves also participate in the process of genre marking, or remarking, as they provide the clues with which the reader will work in order to come to his determination of a particular texts' genre. A reader would probably not label *Molloy* a novel if, for example, it was laid out in verse. On the other hand, the reader would only identify verse as belonging to poetry if he believed that poetry was often written in verse and that, more often than not, novels were written in prose.

Of course, the gesture of conferring the burden of genre marking upon the reader is not unique to Dearlove. It participates in a tradition that is heavily influenced by *Rezeptionstheorie* (Iser and Jauss, for example), which, when later introduced by Jane Tompkins, became known as Reader Response Criticism.[23] Reader Response Criticism is commonly viewed as a reaction against the New Criticism *en vogue* in the mid twentieth century, where the text itself—as distinguished from both the intentions of the author and the expectations of the reader—was considered to be the sole source of the text's meaning. The various interpretations that are often grouped under the umbrella term "reader-response criticism," can differ enormously from one another depending on the type of reader examined—informed, hypothetical, or "real,"—and the particular context that conditions the reader—cultural, political, historical, psychological, linguistic. Each, however, holds the basic premise that, as Riffaterre aptly expresses it, "readers make the literary event."[24]

The reader then approaches the text armed with prior literary experiences that determine more or less how he will read. With respect to genre, one can surmise that a reader's idea of a poem and of poetic language comes from his experience with other so-called poetic texts and his subsequent interpretation of what they all have in common. When reading, he places the expectations that he has amassed over the years on top of the text to see if they match. To focus on genre is thus to engage in a quest for the Same.

Yet, it would seem that when the text matches the reader's expectations of genre, it would not be "remarkable." That a text would correspond to a reader's expectations for a detective novel is hardly worth noting. It would scarcely be significant if the reader's expectations and the text conformed precisely to one another; if a text was, with respect to its genre, generic. It is only when they do not correspond—when a text does not remain within the margins of the genre that it most closely resembles—that the genre of the text calls out for remarking. Or, as Derrida phrases it, "urgent attention is required" only "when genre is *on the line.*" And genre is always on the line.

"*Fort / da*": The Give and Take of Beckett's Genres

Despite the slippery nature of genre and in spite of an awareness of it, Beckett scholars continue to treat it as if it is a priority in his work. Admittedly, there is nothing extraordinary about the predisposition of readers—especially those who read critically, or those who read in order to later write about what was read—to be concerned with the form and language of a text. Trained to read, classify, organize, reorganize, synthesize, and explain what was read, literary scholars are inclined from the start to identify and comment on genre, regardless of the particular text or author. This detail notwithstanding, Beckett's work makes the subject of genre particularly difficult to ignore, for it seems to relentlessly fixate on it.[25] As a result, it obliges the reader to do so as well.

One of the more immediately apparent ways that Beckett calls his reader's attention to genre is by frequently entitling his work after its genre. His one film is simply called *Film*. Two of his radio plays are named *Rough for Radio I* and *Rough for Radio II*. Likewise in theatre, there is *Rough for Theatre I* and *Rough for Theatre II*. Finally, there is the dramatic piece entitled *Play*, which insists all too emphatically on the notion of its genre by repeating it again in the subtitle: *Play: a play in one act*. In each case, the title—which Derrida characterizes as "always unique, like a signature"[26] in that it ought to signal what the work is about—is conflated with its genre.

Conversely, Beckett's equally emblematic tendency to fail to mark the genre of many of his works also evokes the notion of genre in the mind of the reader. For example, many of his plays do not bear the marker "pièce" on the title page, as is customary in French publications. This might not attract much attention, were it not for the fact that out of thirty-two dramatic pieces only fourteen of them are designated as belonging to a particular genre. The eighteen that are signaled (by omission) as genre-less were all written after 1958,[27] perhaps indicating a suspicion on Beckett's part about the legitimacy of such terms. Similarly, many of his prose texts are not designated on the title page as participating in any genre. The inconsistently genre-marked texts of the so-called "trilogy" only add to the confusion, for although *Malone Dies* and *The Unnamable* are both referred to as novels, *Molloy*—the only text of the three to resemble the traditional notion of "novel"—is the only one not to carry this genre marker on its title page. Both the generic titles and the missing or confusing genre markers seem to indicate that the subject of Beckett's work is genre itself, or the lack thereof.

The question remains whether the presence or absence of genre markers on the cover of a text is enough to account for the compulsion on the part of Beckett's critics to wrap themselves up in it when writing about his work. Since those studies that focus on this notion do not restrict themselves to analyzing these types of direct markers, the answer must be no. There is also something about the works themselves that coaxes the reader in this direction. Indeed, scholars classify his texts according to myriad narrative and thematic conventions. The plays are generally said to illustrate the "Theatre of the absurd,"[28] particularly *Waiting for Godot, Happy Days,* and *Endgame.* His novels are thought to exemplify detective novels (*Molloy,* for example), quest novels (*Molloy, Mercier and Camier*), novels of ideas, and novels of manners, and so on.[29] Both his dramatic and his prose texts are often described as belonging to the genre of autobiography; *Not I, That Time, Company,* and *Malone Dies* are frequent suggested examples.[30]

However, like the Murphys, Molloys, Malones, and Watts, who transcend the borders of their own texts in order to appear within the space of each other's stories, Beckett quite often allows his texts to exceed the limitations of their ostensible genres. *Molloy,* for example, relates the story of (at least) two quests: that of Molloy for his mother, and that of Moran for Molloy. Moreover, because Moran is induced to begin his quest at the re-quest of someone other than himself (Gaber) and must follow clues in order to approach his subject, he appears to be a detective. Since his story also bears an uncanny resemblance to that of Molloy (each one prominently features sticks, bicycles, men being killed, disembodied voices, the appearance of a shepherd, etc.), and because he even admits that at least one of the Molloys he is seeking he is "stalking" in his own head,[31] one could imagine that what Moran relates about Molloy is actually autobiographical information. Moran's quest then becomes the quest for the Self. Finally, in view of the fact that the text highlights the mores and values of a society—whether it is a "real," human community or a linguistic one—in which neither protagonist really belongs and yet to which both are ultimately subject, and given that the text endeavors to exploit a plurality of ideas—both philosophical and psychological—one could even say that Molloy is not only a quest-detective-autobiographical novel, but rather a quest-detective-autobiographical-novel of manners and ideas. Is that clear enough?

This is what makes genre in Beckett's work so compelling; it somehow both meets and frustrates the readers' expectations. Much in the same way as his ever beginning beginnings and never ending ends manage to simultaneously construct then collapse limiting boundaries of all kinds, so too does genre in these texts take away from the reader as much and as quickly as it gives. Here, as Derrida observed of genre in general, genre becomes memorable, and thus re-markable, precisely because it departs in some way from the readers preconceived ideas, either by exceeding its limits or by participating in too many different genres at once.

True to form, Beckett's theatre refuses to satiate any appetite for classical theatre. Act Without Words, a play whose very title directly addresses the way in which it resists what some might think of as traditional theatre, is but one example. The play Not I, for its part, challenges our expectations of character by featuring a mouth engaged in a monologue addressed to a "listener," who himself (the gender is unspecified, but the word "auditeur," is masculine in French) is nothing but a silhouette. In Waiting For Godot, it is our yen for coherence and meaningful action in theatre that is denied, for, as Vivian Mercier has remarked, it is not simply a play in which "nothing happens," as so many have said before, but rather a play in which "nothing happens...twice." The same claim could be made about Happy Days, where the principle character "Winnie," finds herself performing the same banal activities—fishing out and examining the various objects in her purse—in both the first and second acts. Yet while the differences between acts one and two in Godot are relatively innocuous—the tree acquires leaves, Pozzo is now deprived of sight and Lucky of speech—the difference between the two acts in Happy Days is a matter of life and death, for from one act to the next we witness Winnie further engulfed in a mound of earth. Alive and still chattering on, she is nonetheless slowly being entombed. Finally, there is Endgame, which, as its title implies, plays with traditional expectations for the type of encapsulation produced when one has a beginning and an end. With its circular discourse and a beginning that is always already an end—nearly commencing, as it does, with "Finished, it's finished, nearly finished, it must be nearly finished"[32]—this is a play that could

Is this the same with repetition in some cases?

begin or end anywhere. And because of the apparent lack of coordination and cooperation in the dialogue (Hamm: "There are no more sugar-plums!" Nagg: "It's natural. After all I'm your father."[33]), when this play is staged, it often does just that: ends at the beginning.[34]

In "Weaving Penelope's Tapestry," J.E. Dearlove contends that although Beckett's texts themselves evoke and then disrupt generic conventions, the success of the stirring up and subsequent thwarting of these conventions depends entirely upon how they are received. Their success depends upon the prior knowledge of the reader. The reader would never know how, or even that, *Molloy* deforms or expands upon the genre of the quest novel if he did not know what that was. It is logical to assume then, as Dearlove does, that "we must know what a detective novel is in order to understand what *Mercier and Camier* denies us; what a novel of ideas implies in order to appreciate the exaggerated claims of *Murphy*; what a novel of manners should do, in order to recognize the omissions of *The Lost Ones*."[35] While Beckett's patent allusions to and subsequent disavowing of various genres may have been written with the intention of exposing the fragility of such conventions, it is only truly achieved with the readers' comprehension of and participation in the subversion.

Of course, the reader that Dearlove refers to is not the average reader. True, the great majority of readers would be able to recognize nods to both the detective and the quest novel. However, in order to grasp the allusions to a novel of manners or a novel of ideas the reader would have had to have slightly more experience with literature and literary terminology. As for autobiography, most readers would be able to recognize the role of the autobiographical writer in the personage of Malone in *Malone Dies*. Likewise, the many references to Irish towns, streets, and proper names scattered throughout his œuvre would surely recall to the reader Beckett's own Irish roots. But they would have to be very familiar with Beckett's life indeed in order to identify the rock diving scene in *Company* as autobiographical. Beckett does not however discriminate. The non-specialized reader—the reader who knows little to no literary terminology and little to nothing about Beckett's own life—is given equal opportunity to participate in the subversion and perversion of genre. For even the most basic of novelistic conventions of plot, distinctive characters, and clearly sequenced events are rendered foreign in these texts.

If one accepts Ian Watt's definition of the novel as the form of writing that owes its shape to nineteenth century realism, and thus to that which attempts to reproduce or re-present "reality," one would have to say that Beckett's prose texts can hardly be referred to as novels at all. That is not to say that many of his works are not greatly reminiscent of this form. There are moments, for example, when *Molloy* seems to be trying to squeeze itself into a novelistic skin; in particular, when Moran's voice of apparent reason and order takes over the role of narrator in the second part of the book. Malone's incessant explanations of the minutia that makes up his daily existence (his writing materials, his stories, his dishes and pots, etc.) certainly seems to be an effort to produce in the mind of the reader a sense of a certain "reality." But few images that correspond to a reader's expectations of mimetic realism do so for very long in Beckett's work. More often than not, as the famous last lines of *Molloy* illustrate, the image is taken back as quickly as it was given. "It is midnight. The rain is beating on the windows. It was not midnight. It was not raining."[36] There is little solace in the narrator's promise of "I'll tell you" when all he is willing to tell is nothing, twice: "I'll tell you nothing. Nothing" (134).

In *Samuel Beckett and the End of Modernity*, Richard Begam expands upon Beckett's tendency to recall for the reader the elements of realism only to quickly dismantle them within the context of one particular text: Beckett's *Dream of Fair to Middling Women*. Quoting Rubin Rabinowitz, Begam notes that the narrator of this text—much like the narrator of all of Beckett's texts, I would add—"refuses to indulge in [...] the artifices of plot manipulation," claiming he is "neither Deus enough nor ex machina enough" to be up to the task. "When the narrator finally does revert to old-fashioned methods," Begam, via Rabinowitz, continues, "he cannot help grumbling. It is with very bad will indeed, he says, that he approaches 'the gehenna of narratio recta.'"[37] Likewise, Beckett refuses to conform to standards regarding typical novelistic characters and refuses to inform his reader of the character's "milieu, race, family, structure, temperament, past and present and consequent and antecedent back to the first combination and the papas and mammas and paramours and cicisbei and the morals of Nanny and the nursery wallpapers and the third and fourth generation snuffles."[38] The subject of his novels is the novel itself, which is to say, its persistent lacing and unlacing of itself. In the end, any reader would find himself preoccupied with trying to identify the margins of these apparently shape-shifting texts. Forced to acknowledge the instability of even his own ideas about representation, he cannot help but pose—to paraphrase Marjorie Perloff—the simplest, though perhaps the most appropriate, of questions: "Just what kind of text is this anyway?"

"Ill Said, Ill Read": Beckett's Poetry, Beckett's Prose

In his seminal *Qu'est-ce que la littérature,* and in a gesture that is strikingly reminiscent of that of Habermas and Genette, Jean-Paul Sartre petitions in the name of "greater clarity"[39] for a leveling between two textual categories. This time it is prose and poetry. And although the objects in question are different for each philosopher, the distinctions that Sartre makes between the functions he desires to remain exclusive to poetry and those he would have belong to prose echo those that Habermas wishes to stabilize for literature and philosophy and those that Genette assigns to *mode* and *genre.* Characterizing prose as, "in essence, utilitarian" (26:10), Sartre calls for prosaic language to be as transparent as a "pane of glass" (18:5). As such, a prosaic word would be recognizable to us "when the word passes across our gaze as the glass across the sun" (27). In contradistinction to prosaic language, where meaning and message is of primary importance, the essential elements of poetic language, that permit it to "represent" as opposed to "express meaning," would be "its sonority, its length, its masculine or feminine endings, and its visual aspect." Its form, therefore, would compose its "face of flesh" (20-21: 6-7). No less than the separation of literature from philosophy for Habermas, clarifying the distinction between poetry and prose is of utmost importance to Sartre. Likened to a textual "cancer," the "deplorable" commingling of poetry and prose that modern literature has become—creating this so-called "poetic prose"—requires, he insists, urgent attention (341:210). If, as Sartre claims, words are "sick," then they must be healed. According to Sartre "It is up to us to cure them" (341:210). What Habermas' language intimates about the "impurity" of genre blending—inevitably evoking an appeal for purity of other kinds—Sartre's lays on the table: "If we want to restore their *virtue* to words, we must carry out [...] an analytical *cleansing* which rids them of their adventitious meanings" (342:211).[40] Beckett might beg to differ.

Not surprisingly, the slippage that occurs within the definition of genre and between seemingly distinct individual genres also manifests itself in the formal or linguistic aspects of Beckett's œuvre. Once again, some thing—here, language—both invites and resists classification. Once again, the reader, knowingly or not, becomes complicit in the act of revealing that any apparent integrity of classifications only masks an inherent weakness within. This has led some critics to wax poetic about his prose, and prosaic about his poetry. Some even observe that it is not that Beckett writes neither poetry nor prose, but rather that he writes both at the same time and in the same text.

In a 1960's review for *Le Figaro*, Claude Mauriac exclaimed enthusiastically, "Samuel Beckett est aussi un poète." In itself this statement may seem less than noteworthy. It is, after all, commonly known that Beckett did write poetry. This was one of his principal endeavors early on in his writing career. However, despite what is implied in the title, this review was not an analysis of any of Beckett's "poetry," but rather a critique of his play *La dernière bande*. Although one might argue that this text contains some "poetic passages," in terms of its layout on the page[41] this text belongs quite clearly to what one would traditionally refer to as theatre.

What makes Mauriac's claim compelling is that it testifies to a general propensity on the part of Beckett scholars to read his prose as if it were poetry, concentrating primarily on its formal elements, and his poetry as if it were prose, focusing almost exclusively on its intended "meaning." This may seem to be an even exchange, but there is a difference between the two situations, and it is a difference of supposed quality. His prose is praised for its "poetic" elements, as one can glean from Mauriac's review, whereas his formal "poetry" is criticized for its resemblance to prose. A. Alvarez, in "Poet waiting for Pegasus," exemplifies this stance by applauding Beckett's prose for having the "subtle artistic tautness one usually associates with poetry."[42] Yet, he denounces Beckett's verse—which he refers to as "a handful of lyrics apart"—for "fritter[ring] itself away in postures and imitation" (21).

This appears to be the general consensus among many readers of Beckett's poetry; that thematically and linguistically it falls short of being "poetic." In his work, *Damned to Fame: the Life of Samuel Beckett*,[43] James Knowlson intimates that Beckett himself may have been in agreement with such a critique. This would appear to explain his desire to change the title of his first book of poetry from *Poems* to *Echo's Bones, and Other Precipitates*[44] in order to render it, as Beckett has said, simply "more modest."[45]

But while his poetry has not inspired much in the way of critical interest,[46] this has not prevented Beckett scholars from seeking, and finding, what they consider to be "poetry" elsewhere in his work. As Johannes Hedberg phrases it, although the "poetic" elements of his poetry may indeed be scarce, "there is no scarcity of poetic passages in Beckett's prose." Lawrence Harvey also refers to Beckett's prose as "densely poetic," in the sense that "narration and dialogue expand at every moment beyond storytelling and communication" to produce what he calls "the distance of aesthetic contemplation [...]."[47] This is particularly curious considering Beckett's well-known desire to distance himself from English precisely because, as he said to Richard N. Coe, "you couldn't help writing poetry in it." Try as he might to resist writing poetry though, his readers still isolate traces of the poetic in his work, even in writings that would, by most standards, be called prose. Perhaps it is because the two types of language are far more implicated in each other than one ordinarily thinks. Echo, in his poem *Echo's Bones*, incarnates in her person this species of linguistic corruption. Spurned by Narcissus, Echo shrivels up until nothing is left of her save her bones (which eventually dry up) and her voice. But while her voice is her own in that it is activated by her, it is a voice that is forever fated to be contaminated by other voices. It is destined to carry within itself the trace of what it once was but is no longer. This may well be Beckett's fate, to have a voice that always bears within itself the memory of another. Indeed, as Hedberg contends, it seems that Samuel Beckett "the poet" is "always there, even when," perhaps *especially* when, "he is at his prosiest."[47]

"Poetic Prose": Reading *Ill Seen, Ill Said* with Marjorie Perloff

Marjorie Perloff's exceptional *Between Verse and Prose: Beckett and the New Poetry*,[48] examines Beckett's language in the short prose text, *Ill Seen Ill Said*. The impetus for her exploration was the publication of *Ill Seen Ill Said* in *The New Yorker* magazine. Particularly problematic for Perloff was the fact that *The New Yorker*–by publishing it in paragraph form accompanied by a cartoon, and by designating it as "prose" in the table of contents–chose to treat this text as if it were a conventional prose piece. All the more perplexing, however, was the fact that on the same page the editors printed Harold Brodkey's *Sea Noise*, which, according to Perloff, is far more conventionally "prosaic" in terms of its language than *Ill Seen Ill Said*, as if it were "poetry."

While Perloff considers the respective classifications of both pieces to be equally erroneous, she is ultimately more concerned with the state of Beckett's text, arguing that it is far closer to poetry than prose. Indeed, she informs the reader that if pushed to choose between verse and prose as a means for defining the language of *Ill Seen Ill Said*, she would favor, at least temporarily, verse. Although she seems to contradict this statement by initially referring to this work in prosaic terms (by speaking of the text's opening "paragraph"), Perloff later describes the opening of *Ill Seen Ill Said* as only a critic accustomed to reading and analyzing poetry could or, for that matter, would do:

"Six dimeter lines, five of them rhyming, followed by three trimeters made up primarily of anapests, the whole bound together by the alliteration of voiced and voiceless spirants [...]." (416)

Later on the same page, she goes on to plot out the rime scheme ("x /x /xx /x /") and lineates the text on the page as if it were a poem. Fully aware of this rough gesture on her part, Perloff does not hesitate to point out her role in the revision and to concede that this text is not *really* poetry either. In order for a text such as *Ill Seen, Ill Said* to conform to the definition of any single mode, it must in fact be altered, for Beckett did not, after all, chose to lineate it. Moreover, the discourse in *Ill Seen Ill Said* hardly conforms to either poetry or prose as it is comprised of a combination of both prosaic and poetic units that often directly follow one another. The result is an amorphous language where poetic expressions such as "Rid with face and hands against the pane she stands and marvels long" are immediately followed by phrases such as "The two zones form a roughly circular whole." Thus, antithetical to one another as the traditional conceptualizations of prose and verse may appear to be, in Beckett's work "free prose [...] is very close to free verse" (425).

There is scant little about the language of this text that can be explained by relying on any one label. While Beckett's narrator makes the occasional nod to direct, clearly prosaic, language, the voice rapidly mutates into "mock Elizabethan pentameter [...], pun and anachronism [...]" (421). The tone, once reminiscent of the language of fairy tales and nursery rhymes, quickly shifts to that of the riddle, then to everyday prose, and so on. What we have then are "bits of flotsam" held together by "the main binding device" of repetition, with sound carrying "the burden of meaning" (421). The result? A "querulous, compulsive, sometimes maddening babble" (422),—one that is *ill said*, and consequently *ill read*—that resembles little we have ever *seen* before.

What the reader must reckon with is something altogether different from both poetry and prose, which, as Perloff notes by way of Northrop Frye, are more akin to "speech on its best behavior," since both types of discourse represent the "expression or imitation of directed thinking or controlled description" and offer the reader a supposed completed work.[50] Instead, what one finds in this text is a type of language that is closer to what Perloff, again citing Frye, refers to as "associative rhythm."[51] More repetitive than prose and (seemingly) less formalized than poetry, associative rhythm imitates everyday speech in which one can witness the coming into being of ideas (Frye 21-22). It represents the text's attempt to come to meaning: an attempt that is ongoing and never manages to achieve fruition. However, as Perloff suggests, while *Ill Seen Ill Said* is certainly neither prose nor verse, it is far too formalized to be considered everyday speech, for "no one surely talks this way." For that matter, Perloff adds, as if anticipating the reader's response, "no one writes this way either" (424).

Ill Seen Ill Said is not the only text of Beckett's that defies our traditional expectations of what we may conceive of as prose. The same can be said of *Company*. Like *Ill Seen Ill Said*, the reader who approaches this text with the idea that prose is, as Northrop Frye defines it, "the arrangement of words [...] dominated by the syntactical relations of subject and predicate" (Frye 21), will be greatly challenged by passages such as the following:

> If the voice is not speaking to him it must be speaking to another. So with what rea-
> son remains he reasons. To another of that other. Or of him. Or of another still. To
> another of that other or of him or of another still. To one on his back in the dark in
> any case. Of one on his back in the dark whether the same or another. So with what
> reason remains he reasons and reasons ill. For were the voice speaking not to him but
> to another then it must be of that other it is speaking and not of him or of another
> still.[52]

Comprised of short, jerky, disjunctive, rhyming, and repetitive phrases, this can hardly be called prose at all. If we accept Frye's definition of "poetry" as "the arrangement of words dominated by some form of regular recurrence, whether meter, accent, vowel quality, rhyme, alliteration, parallelism or any combination of these," the passage I have quoted may seem to be more closely related to poetry than prose.[53] But is it really any more exemplary of poetry than it is of prose? The first line of the passage—"If the voice is not speaking to him, it must be speaking to another"—conforms to the definition of a prose sentence. Moreover, the text is not lineated in the form of a poem, but is instead laid out in paragraph form. Since the language of this work refuses to designate itself as either strictly prose or poetry, the reader cannot help but ask himself, like Marjorie Perloff, "just what kind of *English* is this?" (421).

Whatever one chooses to call either *Company* or *Ill Seen Ill Said*, most would probably agree that Beckett does not disguise but rather displays the inconsistency of the tone and language. This suggests that it is just such "questions of prosody" (423)—indeed, it is the *questionable* nature of prosody— that is the very "subject" of these texts. Perhaps then it would be most appropriate not to attempt to define the language of either work, since both texts defy the gesture of classifying. Perloff would seem to agree when she asks herself if, in the end, it really matters what we call Beckett's texts and those like them, offering instead that we should simply be aware that we are now "living in a world of new literary organisms" (431). She mentions this, however, only after having already committed fifteen pages of text to trying to do just that: to finding *the* right term for the kind of language Beckett employs. Although she characterizes Cohn's term of "lyrics of fiction" as an "apt" term for describing Beckett's work, she chooses nonetheless to apply another—more apt?—label (419). Perhaps in an attempt to link Beckett's language with Frye's conceptualization of associative rhythm, Perloff refers to it as consisting of "associative monologues." Finally, Perloff suggests that, because we cannot deny the existence of new literary species such as what Beckett's late work represents, we might need to reconsider how we categorize writing within the literary canon. One might wonder, however, if it is instead this gesture of classification that ought to be reconsidered. Since such new textual species are hybrids, comprised of several different discourses at once, pointing to something in between poetry and prose, speech and writing—since they resist the most basic assumptions of genre making—perhaps it would be more "apt" to relinquish the idea of genre making altogether. For if we do not, we again are liable to betray the idiom of Beckett's language by assuming that what may be ultimately the unnamable can indeed be clearly named.

"What a Broadening of the Mind":[54] Philosophical Interpretations of Beckett

Arguably, the principal trend in Beckett criticism involves aligning his work with philosophical thought. He has been identified with philosophers from Plato to Spinoza, to Berkeley, Schopenhauer, Badiou, Hegel, Habermas, Heidegger, Merleau-Ponty, Sartre, Levinas, and Foucault, and with philosophical approaches from the pre-Socratic philosophy of Heraclitus and Sophocles, to the modern aesthetic theory of Immanuel Kant and Theodor Adorno.[55] Regardless of the particular philosopher or philosophical approach, each time the association with Beckett is with equal zeal and assurance on the part of the reader.

Until relatively recently, the dominant direction in philosophical readings of Beckett's work has been to link it with phenomenological or existentialist thought. While there are many interpretations that concentrate on other works by Beckett,[56] those focusing on *Waiting for Godot* provide the most fervent examples of existentialist enthusiasm. The basic assumption is that *Waiting for Godot* is a play about the "meaninglessness of existence" that can, and perhaps ought to be, intensely meaningful for the reader or spectator. For critics like Harold Clurman, Ronald Barker, Lawrence E. Harvey, and Colin Duckworth, this play exemplifies the inevitable alienation of existence; in the words of Ronald Barker, the "hopelessness of man's dilemma."[57] For Clurman, *Godot* shows us how it is our destiny to "pass the time [...] waiting for a meaning that will save us—save us from the pain, ugliness, emptiness of existence."[58] Despite the pessimism that the "complete disenchantment at the heart of the play" seems to imply, Clurman still identifies, like many others, a humanistic leaning in the refusal on the part of the author to "honor this disenchantment by a serious demeanor." Evidently in agreement, Colin Duckworth waxes poetic, observing that in *Godot* "the vision is dark, but laughter lends wings."[59] Though the character Godot never arrives, the humor of Beckett's play signals to its readers or viewers that it is nonetheless possible to tolerate human alienation. Accept though we must the meaninglessness of life, we can still retain something of an appetite for living—one which Clurman characterizes as "divine"—through the cathartic possibilities offered by laughter and through an increased consciousness of the "trivia of the day-to-day."

Many criticisms have been leveled against these existentialist-humanist readings.[60] One that is particularly persuasive is Thomas Trezise's *Into the Breach*. Trezise argues that the attempt to root Beckett in humanism by claiming that his texts demonstrate the "redemptive value of laughter," represents nothing less than a willful misreading of the tone and scope of Beckett's work:

> There may well be no writer of this century who has more radically questioned the foundations of humanism than Samuel Beckett and no writer who has spawned a corporation of critics more determined to ignore the consequences of that questioning. This determination frequently surfaces as the professed belief that, in the end, Beckett restores human dignity through his humor—as though the tenor of that humor were self-evident and not in the least subversive.[61]

Trezise's chief objection to humanist readers centers on the way they seem to read but not see. Similar to the situation of one of *The Unnamable*'s narrators, who claims he sees only what is immediately in front of him or close beside him, these readers see only what is directly before their eyes. Since the critical vision is so focused, the total message risks being misconstrued. Or as the narrator of the *Unnamable* adds, "what I best see I see ill."[62] So, like the narrator of *Company*, "with what reason remains he reasons and reasons ill."[63] In other words, the insight such restricted readings provide depends entirely upon a "conspicuous blindness" to all that is in Beckett's œuvre that remains out of the line of vision, here all that demonstrates the very failure of phenomenology.[64]

While one could argue that there could be no critical insight that is not already tainted by critical blindness, this deficiency reaches epidemic proportions when scholars attempt to impose a phenomenological grid on Beckett's texts. Simon Critchley goes one step further by suggesting that it is not just phenomenological readings of Beckett's work—what he calls "the stalest of all the stale philosophical clichés"[65]—but rather all philosophical interpretations that fail in their attempts to account for Beckett's idiom.

"No Happiness": The Failure of Philosophical Interpretations of Beckett

Simon Critchley's "Know Happiness—on Beckett," examines a wide range of philosophical interpretations of Beckett's work. In the end, Critchley comes to the conclusion that whatever the particular interpretation—be it one inspired by "'post-Cartesian modernity,' "sub-Heideggerian interpretation," or "sub-Pascalian absurdist interpretation"—it inevitably fails to explicate Beckett's work.[66] Whatever the approach, it cannot help, as Critchley points out, but "lag behind the text that it is trying to interpret and overshoot it, saying too much and saying too little, saying too little by saying too much" (144). Ultimately, such interpretations end by ascending into the "stratosphere of metalanguage" (101).

To support his argument that philosophical claims in general fail to account for Beckett's idiom, Critchley looks to the words of a philosopher: Jacques Derrida. In particular, he examines Derrida's interview with Derek Attridge (which I referred to in chapter one) where Derrida suggests that the difficulty of interpreting Beckett's work by way of philosophy stems from the impossibility of doing so without in some way betraying the text's specificity, or its particular "signature." Try as one might to identify Beckett's texts with any philosophical tendency, one must ultimately accept the inevitable letdown. There will always be something at the very heart of his work—the very thing that constitutes it as his work—that eludes interpretation.

Of course, Derrida never implies that having a signature that escapes interpretation is unique to Beckett's œuvre. In both *Glas* and "Différance," Derrida has observed that all literary texts have something that eludes the critic. However sound the interpretative grid may seem to be, there is always something that slips through its grasp. The critical apparatus may well isolate something significant about a text, but in order to do so it must inevitably relinquish its hold on what remains. In the words of Derrida, "La matrice transcendantale laisse toujours retomber le reste du texte."[67]

The reason why these interpretations are destined fail is that they cannot hope to account for the inherent doubling and subsequent deceptiveness of language that is at the heart of every text. Every individual text is therefore actually two texts: the first written in the service of "meaning," "reason," and "truth," and the second written in such a way so as to defy these notions. The miscalculation of traditional philosophical analyses—and particularly those relating to humanism, phenomenology, and existentialism—lies in their assumption that they can interpret the first text exclusively and ignore the existence of the second, which is always visible through the "fissures" of the first. The error is in thinking that one can close ones eyes to all that resists interpretation. Or as Beckett expresses it, "the danger is in the neatness of identifications."[68]

"Pigsty Latin and Perjury": Beckett's Perversion of Philosophy

Critchley stresses that it is not simply that Beckett's texts resist interpretation. The uniqueness of Beckett is that he stages this duplicity, pushing the critic, whether philosophical or literary, towards analyses that he cannot hope to sustain. It is not just that these texts make subtle allusions to philosophy and to specific philosophers. They offer themselves generously to the possibility of philosophical interpretations, only to later flaunt their refusal to accept such identifications. *Malone Dies* is a prime example of a text where the "red herrings"[69] are plentiful indeed. In the odd "One day I took counsel of an Israelite on the subject of conation,"[70] Critchley discovers Spinoza with a twist. In the Latin "*De nobis ipsis silemus,*" he spots a nod to Kant, via Bacon.[71] Again here, the tone is hardly that of the original. For Malone, the phrase is just another bit of "pigsty Latin," a little glitter to "sprinkle [...] through the perjury."[72] There is also a thinly veiled reference to Leibniz. The narrator relates the story of a man named Jackson who tries to teach his caged parrot to quote the celebrated philosopher. Initially, the experiment is a success, as the bird manages to repeat the words "Nihil in intellectu." Yet if the reader reads the inclusion of Leibniz's words in this scene as an indication of Beckett's admiration for the philosopher—or *philosophers*, since Leibniz actually borrowed it from the Scholastics[73]—he can only do so for so long. For, according to Malone, "the celebrated restriction was too much for it and all you heard was a series of squawks."[74] The reference eventually lapses into a mockery, just as the parrot's erudite Latin ultimately regresses into so much "squawkery."

Most of these allusions thus turn out to be illusions. That we are incapable of seeing this, at least at the start, and consequently end up "build[ing] up hypotheses that collapse on top of one another," only reveals our very humanity. "It's human," insists one of *The Unnamable*'s narrators, "a lobster couldn't do it" (342). Fortunately, the short interval of time between the offering of the philosophical gift and the text's reclaiming of it makes it hard even for the most resistant readers to ignore the hoax. More difficult to ignore perhaps are what seem to be drawn-out, intentional illustrations of philosophical approaches or personages, like those that recall existentialism outlined above. Another oft-cited example is Beckett's repeated references to Descartes' *Discours de la méthode*. The situation of a man sitting alone in his room thinking, and often writing, is the point of departure for Beckett's poem *Whoroscope*, and for both *Molloy* and *Malone Dies*. Descartes' method of employing systematic doubt in order to ground the self is also borrowed by many of Beckett's narrators. But despite the countless remarks made about the philosopher and his work, it would be a misreading to assume, and thus misleading to say, that Beckett is aligning himself in a definitive way with Descartes. On the contrary, each allusion to Descartes, much like those to other philosophers, seems to be in the service of *rewriting* his thought, or revising it; if not turning it on its head, then at least reviewing it, or viewing it again, as Beckett's narrators are in the habit of saying, "from a certain angle." Far from ever establishing any clear and distinct truths, Beckett's narrators willfully multiply uncertainties. As Molloy freely admits, "perhaps I'm inventing [...] perhaps embellishing [...] perhaps remembering."[75] Far from grounding the cogito, here the Cartesian method of reasoning only leaves the subject on shakier ground. As evidenced in *The Unnamable*, the contemplation of the self begets not one stable subject, but a multitude of characters, including but not limited to Belacqua, Murphy, Watt, Mercier, Camier, Moran, Molloy, Malone, Macmann, Mahood, Worm, and others comprising the general "troop of lunatics" (308), demonstrating how the self is irreparably and always already from the start divided. Goodbye "cogito ergo sum." Hello "fallor, ergo sum!"[76] Here's to an aesthetic of failure, where "to be an artist is to fail, as no other dare [...]."[77]

For Critchley, the only two philosophers whose readings could hope to accurately describe Beckett's texts are Derrida and Adorno. However, he rightly accepts neither uncritically. While Critchley applauds Derrida's designation of Beckett's work as having an illusive "signature" that is bound to forever escape interpretation, he suggests that Derrida himself gives up too quickly on the idea of attempting nonetheless to interpret these texts.

Despite the difficulty of the task, Adorno confronts the unreadability of Beckett's work—and the consequential indescribability—in the fittingly entitled "Trying to Understand Endgame." Employing language that spirals back on itself and explodes in fits and starts, Adorno both states and illustrates the impossibility of ever clearly defining *Endgame*. For in this play, there is no meaning except "meaning's absence." Its "meaning structure" is nonexistent; unless it is that "it has none." Here, philosophy degrades into "culture-trash." Comprehending this play then "can mean nothing other than understanding its incomprehensibility."[78] Nonetheless, Adorno, as others before and after him, continues his attempt to do so, resulting in an analysis that Critchley claims ultimately "tells us more about Adorno's preoccupations than those of Beckett's texts."[79]

"Enlighten Me": The Nature of Reading and Interpretation

Critchley's, Perloff's, and Dearlove's critiques all dovetail around this issue of reader involvement in interpretation. Whether the interpretation is inspired by literary studies, linguistics, or philosophy, it seems that analyses of Beckett's work uncover little more—and yet nothing less—than the very nature of how one reads. All acts of reading are, as Deleuze says of language, "over-burdened" with personal signification before the act ever begins. The history and experiences of the reader predispose him to privilege certain terms and themes at the expense of others, making all interpretations necessarily invested in advance by the specificity of the particular reading subject. Yet, as Nelly Furman points out, that is not to say that reading is an exercise in "unbridled subjectivity," dependent on the whims of the reader alone.[80] Rather, reading is an activity involving a "dynamic interchange" between the author, the reader, and the text. In this relationship, the roles of each can become fused together and thus confused. When writing, the author may have in mind a reader who will read his work, and therefore would act as a reader himself in creating his text. By favoring certain ideas over others, and thus rewriting his own version of the text, the reader shares with the author the act of creation. Finally, since the reader's reading also invariably tells us something about the reader, the reader himself becomes a sort of "text" to be studied in much the same way as a text. Reading, Furman contends, "is no longer just an attempt to decipher; it is simultaneously a gesture of self-inscription."[81] Undoubtedly, this is the condition of all readings. But the situation is exacerbated to hyperbolic proportions when dealing with texts that so readily offer themselves up for interpretation only to immediately recoil back. With Beckett, the reader finds himself tricked into producing interpretations that tell us far less about his work than the actual workings of interpretation.

The French *Robert*[82] defines the verb "to interpret" as the act of "explaining, of making clear (that which is obscure in a text)" ("expliquer, rendre clair (ce qui est obscur dans un texte)"). To interpret is to render something "obscure" which appears to resist analysis more comprehensible, more "clear." In the case of philosophically inspired interpretations, one might even say that to interpret is to "enlighten," which recalls the philosophical "age of enlightenment" of the eighteenth century. This first definition of the word in the *Robert* thus highlights the active role of the subject in interpretation. This vital role is further reinforced in another definition of the term, where the interpreting subject, in order to "interpret," must "give" ("donner") something to the object under investigation. Interestingly, what is "given" or brought to the text is *sens* ("donner un sens à (qqch)"): sense or signification. According to the *Robert* definition then, meaning does not originate within the text itself. Like genre, it seems that meaning comes from without.

Clearly, the definitions from one dictionary, regardless of how good a dictionary it may be, could not possibly account for the long history of hermeneutics in philosophy. The philosophical discussion about the nature of meaning is extensive and thus not something that could be explored in the space of a few paragraphs. However, the *Robert* definitions are relevant in the context of this study. After reading these definitions, it makes *sense* that the philosophically inspired scholarship on Beckett is vast and the existentialist-humanist readings in particular so prominent. After all, what existential metaphysician could resist what one critic calls "this apparent mass of nonsense."[83] Beckett's work simply begs for enlightenment. At least that is how it must seem to those readers who believe that when one reads one will come away from a text with a "message." In this vein, it is possible to see how Beckett's work may not be born of a "deeply felt existential anguish,"[84] as Colin Duckworth claims, but rather that his work *gives birth* to an existential crisis within certain critics already predisposed to search for meaning: one that is then revealed through their interpretations, or even their need to interpret. When Clurman claims that *Godot* illustrates our fate as one in which we are obliged to "pass the time waiting for a meaning that will save us," he is describing a situation that is analogous to that of critics before Beckett's work. They wait for meaning to arrive from on high—from *Godot?*—that will save them from the "pain, ugliness," and apparent "emptiness" of the text.[85] And when a text like *Waiting for Godot* does not offer any relief, any profound message or higher meaning to clarify the obscurities, the critic himself feels compelled to provide one. In the interpretations of Beckett's work, what might have appeared to be a very *human* need to "find" meaning in a text reveals itself to be a very *humanist* need to "impose" meaning on the text.

"Come and Go, Come and Go": Weaving the Beckettian Tapestry

Far from adjusting to any one model of story telling, to the type of language and images that would be appropriate for certain types of texts—whatever that may be—Beckett's works thus evoke the model just enough to act as a nagging memory of what it could have been, and perhaps should have been, but ultimately is not. Dearlove likens this process of evoking genre in order to ultimately thwart it to weaving then unweaving. She relates Beckett's writing to Homer's Penelope, who dissuaded the pretensions of many a suitor while Odysseus was away by vowing to marry as soon as she had finished weaving a tapestry; a task that she succeeded in never completing. During the day hours, she would weave in the presence of the hopefuls so they would believe that she was making every effort to finish her work. But at night, out of their view, she unwove everything she had accomplished earlier. For many readers of Beckett's work, this image is fitting. They may come to the text with certain, perhaps traditional, expectations of genre—expectations that seem, at least temporarily, to be sustained—only to have them spoiled. Is a play still a play when it features no speech, such as in *Act Without Words*? Is a novel still a novel when its narrators are admittedly unreliable and when there is no "story" to speak of, as in *The Unnamable?* Can a text be called "prosaic" if its language is poetic? Is a work still a novel of ideas if all of the references to philosophers and to their words turn out to be perverse re-visions?

Yet—and Dearlove notes this as well—readers who are more familiar with Beckett's work approach his texts with far different expectations. They might anticipate not the reinforcement of traditional notions of genre, but instead the dismantling of such notions. This makes their situation manifestly different than that of other Beckett readers. For if genre is defined as the expectations one brings to the text, and if one's expectations are such that one expects to find transgressions, then Beckett's texts will actually conform to those expectations. Consequently, the definition of genre as something that one brings to a text that would enable one to classify it would also be confirmed. These two different types of readers thus experience two radically different relationships to genre. Whereas Beckett's less familiar readers— because they do not find what they would expect to find—witness an undermining of the notion of genre when reading his work, scholars who are familiar with his work in particular and with modern literature in general, who read these same texts expecting to find something other than conventional genre, participate in sustaining the idea of genre by coming to these texts in a quest for the same. In this topsy-turvy game where genre is, depending on the reader, confirmed and denied, reading becomes, as Barthes has observed about literature in general, at once "an answer that questions and a question which answers."[86]

Despite the title of the article, Dearlove's analogy of the evocation and consequential revocation of genre is largely undeveloped and ends definitively with the unweaving. This is also where Dearlove may well have done an injustice to her own metaphor by not going far enough. For it is not simply that Penelope unweaves, once and for all, what she once wove. In order to ward off the threat of an unwanted marriage, she must weave again. Then unweave, and so on until Odysseus' return. Likewise, Beckett's works evoke genre in order to distort it, so that they may again evoke and then destroy again and so on and so forth indefinitely. The weaving brings on the unweaving, which then, if one hopes to continue the farce, demands reweaving, only to then again undo the threads.

In "Où maintenant, qui maintenant," Maurice Blanchot characterizes this type of back and forth movement—this "movement heurté," this "piétinement de ce qui n'avance jamais"[87]—as the dance particular to all writing, and I would add, all reading, subjects. Like the reading subject, who shuffles between various meanings of words and between divergent interpretations which are constantly folding over into one another, Blanchot's dispossessed writer is destined to forever float between the origin and the end of writing. The situation of Beckett's Malone exemplifies this form of writerly purgatory, for while Malone the character infinitely approaches a physical end to which all beings must go, Malone the writer is condemned to creep incessantly towards an origin marked by self-dispossession, from which all writing comes. When Malone asks himself questions such as "How goes it?," it is therefore only natural that he would in turn respond, "Thanks, it's coming."[88]

As innocuous as this threading and unthreading game seems to be, the stakes are quite high. Much like the tale of *1001 Nights*, where Scheherazade must regale King Shahriyar with continual stories in order to distract him from killing more virgins, Beckett's work is representative of a literature of survival. The *va* and *vient* that is so prevalent—the progression, the "on" that is always countered by the prevention of such forward movement (the period following the "on.")—is what is responsible for the regeneration of language in his texts. One could even say that it is this particular a-rhythmic heartbeat that keeps his work alive, for in order for the text to avoid expiring it cannot simply progress or regress, weave or unweave. In either case the text will eventually reach a limit: a beginning or an end. As Malone repeatedly insists, "In order not to die, you must come and go. Come and Go" (232).

Reading on the Edge of Literature

Staging as they do the very undecidability at the heart of language, Beckett's texts oblige his readers to experience the act of reading and interpreting in an especially intimate way. By enticing the reader to focus on certain aspects of the text—references outside of the text to well-known theories or inside of the text to its very form or language—and by feigning to conform to expectations only to teasingly disappoint them, his work forces the reader to reveal his own preoccupations when taking a text in hand. In so doing, the reading subject becomes a textual object which unveils the desire, whether conscious or not, to uphold certain, rather fragile, conventions—literary, philosophical, or otherwise—which themselves are but the reflection of how we have been conditioned to think in terms of categories, to divide up our world, and if not to find, then to produce meaning. Faced with an œuvre that is in constant motion—confronted by, as Derrida says of Blanchot's writing, "this ellipse unremittingly repelling itself within its own expansion"—the reader's desire must remain unfulfilled. Pressed though we may be to flatten out the "unfolding or coiling up of this text," its "rounds" are made in such a way as to "recoil from any kind of flattening."[89]

Although Beckett's texts urge the reader to acknowledge the "danger" to be found within the "neatness of identification," they do not, nonetheless, exhort the reader to shrink away from the task of enlightenment. Indeed, as Critchley observes, Beckett's work "*demands* a determinate and [...] laborious work of interpretation [...]."[90] In the writings of critics who take the impasse presented by Beckett's work as a sign that there is, as Attridge suggests to Derrida in his interview, "not much left to do,"[91] Critchley sees little more than capitulation. Countering such early forfeiture, he argues that Beckett's works in fact inspire "an *endless* amount of things to say."[92] This may well offer some insight as to the reason why interpretations of his work proliferate despite the refusal of Beckett's texts to justify them; why the industry that Beckett scholarship has become continues to grow even though no interpretation truly ever hits the mark. Perhaps such readings continue to be performed because with Beckett it is always a question, as expressed by Shimon Levy, of "expressing the inexpressible."[93] Or, as Critchley reinterprets it, it is a question of "conceptualizing and communicating that which resists conceptualization and refuses communication." Unreadable, it is inarticulatable. And yet, this is what has leads many theorists to attempt to do so. Incidentally, this is also the condition of possibility for the continual production of "stories" in the trilogy. Beckett's protagonists are able to go on recounting their tales not *despite* the absence of coherent meaning or closure, but *because* of that absence. As one of the narrators of *The Unnamable* argues, it is precisely the search for the "means to put an end to things"—the quest for answers, meaning, and conclusions—that is, in the end, what "enables the discourse to continue."[94] For Critchley, this is the operating mechanism of the trilogy. We might also consider it as that of the critical reader. In order to "convey this radical unrepresentability," both the trilogy and its reader must represent what appears to be unrepresentable. With an end that is unreachable, the narrators' stories and the readers' interpretations simply "go on." To quote one of the narrators of *The Unnamable*, "the essential thing is never to arrive anywhere, never to be anywhere."[95] In the end, what we learn from reading Beckett is that, because we cannot hope to fully capture his idiom, our analyses will never be anything more than meditations, as Derrida has said, "on the line." And yet, since the nature of his work—and, if we agree with Derrida, the nature of literature in general—is to be *on the line*, we will never come any closer to understanding his idiom than precisely when in the precarious position of "kneeling on the edge of literature."

Chapter 3

‡ "This Text Which Is Not One": The Multiplicity of Writing and the Singularity of Translation

In The Beginning: The End of the Book

What is a book? What is a text? What does it mean to "translate" what one wrote? While these questions may seem too evident to ask—and yet perhaps too complex to answer hastily—they are crucial inquiries to make, and particularly in the context of this study. On one hand, these types of queries are important because Beckett's work—with its emphasis on the telling of "stories," the "blackening of pages," and the foreignness of language—endlessly solicits such interrogations. Clearly though, the significance of these questions extends beyond the limits of Beckett's œuvre. Gilles Deleuze contends that inquiries of this sort—that ask what makes a book a book or a text a text—are essentially nothing but the question, "What is writing?" And while he admits that such questions "give rise to the greatest monotonies," and thus to "the greatest weaknesses," Deleuze maintains that they are vital to ask, for as commonplace as they appear to be, they are nonetheless capable of unearthing "the most profound repetitions."[1]

Derrida's *Of Grammatology* also dedicates itself to questions about the nature of writing. As such, it turns out to also be an investigation of the "profound repetitions" of which Deleuze writes. Derrida's primary concern is to distinguish between the traditional mode of written representation and what he perceives as a new genus of textual activity. He differentiates between the notion of a "book" and that of a "text." As the vehicle for conveying classical thought and representation, the "book" is the incarnation of a "perfect totality."[2] It is complete, solid, authoritative and secure in its ability to truthfully represent the "reality" of the physical world.

This idea of the "book" as an autonomous totality derives from the assumption that there are closed, fixed, knowable, "true" structures and points of reference, a conjecture that itself stems from a belief in transcendental signifiers. According to this definition, there is perhaps no better example in Western civilization of the "book" than what is commonly referred to as "the good book." Besides its sobriquet, the Bible is also the "book" *par excellence* because it is devoted primarily to authenticating and celebrating "singularity," in particular, a single God. The opening verses of *Genesis* contain other such "singularities," which—it turns out—constitute the foundations for much of Western metaphysics. There is the establishment of a singular event ("In *the* beginning") that engenders singular acts of creation (of the universe and of mankind). Binary pairs are also brought together. Some twosomes, such as lightness and darkness, are created in order to bestow definition upon the amorphous shape of the world: "And the earth was without form, and void [...] and God divided the light from the darkness [...] and God saw that it was good."[3] Other duos, such as humans and animals, are created only to quickly become hierarchies: "Let us make man in our image [...] and let them have dominion over the fish of the sea, and over the fowl of the air, and over the cattle, [...] and over every creeping thing that creepeth upon the earth."[4] Given the evident similarities between Derrida's notional "book"—which he also refers to as "the first book" and "the mythic book"[5]—and the Bible, it is to be expected that Derrida should describe the task of the former as that of providing the "encyclopedic protection of logocentrism" ("la protection encyclopédique [...] du logocentrisme [...]") and, appropriately, "theology"[6] ("de la théologie"[7]). It appears that whenever we speak of a "book," something sacred is at stake.

Derrida observes that the "book" has been *the* model for written works in Western culture since the beginning of time; so much so that the idea of there being another model, or even an outside of this "book," had been, until the twentieth century, all but unthinkable. It only became possible to imagine another model, and thus to "think outside" of the margins of metaphysics, with the "end of the book," which is to say, with the beginning "*of grammatology*."[8] Setting up what seems to be a binary opposition of his own, Derrida defines the object of grammatology, the "text," as everything that the book is not. Unlike the "book," the "text" does not attempt to conceal the fits and starts involved in the writing process. Instead, it is the mark of the "text" to self-consciously fixate on the act of writing and in so doing to represent, with its "aphoristic energy," the "disruption" of classical writing.[9] In his interview with Henri Ronse, Derrida elaborates on this distinction between the "book" and the "text" by relating the two terms to his own work:

In what you call my books, what is first of all put in question is the unity of the book and the unity "book" considered as a perfect totality [...]. Under these titles ["my 'books'"] it is solely a question of a unique and differentiated textual "operation," if you will, whose unfinished movement assigns itself no absolute beginning, and which, although it is entirely consumed by the reading of other texts, in a certain fashion refers only to its own writing [...].[10]

With its cultivation of paradox, lack of fixed boundaries, nonlinear order and multiplicity, the "text's" primary intention is to arrest the act of reading. But despite the initial claim that the "book" is "profoundly alien to the sense of writing,"[11] these two textual signifiers are not as distinct from each other as they initially seem to be. On the contrary, they are implicated in one another, made of one another, thus forming something akin to a palimpsest. One need only rub the "book" (again)[12] in order to see the trace of what lies beneath. Below the surface, one finds the multiple revisions that the book has undergone, the lack of certainty behind each word, the instability of its margins, its aborted beginnings and abandoned ends—in short, the underside or other side of metaphysical thought and classical representation. What one discovers beneath the "book" is the "text": the evidence of "writing."

Writing on the Edge of Knowledge: The Beginning of the Text

Even the most casual reader of Beckett's work could not fail to notice the resemblance between the above description of the "text" and Beckett's fiction, in particular his so-called "trilogy."[13] In various ways, both unveil all that the "book" attempts to conceal, that is to say the illusions of traditional representation. Perhaps the most salient way in which the trilogy resembles the idea of the "text" is in its compulsive fixation on both the subject and object of writing. Writing is the point of departure for each of the texts. Both narrators of *Molloy* (the title character and Moran) present themselves as under an outside obligation to write. The first narrator's reason for writing is never made explicit, but the narrator of the second part of this text, Moran, tells us he is writing a "report," presumably about the results of his quest for Molloy. The narrator of *Malone Dies* writes, he tells us, as a means of occupying himself while waiting to die. Finally, the ambiguous narrators of *The Unnamable* write in the paradoxical attempt to be done with words.

Admittedly, there is nothing unusual about a narrator who presents himself as a writer. This is so often the situation of narrators that it has become something of a novelistic cliché since its conception; one that Ian Watt suggests dates back to Descartes' *Discours de la méthode*.[14] But the way in which Beckett's narrators are presented as writers, and how they present the act of writing, reveals just how little they conform to the Cartesian model.

One way that Beckett's narrators undermine the classical model of the narrator/writer is by exploiting their distinctive lack of knowledge. The assumption is that one comes to writing having prepared something to say and that one knows this "something" with some certainty. Yet, Beckett's narrators know little of anything at all. Molloy, for example, knows he is in his mother's room, but cannot remember how he got there. He cannot remember his mother's name, her age, or even whether she was still alive when he arrived. Studded with the words "apparently" and "perhaps," this narrator's first utterances are anything but confident of their own authenticity. His decision and ability to write is consequently marred by this uncertainty. He writes but he cannot seem to remember why. At one point he claims to have forgotten how. He cannot recall how to spell, and he has even, on his own admission, forgotten many words. The pages, he informs us, are covered with signs he no longer understands. "The truth is," he admits all too readily, "I don't know much"[15] ("Je ne sais pas grand' chose, franchement"[16]).

This is only the first page of the text. One would imagine that the narrator's knowledge would increase as the text unfolds. Descartes' narrator in *Discours de la méthode* is also less knowledgeable at the beginning of the text than he is at the end. In fact, Descartes' argument depends upon the cultivation of doubt from the very start. But while the first narrator of *Molloy* might seem to be emulating Descartes' classical model—as with regards to the attempt to stabilize the subject discussed in chapter two—nothing could be further from the truth. True, *Molloy*'s narrator, like Descartes', begins with little knowledge, but unlike the latter he never acquires any more. In this lack of knowledge, he even takes a certain amount of pride:

> For to know nothing, not to want to know anything likewise, but to be beyond knowing anything, to know you are beyond knowing anything, that is when peace enters in [...].[17]

What's more, he finishes his journey with as little knowledge as he had at the beginning. But this we know immediately, for the beginning of his narration takes place *after* his journey has ended. His ignorant beginnings were thus always already his ignorant ends.

Although this lack of knowledge is most concentrated in the opening pages of *Molloy*, it is highlighted in many passages of each book of the trilogy. Like Molloy, Malone of *Malone Dies* does not know, for example, how he got where he is, but surmises, also like Molloy, that it was "perhaps" by way of an ambulance (183). The narrators of *The Unnamable* are unsure of almost everything, including who or what they themselves are.

In *Difference and Repetition*,[18] Deleuze argues that this uncertainty is the "true" condition of the writer in general—even of writers who devote themselves to the creation of "books." "How else can one write," he asks in the preface to this text, "but of those things which one doesn't know, or knows badly?"[19] Like Derrida, who insists that we can only read and interpret what we read by positioning ourselves at the very "edge of literature,"[20] Deleuze suggests that we can only write at the frontiers of our knowledge, "at the border which separates our knowledge from our ignorance and *transforms the one into the other*."[21] The sense of authority conveyed by the traditional narrator/writer is thus an illusion. For, "to satisfy ignorance is to put off writing until tomorrow" which is "to make it impossible."[22]

In a dialogue between himself and Georges Duthuit, Beckett expressed the same general sentiment, but with some frustration. He described writing as an activity in which the writer has "nothing with which to express, nothing from which to express, no power to express, no desire to express, together with the obligation to express."[23] One of the narrators of *Molloy* later echoes this opinion, with, of course, some difference: "Not to want to say, not to know what you want to say, not to be able to say what you think you want to say, and never to stop saying or hardly ever, that is the thing to keep in mind."[24]

Yet, the fact that Beckett's "writers" do not conform to the classical model of the narrator/writer does not mean that they do not understand what that model is and at least attempt to live up to it. The narrators of each book of the trilogy are quite aware that they, as writers, have a need for "stories." This is something that they all express—some more ardently than others—on more than one occasion in their respective texts. Molloy, for example, articulates this need to tell stories about cows and the sky within the first ten pages of the opening of this text.[25] In what seems like overkill, Malone of *Malone Dies* considers telling three stories simultaneously about a single subject: a rock. Nevertheless, while each narrator articulates a need for stories and does set out to tell them, none manage to perform this task satisfactorily, either for themselves or for the (traditional) reader. In part, this is because the stories are as uncertain as the narrators relating them. Many of the tales have no clear and distinct point of departure, and thus begin, like *Molloy*, several times. The rare stories that appear to begin with some deliberation are later riddled with uncertainty. The details of Molloy's story about the wandering and nameless "A and C" ("A et B" in the French text) are unclear even to himself:

> The moment came when together they went down into the same trough and in this trough finally met. *To say they knew each other, no, nothing warrants it.* But *perhaps* at the sound of their steps, *or* warned by some obscure instinct, they raised their heads and observed each other, for a good fifteen paces...*But they knew each other perhaps. Now in any case they do, now I think they will know each other* [...] (9, my emphasis).

> Mais le moment vint où ensemble ils dévalèrent vers le même creux et c'est dans ce creux qu'il se rencontrèrent à la fin. *Dire qu'ils se connaissaient, non, rien ne permet de l'affirmer.* Mais au bruit *peut-être* de leurs pas, ou avertis par quelque obscur instinct, ils levèrent la tête et s'observèrent, pendant une bonne quinzaine de pas [...] *Mais ils se connaissaient peut-être. Quoi qu'il en soit, maintenant ils se connaissent* [...].[26]

The rare stories that seem at the outset to be relatively sound often turn out to have no definitive conclusions. A representative example of this is the account of Mahood's homecoming in *The Unnamable*. Mahood recounts what seems to be a very conventional, even "natural"[27] story about a return home. But unlike a more traditional description of this type of story, the one communicated by Mahood has not one but rather several outcomes. In the first resolution, Mahood returns home to find his family—"the whole ten or eleven" of what made up his "kith and kin"—exterminated by the very technical sounding "bacillus botulinus," otherwise known as "sausage-poisoning" (318, 322). Repulsed and saddened by what he finds, the "howls of [his] family [...] and the subsequent stench" (323), Mahood takes his leave without entering the building. In version two of the same story, the account detailing what the narrator insists "really occurred," Mahood again returns to find his family dead on the floor, but instead of respectfully leaving the room he nonchalantly "stamp[s] underfoot" their rotting remains: "here a face, there a stomach, as the case may be, and sinking into them with the ends of my crutches, both coming and going" (323).[28] Finally, he concludes with some irritation that another outcome was always possible: that no journey home ever took place: "But enough of this nonsense. I was never anywhere but here, no one ever got me out of here" (324).[29]

This passage represents just one of the many moments when aporia—or stalemate—enters into the narrative of the trilogy. In the example just mentioned, several possible outcomes to a story are given. Each of these conclusions is plausible on its own, but together they are incompatible. They cannot all be correct. At the same time, it is impossible to decide which should be given priority.

While such deadlocks do occur elsewhere throughout the trilogy, they are most concentrated in *The Unnamable*. The narrator suggests on the first page of this text that aporia is in fact what allows the discourse to begin: "How proceed? By aporia pure and simple."[30] But even before directly making reference to aporia, the narrator of the English version of this text illustrates this concept, so instrumental in the work, with the phrase "I, say I." Richard Begam offers an exemplary reading of this much-cited phrase, and thus warrants direct quotation. He suggests that there are three ways of understanding the first "I" of the equation:

> First, we may read it as an intensifier, an anticipatory repetition that emphasizes the second "I" and is therefore grammatically linked to it, in which event it functions as the implied object of the verb "say." Second, we may read the first "I" as a simple exhibition or representation of the self [...] syntactically unrelated to the rest of the sentence, in which event it functions either as an implied subject, which has no verb or object attached to it or [...] as a fragment without any real grammatical function. Finally, we may treat the first "I" (and for that matter the second) as part of a citational form, reading "I, say I" on the analogy of "cheese, say, cheese" or "no, say, no" in which event what little grammatical determinacy it retained in the second reading is lost, and it ends up functioning neither as subject nor as object.[31]

Begam proposes that even the French version of this expression, "dire je," while it lacks the disruptive quality of the first "I," still retains the effect of *différance* in "dire," which he signals can function as either an imperative or an infinitive, "as either the formulation of a problem (to say I) or an exhortation to speech."[32]

These potential multiple storylines within each individual story represent a refusal on the part of the narrator to allow the reader to become engaged—and taken in—by the illusion of traditional representation. By providing tales with several possible outcomes Beckett's narrators indirectly warn the reader not to forget that what is being described never actually happened; these stories are simple fictions. This revelation is in fact a *fil conducteur* throughout

the trilogy. Early on in *Molloy*, the character/narrator Molloy admits readily to
this conventional deception:

> Every time I say, I said this, or I said that [...] I am merely complying with the
> convention that demands you either lie or hold your peace [...]. In reality, I said
> nothing at all [...].[33]

> Et chaque fois que je dis, je me disais telle et telle chose [...] je ne fais que me plier aux
> exigences d'une convention qui veut qu'on mente ou qu'on se taise [...]. En fait je ne
> me disais rien du tout [...].[34]

This text's second narrator, Moran, also makes continual references to the
trickery involved in representation, as, for example, when he confesses that
what really happened in his story was actually "quite different" than how he
had initially presented it.

It may seem as if the trilogy (and thus, the "text" in general) is concerned
only with revealing what classical representation is *not*. In other words, it seeks
to reveal that traditional stories are *not* re-presentations of reality, that their
narrators are *not* necessarily knowledgeable or in control of their material, and
so on. However, this is just one aspect of what these texts expose. They are
equally concerned with unveiling something affirmative: what classical
representation always concealed, or what it really *is*. While the "book" presents
itself as a mirror, capable of providing the reader with a reflection of an
outside "reality," it is "in reality" made up of words: tricky, slippery, often
deceptive words, but words nonetheless. Moreover, these words have
undergone multiple combinations, substitutions, and revisions before ever
coming to rest in the particular sequence in which the reader eventually finds
them on the page. "Stories" are not simply deposited onto paper and they are
not produced without effort on the part of the writer. The writer's doubts,
hesitations, and changes of opinion—all an inevitable part of the writing
process and yet traditionally concealed from the reader—are highlighted in the
trilogy. Each time the narrators suspend their narratives, which they all do
often, the reader's attention is drawn away from the story and towards the
"writer" himself and the writing itself. Whether it is to beg pardon of the
reader for the minutia of their descriptions ("I apologize for these details,"
63),[35] to provide explanations even to themselves ("But I couldn't. What? Lean
on it. I couldn't. What? Bend it," 77),[36] to make revisions ("No, that won't
do," 189)[37] or even criticize their own work ("This story is no good," 330),[38]

these narrators never allow the reader the luxury of an uninterrupted read. "What tedium," (187/189)[39] as Malone would say.

The writing process is further exposed by the frequent references to the practical concerns of writing. The narrator of *Malone Dies* fixates on the tools of writing: the pens, pencils and carefully ruled exercise books, not to mention the necessary yet elusive stories. In *Molloy*, there is a concentration on grammar, as when Molloy declares that what was written should all be rewritten in the pluperfect. As for the narrators of *The Unnamable*, their main concern seems to be style, evidenced by their admitted dependence on rhetoric (308) and a particular fondness for "colorful language, bold metaphors and apostrophes" (333). Lest the reader choose to stay unaware of the writing process that these texts strive to lay bare, Beckett puts the issue right before his eyes. In all three texts sentences are often left unfinished,[40] punctuation is frequently missing,[41] and paragraph form is often absent,[42] making reading—or at least, reading that remains unconscious of the act of reading and writing—impossible.

The trilogy's highlighting of the writing process allows the reader to begin to see the emergence of the "text" within these "books." In *Writing and Difference*, Derrida explains this moment as something of an epiphany:

> The first book, the mythic book, the eve prior to all repetition, has lived on *the deception that the center was sheltered from play* [...]. Once [a text] is written, *when one can read a book in the book, an origin in the origin* [one becomes witness to] the bottomlessness of the infinite redouble.[43]

When the writing process is uncovered the reader becomes conscious of other fundamental ideas that disrupt the foundations of Western thought. He is made aware of the fact that there is no such thing as a stable center, that no center is "sheltered from play." This awareness is what enables the reader to see an "infinite" doubling of everything. In *Beckett's Fiction*, Leslie Hill characterizes Beckett's trilogy in much the same way. It is a collection of works that, like each of the narrators of these texts, "has its center nowhere and its circumference everywhere." Unlike classical collections of "books" that exhibit a logical, linear order from one book to the next, these texts—with their "intersecting orbits," "flat ellipses," and extremities converging at either end"—behave like the "purgatorial spiral"[44] that is now a familiar Beckettian image.

With the uncovering of the writing process, or the "text" beneath the "book," we also become cognizant of what Derrida calls the disappearance of the "self-identity of the origin." We become attentive, in other words, to the fact that in writing–in language–there may well be no original moments. What we witness is the "origin in the origin," and the "bottomlessness of the infinite redouble."[45] Writing, like knowledge, is multiple. No "book" is ever simply "one."

"Seeing Double": Creation and Repetition

The theory that writing is inherently multiple is one that has been explored by many thinkers in a variety of ways. Vincent Descombes signals two interpretations that have gained the most acceptance among philosophers and therefore stand out as particularly representative. The first interpretation holds that writing must be multiple because it depends upon repetition for its existence. The second interpretation–which is not that different from the first–claims that writing is multiple in that every text represents a dialogue between several voices.

Deleuze suggests that writing owes its existence to repetition by observing that no creative activity can take place and no "novelty" whatsoever can be produced outside of repetition. Expanding upon his own elaboration of Nietzsche's conceptualization of the eternal return,[46] Deleuze claims that since the eternal return selectively eliminates the "weak" (or those elements that are the Same) and allows only the strong (or those elements that produce difference) to survive, "we only produce something new on the condition that we repeat." The "absolutely new" is "nothing but the eternal return."[47]

Although Deleuze maintains that this is the case for creativity in general, his main concern is with the way repetition relates to linguistic creativity. Repetition creates an "after-language" where once all that can be articulated has been articulated, it is repeated. Repeated, that is, with difference, for otherwise we could never recognize it as such. Contradictory though it may seem, it is only this after-language–what Foucault terms alternately "the neurosis of dialectics" and "the second form of words already spoken"–that is capable of producing novelty.[48]

In *Difference and Repetition*, Deleuze illustrates how repetition produces novelty by lacing the text with refrains: groups of phrases that initially seem to be repeated verbatim throughout the work. Yet, these "refrains" are always, in some way, unlike each other. For example, Deleuze's contention that "if we die of repetition, we are also saved and healed by it" reappears approximately fifteen pages later expressed somewhat differently: "If repetition makes us ill, it also heals us; if it enchains and destroys us, it also frees us."[49]

The refrain that appears most often throughout this text is the one in which Deleuze differentiates between the two types of repetition by employing the antithetical structure "One is…, the other is." Although the basic structure of the phrases remains unchanged and thus gives the appearance of being an exact replication of all the other refrains that preceded it, the particular descriptors change from repetition to repetition:

> One is a static repetition, *the other* is dynamic. One results from the work, but *the other* is like the "evolution" of a bodily movement. One refers back to a single concept, which leaves only an external difference; *the other* is the repetition of an internal difference. (20, my emphasis)

> *L'une* est une répétition statique, *l'autre*, dynamique. *L'une* résulte de l'œuvre, mais *l'autre* est comme "l'évolution du geste." *L'une* renvoie à un même concept, qui ne laisse subsister qu'une différence extérieure entre les exemplaires ordinaires d'une figure ; *l'autre* est répétition d'une différence interne [...]. (32, my emphasis)

and several pages later:

> One *is* negative, *the other* affirmative, one conjectural, *the other* categorical. One *is static, the other dynamic.* One is repetition in the effect, *the other* in the cause, one is ordinary, *the other* distinctive. One is horizontal, *the other* vertical. (24, my emphasis)

> *L'une* est négative [...], *l'autre* affirmative, *l'une* est hypothétique, *l'autre* catégorique. *L'une* est statique, *l'autre* dynamique. *L'une* est répétition dans l'effet, *l'autre* dans la cause. [...] *L'une* ordinaire, *l'autre* remarquable et singulière. *L'une* est horizontale, *l'autre* verticale. (36, my emphasis)

Repeating many of the same words while imparting difference, by adding and subtracting new phrases or descriptors, this text appears to be building itself *of itself.*

There is a similar principle at work in many of Beckett's texts. Steven Connor likens this complex play between reduction and addition in Beckett's texts to the child's *fort/da* game in Freud's *Beyond the Pleasure Principle.* Freud maintains that when the child continuously throws out and retrieves a wooden spool tied to a string he is in effect illustrating the "dialectic of mastery and loss, pleasure and unpleasure," peculiar to the repetition compulsion. For Connor, this "game of psychic control and release" in

Beckett's work translates into one in which to repeat, and thus to say less, "seems uncannily, always to involve saying more."[50] Repetition enables the text to continue even when there's little left to say.

This operation is particularly evident in Beckett's *Company*. In contrast with the trilogy whose lengthy, marathon-like sentences and complex syntax leave even the most persistent readers feeling caught up in a whirlwind of seemingly infinite babble, *Company*'s forty pages of rather simple vocabulary set in paragraph form is—at the outset—literally a sight for sore eyes. But appearances can be deceiving. The short length of the text and the abundant blank space between paragraphs only give the illusion of clarity. The same is true of the ostensible simplicity of the language. Comprised of what seems to be no more than a handful of very elementary words that are used over and over again, this text initially promises an uncomplicated and somewhat predictable reading experience. Yet despite this early impression, the reader finds no respite in the outwardly straightforward, repetitive words, or in the narrator's assurance that there is—in life or in language—a "nought" from which to start "anew."[51] Such manifestations are all little more than the "figments" of which the narrator is so fond, the "fables" (46) one uses to convince oneself that one has some control over language.

Carla Locatelli interprets the deceptively minimal form and repetitive language of *Company* as an effort on Beckett's part to "unword the world." But a characterization such as this that equates simplicity with diminishment does not accurately describe what takes place in *Company*. If the language of this text is simple, it is in order to reveal what S.E. Gontarski has called its "tenacious power to represent" even when language is—perhaps especially when it is—"reduced, denuded and stripped bare."[52] Far from "unwording the world," the technique of repeating a few basic words—"with only minor variants"[53]—allows for a gradual accumulation of language. In effect, the text produces itself by continuously reusing words and expressions that had previously been employed. The first few lines of *Company* exhibit this phenomenon quite clearly:

A voice comes *to one in the dark*. Imagine. *To one* on his back *in the dark*. This he can tell by the pressure on his hind parts and by how the dark changes when he shuts his eyes and again when he opens them again. Only a small part of what is said can be verified. *As for example* when he hears, You are *on your back in the dark*. Then he must acknowledge the truth of what is said. But by far the greater part of what is said cannot be verified. *As for example* when he hears, You first saw the light on such and such *a day.* Sometimes the two are combined, *as for example, You first saw the light on such and such a day* and now *you are on your back in the dark.* (my emphasis)

Une voix parvient à quelqu'un dans le noir. Imaginer. Une voix parvient à quelqu'un dans le noir. *Le dos* pour ne nommer que lui le lui dit et la façon dont change le noir quand il rouvre les yeux et encore quand il les renferme. Seule peut se vérifier une infime partie de ce qui se dit. *Comme par exemple lorsqu'il entend,* Tu es sur le dos dans le noir. Là il ne peut qu'admettre *ce qui se dit.* Mais de loin la majeure partie *de ce qui se dit* ne peut se vérifier. *Comme par exemple lorsqu'il entend,* Tu vis le jour tel et tel jour. Il arrive que les deux se combinent *comme par exemple,* Tu vis le jour tel et tel jour et maintenant *tu es sur le dos dans le noir.* (my emphasis)

The expression "à quelqu'un dans le noir" from the first phrase of the French text remains unaltered in the second phrase. Yet this "same" phrase in the English version—"to one in the dark"—undergoes a major alteration in the next phrase. It is divided, added on to, and reformulated to create the second phrase of the text: "*to one on his back in the dark.*" Several phrases later, the first phrase of the French text (and the second of the English) becomes "Tu es *sur le dos dans le noir*" ("you are *on your back in the dark*") only soon to be transformed—with the addition of two other previously used phrases—to "*comme par exemple, Tu vis le jour tel et tel jour* et maintenant *tu es sur le dos dans le noir*" ("*as for example, you first saw the light on such and such a day* and now *you are on your back in the dark*").

It is significant that this creation by way of recycling old material from the first few pages of this text is not an anomaly in *Company*. The entire short story is generated in this same manner. Like its "crawling creator" who slides around in the dark unimpeded, the language of *Company* continues to regenerate itself indefinitely and seemingly with no obstacles to deter it. There are, however, moments when the language builds so quickly that the words themselves collide, producing sentences that defy the rules of syntax. One such instance—where verbs, prepositions and their referents run out of control producing something akin to a linguistic pile-up—can be found as early as the seventh page of this text: "Were it not *of him to whom it is speaking speaking* but of another it would not speak in the second person but in the third" (7, my emphasis).

The words and expressions of this text regenerate and weave themselves together in new configurations so rapidly that they instantly fill up what originally appears to be any available space on the page. The spaces separating paragraphs from one another seem suddenly to be crammed with words. At the end of the text, even the silence evoked by the word "alone"—itself alone on a line—does not remain that way long. After reading nearly eighty-eight pages in the French text (and forty-three pages in the English) of what seems to be unlimited variations on the same theme, it would be difficult for any reader to prevent himself from repeating the narrative discourse, even if only within the recesses of his own mind. Thus, when the text ends with "Alone.," the reader, seconds later, is compelled to respond, "on your back in the dark," taking up where the text appeared to leave off—filling the silence with words— thereby enabling it to begin again.

"Hearing Double": The Many Voices of a Text

The second most common way in which theorists have interpreted the notion that writing is multiple concerns the idea that no one mind is ever responsible for the creation of a text. Writing is the product of a multitude of "voices." In one of the two introductions to *Le même et l'autre*, Descombes not only explains this theory, but he also uses it to justify his choice of certain figures to represent modern French philosophy. Descombes argues that the choice should not be based on who wrote the most "original" work because no real "originality" exists as such. No text is born of nothingness. What appear to be "new" ideas are the product of other ideas that once preceded them, what Blanchot refers to as the "le rumeur."

For Descombes, the great philosophers are not, therefore, those one would commonly think of as the most "original" or "revolutionary" in the sense that their thinking is radically innovative. Rather, the exemplary representatives of French philosophy are the philosophers who are revolutionary in that they participate in a continuously revolving circulation of ideas—who directly confirm already existing knowledge. Quoting Merleau-Ponty, Descombes suggests that a philosopher can be considered notable if what one feels in reading his work is less the sentiment of having read something new, than that of *recognizing* what one *expected* to find.[54] The text with which "one falls in love" is therefore necessarily the text through which what one continuously learns is what one already knew (14).

Certainly, this is not the same thing as suggesting that great philosophical texts duplicate other previously written texts in their entirety. They do not simply re-present the "already thought thoughts." Returning to Deleuze's conceptualization of novelty, one cannot produce a new text by remaining entirely and slavishly faithful to an old one, for a new idea or text can only come into being as the result of a certain difference. This difference, which Descombes calls a "betrayal," is what enables one to tease out the "unthought" from that which was previously thought: "un certain *impensé* [...] inhérent à ces pensées" (15). In this sense then, all written works—all ideas whatever they may be—are the product of a plurality of voices. While this is theoretically the case for all texts regardless of the author, at one time or another Derrida, Deleuze and Beckett all seem to take this literally. Derrida illustrates this idea by writing essays in which he highlights the interplay between many different textual voices. In "Tympan," his own writing shares the page with that of Leiris. In *Glas*, the words of Hegel meet those of Genet. As mentioned in chapter one, "The Double Session" is the result of his voice mingling with those of Plato and Mallarmé. Reading Derrida's work becomes an exercise in reading in what he refers to as "the fold." Deleuze, for his part, is so well-known for his many collaborative projects with Félix Guatarri[55] that one critic has even referred to them as the "Gilbert and Sullivan" of contemporary philosophical writing.[56] *L'anti–Oedipe; Capitalisme et schizophrénie, Kafka ; Pour une littérature mineure, Rhizome, Mille Plateaux - Capitalisme et schizophrénie 2*, and *Qu'est-ce que la philosophie* are examples of their particular species of dialogic exchange in which each wrote one section of the work on his own, then exchanged that section with the other author to be developed. To paraphrase Jean-Jacques Lecercle, in each instance, it is a case of a text (Deleuze) rewriting itself under a different name (Guattari)—and vice versa. Here, as in the work of Derrida, philosophy is not simply "a kind of writing." Like every text, philosophy is a kind of *re*-writing.

Beckett reveals the innately plural nature of the narrative voice in a variety of ways. As previously referenced, he does this by employing multiple narrative voices, such as those competing for space in *Molloy* and *The Unnamable*. What makes Beckett's work notable, however, is not so much that his texts often have several narrators, which is not uncommon in twentieth century literature, but rather that these various voices do not simply narrate in a vacuum; they seem to communicate.

In many ways, *Molloy* would seem to defy this notion of communication, for, at least on the surface, it is a text that is divided into two distinct sections seemingly joined together as an afterthought. In part, one would read this text as cleaved in two because the author or the publisher labeled the second half of the text as "Part two." Although it is not designated as such, one would then deduce that the first part of the text would then be "Part one." These sections also appear to be separate pieces because each of the two parts is narrated by a different narrator with a distinct style that is reflected in the way in which his discourse is laid out on the page. The Moran narrative, the second of the two, is written in traditional paragraph form. In contrast, Molloy's account is related without any paragraph breaks whatsoever. The first half of the English text is in essence one thirty-page long paragraph.

Despite their apparent irreconcilable differences, these narratives have much in common. Firstly, each narrative shares many of the same central objects, among them bicycles, crutches, and sticks. Each also features similar types of people, such as Gaber who is supposed to collect Moran's report and always wants a beer, and the man who retrieves Molloy's papers who is equally thirsty, but never specifies his drink of choice. In addition, there is a resemblance in the adventures supposedly experienced by the principal characters of each part of the text. Both narrators are on a quest that is never achieved: Molloy's search for his mother and Moran's search for Molloy. Both kill a man, hear voices inside their heads, and see a shepherd. Finally, they both experience progressive physical degeneration—beginning in the legs—which ultimately lands them in bed, paralyzed and writing.

Taking into account both the divergences and the correspondences between the two parts of this one story, one cannot help but wonder about the relationship between the two parts. Are Molloy and Moran one and the same person, but at different moments of their life and at varying states of mental and physical well-being? If so, which of their stories logically precedes the other? Is it the more traditionally structured narrative of Moran—in other words, "Part Two"—or the thorny and difficult-to-follow account of Molloy; a difficulty that becomes literal for Moran who never manages to catch up to him? Or are they the same person but living in alternate realties? If so, which is the "original" and which is the "copy"?

These questions become more challenging when one takes into account the fact that the two parts of *Molloy* "correspond" not only in that they resemble each other, but also in that they communicate *with* each other and even *for* each other. Each narrator, at once, tells his own "story" and that of the other narrator. They are each subject and object. Neither one nor the other can claim priority, at least not for long. One might argue that it is only natural that the two narrators of *Molloy* would turn out to be implicated in each other's stories since both are already contained within the same literal margins and under the same title. While this is a reasonable comment to make, it should be noted that Beckett permits this type of margin hopping not only between two narratives of a single text, but also from one text to another. Just as the name "Watt" resonates all throughout the novel bearing that name, the names "Molloy" and "Malone" reverberate throughout the trilogy. Molloy's name is recalled in the English words "mollify" and "moly," as well as in the names "Molly," "Mollose," "Molloc," "Mellose," and "Mrs. Loy." The name "Malone" and variations on this name appear several times in *The Unnamable* and are even echoed in ordinary expressions such as "*me alone.*" Favorite words such as "on" (employed as a self-sufficient phrase, "on.") and expressions such as "what tedium," and the previously mentioned "come and go" are similarly replicated throughout the Beckettian œuvre.[57] The persistent self-referential citations testify to Beckett's predilection for a peculiar brand of plagiarism: "that most necessary, wholesome and monotonous plagiarism [...] of oneself."[58]

Besides the reiteration of particular objects, characters, and words, there are also instances of entire phrases in one text that bear an uncanny—though not identical—resemblance to those found in another text. A striking example of this concerns the narrator's musings at the beginning of *Molloy* about how he eventually ended up in his mother's home:

> I am in my mother's room. It's I who live there now. I *don't* know how I got *there.* *Perhaps in an ambulance, certainly* a vehicle of some kind.[59]

> Je suis dans la chambre de ma mère. C'est moi qui y vis maintenant. *Je ne sais pas* comment j'y suis. *Dans une ambulance peut-être, un véhicule quelconque certainement.*[60]

Apart from the narrator's odd lack of knowledge about his own experiences, there is nothing particularly remarkable about these phrases. The vagueness of the details describing what happened only makes the statements appear even less significant. Yet in another text—*Malone Dies*—these words come back to the reader like a faint and faraway memory:

> ...this is just a plain private room apparently, in what appears to be a plain ordinary house. I *do not* remember how I got *here.* *In an ambulance perhaps, a vehicle of some kind certainly.* (183, my emphasis)

...c'est une chambre de particulier ordinaire dans un immeuble courant apparemment. Je ne me rappelle pas *comment j'y suis* arrivé. *Dans une ambulance peut-être, un véhicule quelconque certainement.*[61]

Like Molloy, Malone begins his narrative by attempting to describe his whereabouts, which are even less precise than those of Molloy, finding himself in "une chambre de particulier ordinaire," in "un immeuble courant apparemment" ("just a plain private room" in a "plain ordinary house"). What follows is even more notable, for it appears to be an exact replication of the words voiced by Molloy at the beginning of that text. However, while the descriptions of how each of the narrators arrived in their respective rooms are again similar they are not identical. Molloy's informal and less precise "je ne sais pas comment j'y suis," becomes the more eloquent and exact "je ne *me rappelle* pas comment j'y suis *arrivé.*" The transformations in the English versions of these two texts are even more surprising. Molloy's casual contraction "don't" becomes the more elegant "do not" for Malone. Molloy's distant "there" is changed by Malone to the closer "here." Finally, although both narrators employ the odd combination of "perhaps" and "certainly" in the same phrase, they place the two words in different positions. Both words appear earlier in Molloy's description than in Malone's. Yet, unlike the communication between the two narrators of *Molloy*, the interaction between the first narrator of *Molloy* and the narrator of *Malone Dies* would most likely only be appreciated by a reader who reads both of these texts within a relatively short period of time. Likewise, the difference that is communicated from text to text—and the linguistic fine-tuning that seems to occur in the transfer of information from one book to the next—will only be identified by the reader who places the texts side-by-side and compares them by reading them again. The exchange between the two books depends upon the extent to which the reader participates in the dialogue.

The gesture of revealing that texts are always, somehow, multiple is quite similar to that of cultivating paradox within a narrative. They are both strategies intended to arrest conventional ways of reading, and both manage to dismantle the traditional conceptualization of the "book" as a self-sufficient, "pure" totality. When several possibilities are offered—whether they come in the form of aporetic discourse or as several possible outcomes for a story—it becomes difficult for the reader to decide which option or possibility should take precedence over the others. In a sense, this is also the result of incorporating a plurality of voices in a work and allowing them to correspond with each other from text to text. If, in order to fully understand what one text has to offer, we are required to look to a second and vice versa, then neither of the two texts was ever actually "complete" to begin with. Paradoxically, what this means is that written works will always require the supplement of other texts in order to be whole. Perhaps then, there is no "book," no "whole," no original moments—no "theology"—to protect after all. Maybe nothing is sacred. "Let there be light," as the narrator of *The Unnamable* says, "or let there be none." This is writing. And writing is repetition.

"The Tower of Babel": The "Origin" of the Multiplicity of Language

"In the beginning God created the heaven and the earth [...] And the whole earth was of one language and of one speech."[62] According to this passage in the King James version of the Book of Genesis (1611), this period was characterized by a state of innocence akin to that experienced by Adam and Eve before original sin. Unified by a common means of communication, humankind was—for all intents and purposes—"one": "And the Lord said, Behold, the people is one" (11.6). Humans also shared a common vision: to surpass their proper limits by building a spiraling tower whose top would "reach unto heaven [...]." Alas, due to their inability to be satisfied with their own "oneness," and their need to approach *the* "one"—*the original* origin—this singularly blissful state of singularity was not to last. In attempting to pierce through the heavens, humankind brought upon itself the wrath of God:

> And the lord came down to see the city and the tower, which the children of men builded. And the Lord said, Behold, the people is one, and they have all one language; and this they begin to do; and now nothing will be restrained from them, which they have imagined to do. Go to, let us go down, and there confound their language, that they may not understand one another's speech. So the Lord scattered them abroad from thence upon the face of all the earth [...]. Therefore is the name of it called Babel; because the Lord did there confound the language of all the earth; and from thence did the Lord scatter them abroad upon the face of all the earth. (II: 1-9)

In the *Cratylus* and *The Republic*, Plato reminds us of the still relevant severity of this other "original sin." If one approaches an origin or an original entity—such as a God or an idea—too closely, one threatens the very identity of this original thing, the very *originality* of this origin. Emulation gives way to consummation, as the copy comes to stand in for and replace the original entity. Yet at the same time, if one strays too far from the origin—imitating it, but only moderately—one no longer remains its faithful servant. One becomes oneself, "original." In the end, both conditions are equally menacing to the original idea or entity, for in each case the origin is in danger of losing what constitutes its being and risks being replaced by its likeness, or "copy."

This "dangerous supplementarity" is averted in *Genesis*. God's singularity remains intact, at least in the beginning. The "Lord" frustrates the plan to complete the tower and exacts payment from humankind for its transgression of having even begun the task. The price humanity pays for its attempt to reach the "origin" is, appropriately, its very "oneness." Once linked by a common dwelling, human beings were henceforth scattered across the earth and separated from each other physically. Once unified intellectually by a shared language, the human race was now subjected to a multiplicity of tongues and doomed to live in a state of perpetual misunderstanding. This "Babel"—both the linguistic confusion and the city after which it was named—became the foundation upon which the Lord erected the "beginning of His kingdom."

If we take this passage in *Genesis* for the gospel truth, we might also understand it as a decisive moment in the history of interpretation. The creation of "Babel" gave birth to a need for translation. An explicit need, that is, for translation actually predates the apparition of multiple languages. One could say that translation in fact came into existence the moment an idea was first represented as a pictogram. In order to get from the idea to its reproduction—to cross that interval between the thought and its sign—one must subject the idea to an operation of translation. In this sense, all images, language, and texts are already translations.

While Derrida refers to this "first" act of translation as the real "original sin,"[63] because it was the first time mankind attempted to approach and even supplement its God, it also, paradoxically, served to guarantee God's "original" status. In effect, as Derrida explains it, the entire "theme" of a transcendental signifier—the idea of a God, a truth, a beginning, and so on—came into being within the horizon of what he refers to as an "absolutely pure, transparent and unequivocal translatability."[64] Translation establishes the identity of an "original" entity because in translating—in producing this "original" entity again—one authorizes its position as "the first" of two things. The translation itself, whether it is of a metaphysical or textual entity, is but a copy, depending on the "original" object for its existence. But if translation sustains the traditional coupling and hierarchy of the "origin/copy," it also undermines it. As Derrida observes, the "original" is just as dependent upon the translation as the translation is on the original:

> If the structure of the original is marked by the requirement to be translated, it is that in laying down the law the original begins by indebting itself as well with regard to the translator. The original is the first debtor, the first petitioner, it begins by lacking and by pleading for translation.[65]

The original—whatever it may be—is "original" in that it is the "first petitioner." The translation is left to re-petition, or repeat. But what the original "petitions for," what it requests and requires in order to sustain its original status, can only be granted by the translation. It was thus always already secondary to its translation. Translation, like repetition, overturns this common "origin/copy" hierarchy, revealing that the boundaries distinguishing the two terms were always too weak to prevent the properties of one from leaking into the other. The "original" entity is as secondary as the "copy" is original.

With respect to literature, a translation cannot then be a simple copy of some "ever-engendering Urtext."[66] It cannot draw too closely to this original, for if it did it would not be recognizable as a translation, and then would be incapable of guaranteeing its own identity or that of the "original." In order to confirm its own "originality" as well as that of the "original" text, the translation must be different.

As Derrida explains it, while translation is indeed re-presentation, an "infinitesimal and radical displacement" does occur.[67] By virtue of the fact that it entails the transfer of information from one language to another, any translation already produces difference, but the difference is not just one of differing signifiers. To believe that only the signifiers undergo a transformation in translation depends upon an understanding of translation as pure substitution. For Philip E. Lewis, this is the case. Since priority is given to the re-presentational process, the "textual work," which he refers to as the work in which "the signifiers of the original are linked to one another and in which that more or less poetic activity [...] takes place,"[68] is subordinated to the "meaning" of the words. For Derrida, this amounts to nothing less than putting one's faith in the "doctrine of the immunity of the signified from the signifier," for the assumption is that the meaning of a word or text can remain more or less unaltered when transposed from one language to another. Yet, in transposing information written in one language to another, one inevitably changes the information itself in some "infinitesimal" way. Something is always lost—or gained—in the translation.

Traduttore, Traditore: Derrida on the Impossibility of Translation

As any multi-lingual person knows, translation as an exact and transparent transposition of signification from one language to another does not exist as such. There is always something that bars its passage. In his essays "Shibboleth" and "Ulysses Gramophone," Derrida examines the various obstacles to translation. Among the barriers mentioned are neologisms, signatures, proper names, aporia, and general impasses: in effect any "difficult passage," or "*no pasarán.*" The hurdle he is most concerned with in both essays is "Babel" because it represents *the* "possible impossible step,"[69] the impasse *par excellence*:

> Babel is [...] beyond hope of transaction, tied to *the multiplicity of languages* within the uniqueness of the poetic inscription; *several times in one, several languages in a single poetic act.*[70]

"Shibboleth" is Derrida's homage to the poet Paul Celan and to the resistance his poetry offers to translation. Derrida suggests that it is the very signature of Celan's poetry, its "here-and-nowness," that is responsible for this resistance. Babel, or the combination of "several languages in a single poetic act," is its principal component.

The particular poem in which Derrida locates this multiplicity of tongues is entitled, interestingly, *IN EINS—In One*. This poem, which starts in German, but which also features Hebrew and French, not to mention the words "*no pasarán*" and "Babel," is for Derrida the incarnation of "multiple singularity" (398): "*several times in one, several languages in a single poetic act*" (408). To demonstrate this poem's untranslatability, Derrida examines several versions. In the French incarnation of *In Eins*, the German expressions are translated into French, while the words *shibboleth* and *no pasarán* are left untranslated, respecting the foreignness of the words. However, the French translation becomes problematic when the translator is confronted with the French language itself. In other words, the greatest obstacles for the French translation are the words that had been written in French in the "German idiom of what one calls the original version." If the French words "Avec toi/Peuple/de Paris," are left in French in the French translation, the translation would efface "the very thing which it preserves" (408), the foreign effect of the French. This is the moment of impasse.

"Ulysses Gramophone" also illustrates the particular impediment posed by the multiplicity of languages. Derrida begins this essay with an example of a single phrase composed in two languages. The phrase opens in French, then finishes in English: "Oui, oui, you are receiving me, these are French words."[71] This sentence is clearly untranslatable, because to translate "oui, oui" into English—to change the phrase to read "yes, yes, these are French words"—would be, as Derrida asserts, both absurd and illegitimate. He then compares the problem posed by this phrase to a similar impasse he locates in Descartes' *Discours de la méthode*. At the end of the French original of *Discours de la méthode*, Descartes explains why he chose to write in French. This explanation is omitted in the Latin translation. For Derrida, this makes perfect sense, for, "what is the sense of writing a sentence in Latin, the gist of which is: 'the following reasons illustrate why I am now writing in French.'" He continues in greater detail:

> An act which in one language remarks the language itself, and which in this way affirms doubly, once by speaking it and once by saying that it has thus been spoken, opens up the space for a re-marking, which, at the same time and in the same double way, defies and calls for translation. (257)

It is this affirmation of a language through itself—this multiplicity of tongues within a single poetic inscription, this Babel—that is ultimately untranslatable. And yet, it is precisely the *untranslatable* that is, in the end, "the only thing to *translate*, the only thing *translatable*." Then, in what passes as an attempt to clarify the situation but which actually seems itself to plead for translation, he adds, "what must be *translated* of that which is *translatable* can only be the *untranslatable*." As Beckett's Malone says, "that's it, babble."[72]

"That's it, Babble": Translation and Difference in Beckett's Work

Like the examples provided by Derrida in *Shibboleth* and *Ulysses Gramophone*, Beckett's texts and translations, governed as they are by aporia and neologism, self-consciously underscore the notion of "untranslatability." Riddled with expressions in foreign tongues—German, French, English, Italian, and, what seems to be his favorite, "pigsty Latin" (329)—his work is a virtual tower of Babel. As such, Beckett challenges translators to consider what merits and does not merit translation. The titles of his texts are a case in point. Many of the titles are proper names, which are generally never translated. However, the particular names employed often resonate with a specific national identity. Names like Murphy, Molloy, and Malone are relatively common in the Anglo-Irish world but not elsewhere. If these titles remain unchanged in German translations, they would impart a foreignness to the German text that they would not have had in the English version. There are also the titles that do not seem to belong to any language, the title of the French text *Bing*, for example, which is not even a word and hardly a name. It is a sound, perhaps. One might then assume it would be universal, and have no need for translation, certainly not from French to English. Evidently for Beckett, that is not the case. In English, the title of this text is *Ping*. This is the bi-product of Babel: "Heavenly father, the creature was bilingual!"[73]

Beckett's translations, which he almost invariably participated in if not performed entirely himself, stage the inescapable difference produced by translation. In the words of Tom Bishop, they illustrate the fact that a translation is not merely a "superfluous addition" to some original text, but an actual "expansion of the work itself."[74] Not that Beckett viewed translation as a stimulating creative endeavor. For Beckett, the hopelessness involved in this type of work was a source of limitless frustration. In a 1957 letter written to Thomas McGreevy, Beckett expressed his mounting dissatisfaction with this task:

> Translation of *All that Fall* into French and German, of *Fin de Partie* into German and English, of *L'Innommable* into English, of *Malone meurt* into German and *Echo's Bones* and other odd poems into German and sick and tired I am of translation and what losing battle it is always. Wish I had the courage to wash my hands of it all. I mean, to leave it to others and try to get on with some work.[75]

But the fact remains that he did not "wash [his] hands of it all," and continued until the end of his days to translate his own work. According to Leslie Hill, only twice did Beckett abstain from participating in the translation of one of his texts. Robert Pinget is given exclusive credit for the French translation of *All That Fall*, and Alain Bosquet translated several of Beckett's poems on his own. Five of Beckett's texts were translated in collaboration with other translators: *Cendres* with Pinget, *L'Expulsé* and *La Fin* with Richard Seaver, and the French *Watt* and *D'un ouvrage abandonné* with Ludovic and Agnès Janvier.

Beckett alone was responsible for the French and English translations of the remainder of his œuvre.[76]

As the author of these texts, and thus more familiar with the "originals" than anyone else, one would suppose that Beckett would be more capable than any other writer of reproducing the signature of his work in a translation. Indeed, many critics have commented upon his uncanny ability to compensate for different cultural contexts, colloquialisms, and puns in his translations.[77] However, coming close to the "original" is much more the exception in Beckett's translations than the rule. In truth, the majority of his translations differ markedly from the "originals" upon which they are based. Many of his translations diverge from the "original" texts with respect to length. By and large, Beckett is much less wordy in French than in English. Rabinowitz notes that *Company* is an exception, as seventeen sentences of the English text were omitted in the French.[78] Connor estimates that the move from French to English of *Mercier et Camier* resulted in a twelve percent loss of the "original" French text.[79] There are also significant changes in meaning that arise in the shift from the "original" to the translation. According to Brian Fitch, seventeen of the seventy sentences in the French text *Bing*–approximately one third of the text–were subjected to considerable modifications in meaning when translated into the English *Ping*.[80] More extensive changes can be found in the *Still/Immobile* pairing, where some two thirds of the sentences are altered. This time, however, the direction of the language exchange is the opposite of *Bing/Ping*. Here the transformation was from English to French and not French to English (82). There are also substantial alterations in tone in the translations. Where the French is often more comical, subtle, and expansive, the English texts exhibit a tendency toward a deepening pessimism and progressive degradation. Connor notes many examples in *Premier amour* of the worsening of a situation when it finds itself translated into English. In this text, an already exaggerated rumination about foot problems that is described in the French as involving a corn, a cramp, a bunion, an ingrown nail, a blain, a trench foot "and other curiosities," grows in English to include additional grievances about "the kibe, the hammer toe, the fallen arch, the club foot, duck foot, goose foot, pigeon foot," and "flat foot."[81] It is as if the movement alone from one language to another was enough to amplify the characters pains.

With the multitude of excisions, additions, and general distortions, Beckett's translations come to seem less like translations and more like revisions. Or as Fitch expresses it, with Beckett's translations it is less a matter of *redoing* a text (as in exact duplication), as it is of *recasting* it in a different role.[82] In the English *Waiting for Godot*, one obvious recasting is where Lucky mentions the philosopher Berkeley, but in the French he opts for Voltaire.[83] Initially this amendment may seem fitting, for the English readers may not respond in the same way to the name Voltaire as they would to an Anglo-Irish philosopher. Similar changes occur elsewhere in the trilogy, as when the name "Mme Louis" in *Malone meurt* mutates into "Mrs. Lambert" in the English *Malone Dies*. But while Voltaire and Berkeley are both eighteenth century philosophers, and thus perhaps justifiably interchangeable for this reason, they are very different men and philosophers indeed. Berkeley was known for his connection to idealism and empiricism, and Voltaire was a skeptic. Berkeley was a devoutly religious Bishop and Voltaire, a deist who vehemently opposed institutions in general and the Catholic Church in particular. This swapping of one philosopher for the other does not, therefore, seem to be the equitable type of exchange that takes place in the substitution of Mrs. Lambert for Mme. Louis. Instead, this replacement seems as gratuitous as that of "A and C" in the English version of *Molloy* for "A and B" of the French text.

These kinds of changes could only come from a translator who was also the author, and this is the advantage that Beckett not only had, but flaunted. No ordinary translator could introduce such changes in the translations without risking criticism. Such extensive alterations would most likely elicit anger from the author for having distorted his text or from the reader who would perceive the changes to be errors. Richard Seaver, who collaborated with Beckett on the English translation of *La Fin*, remarked that during this experience Beckett the creator was much more present than Beckett the translator. Rather than making a concerted effort to remain as faithful to the "original" text as possible, Beckett went out of his way to make the differences in the translation apparent to the bilingual reader: so much so that what they ended up with was not a translation but a "complete redoing of the original, [...] a completely new creation."[84]

However, while Beckett took pains to reveal the "originality" and singularity of his translations, he also made sure to emphasize that they were at the same time still dependent upon some other earlier text and vice versa. Henri Meschonnic describes this as the fundamental nature not just of translation but of writing in general, stating, "To say that the writer goes from the real to the book, and the translator from a book to another book, is to not be aware

of what we know today, that there have always been books between the experience and the book."[85] In the introduction to her English translation of Derrida's *La Loi du genre* entitled *Why I Write Such Good Translator's Notes*—a
translation and translator's introduction that actually *precede* the "original"
French text in *Glyph*—Avital Ronell, points out that all texts and their translations call out to one another and to the translator by "secretly exchanging and
renewing vows of constancy" with the other text's language. In other words,
texts and translations always, in some small way, remind the reader of the existence of another absent text. Ronell suggests that in certain cases the language
of the absent text, whether that of the original or the translation, remains so
present that each language seems to stand in "perpetual anticipation of passing
into the other language." The particular example Ronell draws upon is Derrida's claim that the law of genre wants "to be born like a person/like no one."
The uncertainty as to how the phrase should be translated stems from the fact
that the French "naître comme personne" has several possible meanings. Since
the word "naître" recalls phonetically the word "être," and since "personne"
could mean either "person" or "no one," this phrase could be translated in a
variety of ways. The Law simultaneously "wants to be born, wants to be, or
does not want to be, like anybody, unlike anybody, a nobody and so forth."[86]
"Innumerable babble,"[87] Beckett's English speaking Malone would say.

Beckett's texts and their translations perpetually dialogue with each other,
and thus constantly remind the bilingual reader of the other absent text. This
is particularly true of the French and English texts and translations, perhaps
because he wrote the majority of his work first in one of these two languages.
Whether one is reading the "original" text or the translation, one is often left
with the uncanny impression of having caught a glimpse of a French text
beneath an English one, and an English text within the French. The trilogy is
exemplary of such linguistic cross-referencing, for while each text was first
written in French, they all constantly hint to the existence of an English
"version." For example, none of the proper names of the characters—Malone,
Molloy, etc—are of French origin. Certain expressions used by both the
characters and the narrators often seem so foreign to the language in which
the text was written that they too point to a culture that is not consistent with
that of the language of the text. Leslie Hill offers as an example how an
Irishman in *Molloy* repeatedly refers, as if it were an everyday dish, to "Irish
stew." This same man also informs us, in French, that "da, dans ma région
veut dire papa."[88] The confusion is two-fold, for as Hill observes, while the

Irishman is "compelled to narrate his life within words not his own," the French-speaking narrator likewise is obliged to exist in a "pseudo-Irish world."[89] There are so many Irish references in this French language text that even the French reader cannot help but feel like what he is reading is but "so much Gaelic"[90] to him.

Similarly, there is a denaturalization of the English language in many of Beckett's English texts, recalling the presence of an absent French "translation" or "original." Perhaps the most conspicuous example of this is in *Mercier and Camier* when Mercier says to the owner of a bar "Your whisky likes us," which might suggest that the French would read "Votre whisky nous aime." However, although this translation would make sense—despite the awkwardness of the statement in both English and French—the French *Mercier et Camier* actually reads "Votre whisky est succulent."[91] For Walter Benjamin, this is the defining trait of translation: to expose itself as foreign. Rather than disappearing around the content, the language of the translation "envelops its content like a royal robe with ample folds." This, it cannot help but do, "for it signifies a more exalted language than its own and thus remains unsuited to its content, overpowering and alien."[92] Ultimately, both English and French come to seem so unfamiliar under Beckett's pen that the reader might wonder if, like Moran, he had always understood these languages "all wrong perhaps."[93]

"What Truth Is There in All This Babble?":[94] The Search for the Origin

The way in which Beckett's texts and translations differ from and yet depend upon each other reveals a general lack at the center of both the original and the translation. Ultimately, neither one can make authoritative claims for its own autonomy. Each requires something from the other text, something supplemental, in order to come close to being "complete." But even with the addition of this supplement, "completion" will never be attained, for paradoxically, the moment the supplement comes into being, the "original" text is exposed as incomplete and provisional.

What we learn from Beckett's writing and translation is that the world is a text and this text is nothing but a play of differences. The promise of an "end" remains unfulfilled. There is only the possibility of further texts behind the "books," translations behind the texts, and versions of translations behind the translations, with no end in sight. Similarly, there is the suggestion that there is no purely "original" entity or moment that is not also contaminated by multiplicity. The singular "book" is inhabited by texts and the "original" text could not even exist, could not be original as such, were it not for translation. Here, we find ourselves caught up in a hall of mirrors. The search for some "truth" in "all this babble" remains unfulfilled, for there is none to find. "Masks," as Deleuze says, "do not hide anything but other masks" and the only illusion "is that of unmasking."[95] At the end of the day, the search for the "truth," the "one," or the "origin," is a lost cause. If one hopes to go back "from the supplement to the source" one will be disappointed, for, as Derrida says, "there is a supplement at the source."[96] "In the beginning, repetition."[97]

Chapter 4

‡ "The Ether of Metaphysics": Repetition and Presence on Stage and Page

> "Le grand remède aux misères de ce monde, c'est l'absorption dans l'instant présent."
> –Jean-Jacques Rousseau[1]

"Je ne peux pas continuer, je vais continuer": Beckett After *The Unnamable*

Beckett published *L'Innommable* in 1953. This last book of the trilogy was also Beckett's last so-called "novel." Three years later, in an interview with Israel Schenker, Beckett explained the move away from novel writing as inevitable after the trilogy. After writing texts in which there was "no 'I,' no 'have,' no 'being,'" there was, as Beckett said, truly "no way to go on."[2] Despite this claim, Beckett, like the ever-running discourse of *The Unnamable*, did indeed "go on." During the same period in which Beckett stopped writing novels, he began writing extensively for the theatre. Since then, many critics—among them Bruce Kawin, Enoch Brater, Ruby Cohn, Shimon Levy, and Sidney Homan—[3] have come to believe in varying degrees that the "coincidence" of Beckett's last novel with his increased interest in the theatre was no coincidence at all; that it represented a "natural" progression in his career, "the only direction in which a development was possible."[4] Having just completed several novels increasingly dominated by a sense of absence—the absence of "I," of "have," and so on—Beckett, it is often suggested, looked to the stage in search of what had become increasingly elusive in his novels: what Kawin calls "its flawless present tense."[5]

There is some evidence to support the claim that Beckett himself viewed his work after *The Unnamable* as indicative of a general turn from the inherent "lack" of the novel towards the "presence" of the theatre. Apart from *En Attendant Godot*, which was published in French in 1952, the majority of Beckett's dramatic texts were indeed composed only after the trilogy had been completed. Perhaps more striking, as Steven Connor notes, the suggestion that Beckett looked to the theatre in search of a "presence" not found in the novel was actually made first by Beckett himself. In Michael Haerdter's *Materialien zu Becketts Endspiel*, Beckett states: "Theater ist für mich zunächst eine Erholung von der Arbeit am Roman"[6] ("Theatre is for me initially a relief/rest from the work of the novel"). Beckett goes on to explain that this is not because he thought it easier to write theatrical texts than novels, but rather because the theatrical performance fulfills a need that novel writing does not: "Man hat es mit einem bestimmten Raum zu tun und mit Menschen in diesem Raum" ("One is dealing with a specific space, and with human beings in this space.").[7] Although it might seem as if Beckett is articulating a philosophical declaration about the nature of presence and being in that his statement is clearly a generalization ("One...human beings"), there is little in the interview to justify such a reading. Instead, it appears that Beckett is expressing a desire for representation by way of moving, possibly speaking bodies, in other words, a wish to participate in a rather commonplace identification of the theatre as the privileged space of group presence. After immersing himself in the extreme isolation and claustrophobia associated with the prose of the trilogy, Beckett, it seems from his statement, simply found relief in the physical presence of bodies on stage.

"Being There": Presence and the Body

The designation of the theatre as the space in which "metaphysical plenitude"[8] reigns is a common identification in Western thought. The assumption is that the theatre permits—and in the case of traditional theatre, even demands—the presence of actual moving, speaking bodies on stage. That the theatre is also simultaneously a space of non-presence, in that the people on stage are acting and the events portrayed are not "real," goes without saying. However, the actors are nonetheless still physically present on stage, and actions are performed on that stage and in the present time of the production. Thus, regardless of the fact that what is being presented is simply "pretend," the audience experiences the production in a way that is more directly assessable to the senses than its more cerebral prose counterpart. The determination of the theatre as the privileged space of presence for such reasons amounts to the simple—even simplistic—equating of "presence" with "being." This is the ostensible reason underlying the primacy of performance that was even more in vogue in experimental theatre of the late 1960's and 70's: performance is privileged because what takes place in the staging of a text appears to be nothing less than a miracle. To stage a theatrical text, to put it physically before an audience, is to seemingly *embody* it or resurrect it before that audience. In this not-so-distant relative of Berkeley's "Esse est percipi," acting out a written text on stage is to bestow upon it flesh and therefore life.

In "Notes from the Underground," Herbert Blau suggests an unspoken dialogue between Beckett and Antonin Artaud, perhaps the most well known French playwright to have attempted both to access and exploit a supposed natural presence of the theatre. In fact, Blau describes Beckett's *Endgame* as more than simply *evocative of* Artaud's theatre, but rather *as* Artaud's theatre. Here, he claims, "We *are in* Artaud's Theater of Cruelty, at the dark root of the scream, the unbearably humane."[9] Before examining the extent to which this statement about the correspondence between the works of these two playwrights is legitimate, it is necessary to first recall the theoretical basis of Artaud's concept of the theatre. In "Production and metaphysics," Artaud characterizes his conceptualization of a "fully present theatre" as a "theatre of cruelty." By naming it thus, Artaud was not advocating subjecting the audience to depictions of sadistic or "cruel" actions on stage—not necessarily, in any case. Instead, he was expressing a concern for the relationship between the spectators and the production. He suggests that dramatic works should permeate the audience like a "full," "physical" "shock" to the senses, so that the spectators would be permitted to experience the "presence" of the theatre in an extremely intimate, visceral way. Artaud argues that if one allows the stage to "speak its own concrete language," the audience will be able to experience even the language of the production in a "completely tangible manner." Yet, the stage can "speak its own [...] language" and thus can achieve the fullness of presence only if it is independent of the "tyranny of the text"[10] and thus free from re-presentation. Reminiscent of Jean-Jacques Rousseau's idealized, non-representational theatre,[11] Artaud's Theatre of Cruelty is not a representation at all, which is in part what makes it impossible to achieve: "It is life itself, in the extent to which life is unrepresentable."[12]

Many eminent Beckett scholars—among them Enoch Brater and Hugh Kenner—have suggested that Beckett's theatre also underscores a sheer, physical "presence," albeit in a less extreme fashion than in Artaud's theorizations. Perhaps the most prominent of critics who have made this claim is writer Alain Robbe-Grillet. Robbe-Grillet claims that by highlighting physical presence, Beckett's plays stage the very essence of the theatre. In his article, "Samuel Beckett, ou la présence sur la scène,"[13] Robbe-Grillet suggests that by stressing the fundamental nature of the theatre, Beckett is also (re)presenting the "essence" of the human condition. As his primary example, Robbe-Grillet focuses on Beckett's *En Attendant Godot* which he views as representative of the Heideggerian conceptualization of the human condition as "Dasein," or "being-there." With almost no personal background and with seemingly nothing to do but wait, *Godot*'s Vladimir and Estragon appear to be, as Sidney Homan reminds us, "HERE."[14] As Robbe-Grillet puts it, they are simply and "irremediably present." Though they may have little in common with anyone we might know in "real" life, they do seem to share at least one thing with the human condition: the "primary quality" of *being there*.[15]

Four years after the publication of Robbe-Grillet's *Pour un nouveau roman*, Jacques Derrida also examined the association of being and presence in philosophy, but with decidedly more suspicion than Robbe-Grillet. For Derrida, the association of being with presence carries with it greater consequences than that of simply establishing a link between so-called pure presence and the human body, which is, for Derrida, what makes this association particularly dangerous. Once established, this determination allows for the possibility of inaugurating a set of subdeterminations. Among them, Derrida lists "presence of the thing to the sight as *eidos*, presence as substance/essence/existence [*ousia*], temporal presence as point [*stigmè*] of the now or of the moment [*nun*], the self-presence of the cogito, consciousness, subjectivity, the co-presence of the other and of the self, intersubjectivity as the intentional phenomenon of the ego, and so forth."[16] Simply put, once presence is linked to Being, a surplus of general principles of metaphysics can henceforth be posited, and all notions that complicate these principles can be disregarded. The moment presence is determined as "being," we become anesthetized to anything that disrupts the assumptions that are born of this association. For Derrida, the coupling of being and presence is nothing less than "l'ether de la métaphysique."[17]

"Being? Where?": The Absence of Presence in Beckett's Theatre

The question remains as to whether Beckett's theatre intends to exploit a "pure presence" or whether it instead means to expose it as an illusion. In order to answer this question, several points must be taken into consideration. First, no play that derives from a text can logically be considered to represent "pure presence," since it relies on something prior to itself for its existence. In order for presence to be "pure," by definition, it cannot be tainted by anything that is not itself. It must be its own origin and end. It goes without saying that Beckett's staged plays are all the product of a text. Secondly, much of what appears to be indicative of pure presence in his work is the result of detailed stage directions in the script. For example, if the director remains true to the text, as directors such as Roger Blin and Alan Schneider often did,[18] every pause a character makes on stage can be found already recorded in the script. In some plays, such as *Happy Days*, there are hundreds of pauses; all of which are scripted:

> ...I have the whole—[*Pause. Puzzled.*] Them? [*Pause.*] Or it? [*Pause.*] Brush and comb it? [*Pause.*] Sounds improper somehow. [*Pause...*] What would you say, Willie? [*Pause...*] What would you say, Willie, speaking of your hair, them or it? [*Pause.*] The hair on your head, I mean. [*Pause...*] The hair on your head, Willie, what would you say speaking of the hair on your head, them or it? [*Long pause.*][19]

In the case of *Footfalls*, even the steps taken are accounted for in the stage directions:

> Pacing: starting with right foot (r), from right (r) to left (L), with left foot (l) from L to R. Turn: rightabout at L, leftabout at R. Steps: clearly audible rhythmic tread.

The stage directions are later brought to the spectator's attention, for the steps are then measured and voiced by the characters themselves:

> One two three four five six seven eight nine wheel one two three four five six seven eight nine wheel.[20]

Even where the pure presence seems to be, if not to be presented, at least re-presented in Beckett's theatre, it is never truly "pure." Presence is exposed in his work to be contaminated by, even produced by, repetition. As previously noted, Vivian Mercier has called *Waiting for Godot* "theoretical impossibility," for it is a play in which not only "*nothing* happens,"[21]—which would highlight the presence and present of the moment—but rather in which nothing happens "*twice.*"[22] Clearly, Mercier does not mean to say that literally *nothing at all* happens in the play. That actions are performed, speech is articulated, is indisputable. Vladimir and Estragon wait on a road by one leafless tree for the coming of Godot. They talk to pass the time, meet Pozzo and Lucky, watch the former coerce the latter into performing a variety of commands, and meet a boy who informs them that Godot is busy and will instead come tomorrow. But as Ruby Cohn notes and the title of the play suggests, the reason that some readers and critics have labeled *Godot* as a play "about nothing," is because the most evident "action" of this play is not an action *per se* but rather a state—that of waiting: "[...] they keep their appointment and they wait. Night after night, they keep their appointment, and they wait."[23] Echoing Robbe-Grillet, Cohn adds that *Godot*'s "*thereness* unrolls before our perceptions" (138). Cohn maintains that there is in fact actually as much "doing" as "being" in *Godot*, but the doing and being is "constantly threatened by Nothing" (134). Both Cohn and Martin Esslin insist that the apparent stasis in a play like *Godot* might even be better described as less a study on Nothingness than an amplification of the dramatic form, a "maximal intensification of the tensions that make conventional plays dramatic."[24]

Whatever the particular interpretation of the "events" of *Godot*, the virtual lack of so-called meaningful action that is described by Cohn as frequently having an "improvisational quality,"[25] accompanied by a focus on the dramatic form, seems an attempt on the part of the playwright to render the notion of presence—presence of being and present in time—immediately perceptible to the audience. Even Cohn has referred to *Godot*, *Endgame*, and *Krapp's Last Tape*, as plays that offer not only "endless continua" but also "different images of an unending present."[26] However, there is an equal emphasis on repetition in Beckett's plays that complicates such a reading. Besides the innumerable words and phrases that are repeated verbatim in *Godot*, Act two is so strikingly similar to Act one that it reads as a virtual duplication of all that preceded it. Admittedly, the tree now has leaves on it, signaling the passage of time from the first to the second Act, and Pozzo and Lucky's relationship takes on a decidedly less vaudevillesque and more sadistic tone. Yet the symmetry between the two Acts remains startling: Vladimir and Estragon find themselves again on the road, by a tree, in the company of Pozzo and Lucky, later of the boy who informs them again about Godot's plans, and all the while they wait. Cohen extends the list of repetitive gestures: "In both acts they comment on their reunion, they complain of their misery, they seek escape into games, they are frightened by offstage menace, they try to remember a past, they stammer a hope for a future, they utter doubts about time, place, and language, they wait for Godot."[27] Or as Mercier writes, nothing happens twice.

Far from affirming a sense of a pure presence, the reprisals of these seemingly innocuous and uneventful actions suggest instead the theoretical impossibility of such purity. Steven Connor explains this in Heideggerian terms. At the beginning of the second Act, the audience witnesses what seems to be a near repetition of the first Act. Yet, as Connor argues, we are only cognizant of the return of Vladimir and Estragon's "being-back (on stage)-again," or even their "still-being-there" at the beginning of the second Act "because of our awareness of the break that has taken place between the first two Acts." The break or "absence" that marks the first Act as, at once, the same as and different from the second Act, is enough to allow the "shadow of absence or non-being to fall across the fullness and simplicity of Dasein."

Herbert Blau contends that no modern drama is "more sensitively aware of the presence of an audience or its absence" than Beckett's Godot.[28] I would suggest that Godot is not an exception. I would also add, like Connor, that this sensitivity extends far beyond the level of the audience. Beckettian presence depends upon absence, just as absence in his work relies on presence for the perception of its very existence. Beckett offers his audience an absence which, in the words of Enoch Brater, takes on "a hovering presence."[29] In Happy Days we are only aware of Winnie's "present" or her condition of "still-being-there"—buried in the mound of dirt, rattling on about the objects in her purse—because of the absence involved in the change in Acts. Presence in this play, as well as in Godot—a play in which the title "character" himself is never "present,"—can only be perceived by way of its contamination by something "other" than itself.

Derrida argues that any desire for a pure presence, such as that invested in Artaud's "theatre of cruelty," is destined to remain unfulfilled precisely because there is no such thing as "pure" presence to begin with[30]: "Presence, in order to be presence and self-presence, has always already begun to represent itself, has always already been penetrated."[31] Thus, the extent to which Artaud wanted to save the "purity" of presence untainted by "interior difference" and repetition is the extent to which he simultaneously "desired the impossibility of the theatre" (249). Derrida is quick, however, to note that Artaud knew this "better than any other." He knew that the theatre of cruelty would always be "the inaccessible limit of a representation which is not repetition, of a re-presentation which is full presence, which does not carry its double within itself as its death, of a present which does not repeat itself, that is, of a present outside time, a non-present" (248).

The appearance of a "pure present," what Vincent Descombes refers to as the Husserlian "présent vivant," is just that: appearance. It is an illusion constructed in order to support phenomenological and metaphysical thought, in particular, the idea that one can distinguish between an original entity and one that is derived. In order to effect a deconstruction of this so-called "Husserlian principle of principles," Derrida counters it with his own "principle of non-principles." This "principle of non-principles" is strikingly similar to Gilles Deleuze's "paradox of coexistence." As Deleuze articulates it, duration never describes what "is," because that would mean that it names what "exists." Identifying what "exists" is impossible, for in order to do so one would have to freeze the time of the object in question. The "paradox" is therefore the following: in order for a present to be a present as such—to be identified as existing—it must also not be present. Here, one can only conceive of a present or presence either immediately before or immediately after it has happened. The present can only be conceived of as "present" belatedly, and thus, as Derrida claims, any present that does not "carry its double within itself as its death," is a present "outside time." "The "present" is always already "non-present." As Descombes explains it, this belated present is thus even responsible for producing history: "There is only history, because, from the origin onwards, the present is, so to speak, always delayed with regard to itself."[32] Whether it is in relation to the present time or the presence of the physical body, "pure presence" is no more than a fantasy. This is not to say that presence is absence. It is, says Derrida, instead "a trace which replaces a presence which has never been present" (297). It cannot be re-presented on stage—not by Artaud, nor by Beckett—because "pure" presence is not capable of being *presently present.*

"Writing is Dirty, Speech is Clean": The Moralization of Speech and Presence

If the theatre can be perceived as the space of "pure presence" because it allows spectators to witness the presence of physical bodies on stage acting out a text in the present time of the production, it is no less possible to make this same connection between the supposed presence of the speech act in the theatre. The stage permits for the possibility of the articulation and reception of speech, which has historically been associated with presence. This correlation between the speech act and presence stems from the perception of the body as the original intentional context of the "message" or "idea." When one verbally articulates a message in the *presence* of and in the *present time* of another person, there is less chance of the message being misinterpreted than if the message had first been written and read at a later time. The implication then is that the body, as the source of the verbal message, is the site at which the "truth" of a message originates.

There is, of course, nothing "original" in characterizing the speech act as representative of presence and the written word as inhabited by absence. Philosophers from Plato, to Malebranche, to Descartes, to Leibniz, to Condillac, to Rousseau, and so on, have long made this claim. They argue that writing depends on absence for its very being, since it would not be "present" at all if it were not needed to account for some "originary absence."

In *Of Grammatology*, Derrida interrogates the origins of such an originary absence linked to the written word. Readers who are familiar with Derrida's work will certainly need no introduction to such a canonical text as *Of Grammatology*. However, an elucidation of certain aspects of this text will prove useful in the context of this study. In "From/Of the Supplement to the Source," Derrida explains the inauguration of the association of writing with absence by stating that:

> ...it is at the moment that the social distance [...] increases to the point of becoming *absence*, that writing becomes necessary. [...] When the field of society extends to the point of *absence*, of the *invisible*, the *inaudible*, and the *immemorable*, when the local community is dislocated to the point where individuals *no longer appear* to one another, become capable of being *imperceptible*, the age of writing begins. (281–282, my emphasis)

> ...c'est au moment où la distance sociale [...] s'accroît jusqu'à devenir *absence*, que l'écriture devient nécessaire. [...] Quand le champ de la société s'étend au point de l'*absence*, de l'*invisible*, de l'*inaudible*, de l'*immémorable*, quand la communauté locale est disloquée au point que les individus *ne s'apparaissent plus les uns aux autres*, deviennent sujets d'être *imperceptibles*, l'âge de l'écriture commence. (399, my emphasis)

While communication in the way of gestures or speech is considered "fully present" and even "originary" (18) because it is intended to be used in the *presence* of the destinator, writing is meant to signify in the *absence* of both the destinator and the locutor. One might imagine that writing would then at least be privileged as an invaluable form of communication *in absentia*. Yet, this has not been the case in Western thought. Instead, writing has been regarded not only as the weaker counterpart of speech, but even as a degenerative form of communication, fraught with risk and a potential for perversity, only to be used when absolutely necessary, and only in the "absence" of speech. Derrida claims that this has always been the status of writing in the history of metaphysics: it is but "a debased, lateralized, repressed, displaced theme [...]" (270). The Swiss linguist Ferdinand de Saussure offers one reason for the secondary status of writing in Western thought. While the oral sign is the sign of the "inner meaning" of the original thing or idea, the graphic sign is but a sign of the oral sign, and as such it is one additional step removed from the original idea. Thus, although both speech and writing are supplements for some original entity, writing is, as Derrida expresses it, "the supplement par excellence" because it "marks the point where the supplement proposes itself" not simply as a supplement, but as a "supplement of supplement, sign of sign, *taking the place of* a speech already significant." Writing "marks the place of the initial doubling" (281).

Unlike Derrida, Beckett does not explicitly theorize writing as a supplement. There is, nonetheless, a significant amount of supplementing that takes place on the level of the characters and particularly in Beckett's novels. The names of the characters in *Molloy*, for example, are substituted for one another willy-nilly. Molloy's mother is "Ma, Mag or the Countess caca."[33] Mrs. Loy, for her part, becomes Mrs. Lousse, Sophie, who is then confused with Edith, also known as Ruth, who is indistinguishable from Molloy's mother, and so forth:

> "[...] I am tempted to think of them as one and the same old hag, flattened and crazed by life. And God forgive me, to tell you the horrible truth, my mother's image sometimes mingles with theirs, which is literally unendurable, like being crucified." (59)

However, the real "supplement par excellence" is Molloy himself. For Lousse, he takes the place of her dog, much in the same way "as [the dog] for her had taken the place of a child" (47). With his mother, Molloy participates in something of an exchange. First, it is an exchange of equivalency, where each could be the other: "We were so old, she and I [...], we were like a couple of old cronies, sexless, unrelated, with the same memories, the same rancours, the same expectations." Next, it is an exchange of another sort: "I took her for my mother," he claims, "and she took me for my father" (17). Yet, at the temporal end of his voyage—the proper beginning of his official narration and the novel—he ceases to stand in for his father, and instead replaces his mother. Although Molloy fails to find his mother—the object of his errant quest—in that he never actually reaches her, he does succeed to a certain extent by standing in for her. "I am in my mother's room," begins the text, "I sleep in her bed. I piss and shit in her pot." "I have," he informs us, "taken her place" (7).

Derrida notes, then again, that supplementarity is more often than not characterized as being far from innocuous. He argues that writing is not thought of as a simple supplement to speech, but rather as "*the dangerous supplement*." Although these examples of "place-taking" in Beckett's *Molloy* seem to be included more for amusement than anything else, they hint at an underlying darkness involved in supplementing, for the majority of these examples seem to require the death of some person or thing in order to take place. Molloy is only able to take the place of a father who is dead, an equally dead dog, and an "apparently" dead mother, though he is unsure whether or not she is indeed dead "enough to bury" (7).

There are several reasons for the designation of writing as a "dangerous supplement." The practical explanation states that if a person is not present when what he has written is read, he cannot be sure that the message has been interpreted as it was intended. To commit one's thoughts to writing then is to put one's message *in danger* of being misunderstood; it is to *risk* the "truth" of the original utterance. Every instance of writing accuses the absence of this original context and thus accuses the absence of the "truth" of the original context. Thus, Derrida insists that "the history of truth," of "the truth of truth," has always been the "debasement of writing."[34]

Derrida admits that there are "practical" reasons why writing has been traditionally viewed as less desirable than speech. Here he provides the example of Rousseau's condemnation of writing in "The Social Contract," where representation leads to the loss of personal freedom: "the moment a people allows itself to be represented, it is no longer free; it no longer exists." But while this is true of all forms of representation, it is because of the written word—the "decree" that can be substituted for a law—that "the general will becomes mute." Threatened in advance by "the letter," the body politic "begins to die as soon as it is born, and carries in itself the cases of its destruction." As Derrida concludes, writing is for Rousseau the very "origin of inequality" (297).

Yet, as Derrida insists, the real reason for the secondary status of writing—why it is indeed characterized as perilous in comparison—is ultimately mythic and moral. The sign "is always a sign of the Fall." Any absence "always relates to distancing from God" (283). For Rousseau, this translates to a fall into depravity. The "noble savage" of the "Discourse on the Origin of Inequality" loses his nobility and innocence with the advent of civilization, representation, and in particular, writing. Rousseau suggests that any representation clumsily and excessively conceals or "masks" something "natural," and in so doing, renders that original and "natural" thing "civilized," that is to say, frightening, even perverse. As an example, Rousseau brings up the case of nudity in art. Nudity, in itself, is a "natural" state. Thus, artistic representations of nudity are not in and of themselves perverse. But if some small item of clothing is added to the representation of the nude—masking one part of the body but not another—the image is corrupted. "Statues and paintings only offend the eyes when a mixture of clothing renders the nudity obscene."[35]

Rousseau employs this same argument in his critique of the theatre. He explains that one must allow "a lively and frolicsome youth" to partake of innocent and "natural" pleasures such as public gatherings in "open air" festivals "without object [...] without sacrifice [...] without expense [...] and above all without masks." He warns that if we do not allow youth such innocent pleasures, they invariably "substitut[e] more dangerous ones [...]." One way or another, a choice will be made; children will chose to take part in activities that take place out in open, public spaces, or in private, concealed spaces. For Rousseau, the appropriate decision is quite "clear." While innocent joys "evaporate in the full light of day," vice "is a friend of shadows" (308). For Derrida, the underlying message of Rousseau's argument against concealment is ironically just as transparent. Any "condemnation of masks," he argues, is also "an ambiguous condemnation" of writing (353).

"Speaking is Dirty, Writing is Clean": Revisiting the Speech/Writing Polarity

In a television interview with Claire Parnet, Gilles Deleuze uttered the now (in)famous phrase with which he will perhaps forever be associated: "Speaking is dirty, writing is clean" ("parler, c'est sale, écrire, c'est propre"). Notwithstanding the evident incongruity of actually *speaking* such an utterance, Deleuze's aim was to launch a critique against all so-called intellectuals who waste their time speaking instead of thinking by participating in opportunities for "babble," otherwise named "colloquia," rather than carefully organizing and writing down their thoughts. However, in uttering the phrase "Speaking is dirty, writing is clean," Deleuze also manages to unsettle the age-old speech /

writing hierarchy by turning it on its head. Here, it is speech—not writing—that is not only inadequate but even perverse or "dirty."

In "La différance," Derrida also sets out to undermine these age-old assumptions about speech and writing by demonstrating the inability of speech to account for meaning or for the intent of the speaker. The example he employs is the word "différance," which, depending on whether it is spelled with an "a" ("-ance") or an "e" ("-ence"), could mean either "to differ" or "to defer." What makes this word particularly important for his argument is that the difference between the two words—"différance" or "différence"—cannot be heard. It can only be seen. The difference is therefore solely graphic. Thus, when uttering these words in a speech—which Derrida does, as "La différance" was originally delivered as a speech—there is no way of knowing which meaning is being referred to: "Je ne peux en effet vous faire savoir par mon discours, par ma parole à l'instant proféré de quelle différence je parle au moment où j'en parle" (4). In speech, the "a" remains "silent, secret and discreet as a tomb" ("il demeure silencieux, secret et discret comme un tombeau"). Immediately perceptible in writing alone, this one letter manages to effect a privileging of the written word and to topple the speech/writing hierarchy. As such, this seemingly insignificant "a" has the power to bring about the "death of a dynasty" (4).

Yet, despite their common suspicion of the speech/writing binary opposition, Deleuze and Derrida remain very different thinkers, and this difference extends itself to the way in which each problematizes this hierarchy. Where Deleuze reverses the hierarchy—which disturbs the balance of power, but still leaves the hierarchy intact—Derrida destabilizes the hierarchy itself by demonstrating how it is ultimately impossible to decide which term has more power. Simply put, perhaps neither speech nor writing can lay exclusive claim to presence, or for that matter, to absence either.

Derrida comes to this conclusion after investigating the definition of the sign itself. Every sign is a substitute for the thing, idea, or person it represents. An oral sign, like its written counterpart, is but a signifier "whose signified is another signifier and never the thing itself" ("dont le *signifié* est un autre *signifiant*, et jamais 'la chose même,'" Descombes 172). Regardless of whether it is graphic or oral, the sign can therefore *never* truly lay any claim to presence, because, as Derrida states:

> The sign is usually said to be put in the place of the thing itself, the present thing, "thing" here standing equally for meaning or referent. The sign represents the present

in its absence. It takes the place of the present. When we cannot grasp or show the thing, state the present, the being-present, when the present cannot be presented, we signify, we go through the detour of the sign. (9)

Le signe, dit-on couramment, se met à la place de la chose même, de la chose présente, "chose" valant ici aussi bien pour le sens que pour le référent. Le signe représente le présent en son absence. Il en tient lieu. Quand nous ne pouvons prendre ou montrer la chose, disons le présent, l'étant-présent, quand le présent ne se présente pas, nous signifions, nous passons par le détour du signe. (9)

If the sign represents a present, it can therefore only be a differed presence. All signs, even those belonging to speech, are conceivable "only on the *basis* of a presence that [they] defer and *moving toward* the differed presence that [they] aim to reappropriate" (9).

The absence of presence is not the only property speech and writing have in common. As a result of this lack, they also share the quality of iterability. Due to the potential for its message to be taken out of the particular context in which it was written (i.e., its potential for repeatability), writing has always been conceived of as "dead" or contaminated by absence. Speech, on the other hand, is considered to be squarely set within its original context. Thus unlike writing, which is thought of as nothing but the "sign of a sign," speech supposedly resists facile quotation. Derrida suggests, however, that the possibility of extraction and "citational grafting" may well constitute not only the condition of writing, but of all language:

Every sign, linguistic or non-linguistic, spoken or written [...] can be cited, put between quotation marks; thereby it can break with every given context, and engender infinitely new contexts in an absolutely nonsaturable fashion.[36]

Tout signe, linguistique ou non linguistique, parlé ou écrit [...] peut être cité, mis entre guillemets; par là, il peut rompre avec tout contexte donné, engendrer à l'infini de nouveaux contextes, de façon absolument non saturable.[37]

This possibility of being severed from its referent, "cut off from its alleged 'production' or origin," marks every sign, even if oral, as a "grapheme"; it constitutes all signs in advance as writing.[38] Regardless of how much one would like to believe that speech is exempt from the constraints of writing, and is independent of writing, the facts are inescapable. Rousseau is the preeminent example, for though he praises the healing properties of presence and speech, he is obliged to concede his own dependence on writing in order to make these thoughts known. Plato too shows his hand in this way, for though the *Symposium* is presented in dialogue form, it was always, and only, a written work. Finally, speech in the theatre is always already simultaneously present and represented. Speech and writing are implicated within one another, and the only "illusion" is that "they are two" (*"qu'ils font deux"*) (5).

"Play It Again, Sam": Presence, Speech and Repetition in Beckett's Theatrical Productions

Beckett's so-called "turn" to the theatre could be perceived less as a desire to simply be in the presence of bodies on stage as a wish to distance himself in a definitive manner from the tyrannical drudgery of the written word.[39] Beckett implied as much when telling Colin Duckworth that he began to write *Godot* "as a relaxation, to get away from the awful prose I was writing at that time."[40] Yet the idea that Beckett "turned" to the theatre and away from prose decisively in search of the presence of speech is problematic. While Beckett did concentrate more energy on writing for the stage after completing the trilogy, by no means did he give up writing prose altogether in order to do so. In fact, he continued to write and publish a significant amount of short prose well into the 1980's. The idea that Beckett turned to the theatre to the exclusion of other writing—that there was some evolutionary "progression" from prose to the theatre—is then simply inaccurate and can only be explained as the result of a willful disregard of at least half of the work he produced from the mid 1950's until his death.

More importantly, Beckett's treatment of the speech act on stage reveals that he is as suspicious of its supposed natural primacy or claim to presence as he is of the notion of presence itself. His extensive use of silence in both his plays and films suggests this quite readily. *Act Without Words, Nacht und Träume*, and *Quad* are all productions—the first a play, and the other two telefilms—in which no words are ever uttered. No speech is present. *Film*, on the other hand, features one word, but it is a word that is meant to produce silence alone: "Shhhhh." Even the plays and telefilms that feature a substantial amount of dialogue manage to question the primacy of speech. The countless refrains uttered by characters like Vladimir and Estragon in *Godot*, Winnie in *Happy Days*, and Hamm, Clov, Nell, and Nagg in *Endgame*, undermine any sense of originality in speech. In certain plays, *Endgame, Cendres*, and *Happy*

Days, for example, there are so many pauses incorporated into the script that they rival the words that are actually spoken.

Of all of Beckett's plays the one that most calls into question the link between speech and presence is *Krapp's Last Tape*. *Krapp's Last Tape* is the "story" of a man who, on his birthday, ritualistically takes out his tape recorder in order to listen to past recordings of his own voice—recordings made on previous birthdays—and to tape present-day impressions of his life and state of being. Initially, thus, this appears to be a play about the "present," in particular, about the possibility of accessing the present long after the present has ceased to be. By listening to recordings of a past-present in the present-present, and by taping the present-present that is also projected as a future-present, Krapp appears to have found a way to still time and to live in a perpetual present. This impression is deceptive. While it would seem that a tape-recorded version of past events could capture a presence that writing could not (if only by bringing the actual voice of a present long since past into the actual present), this is not what takes place in this play. For, although the recorded voice of Krapp as a young man has indeed been fixed within the present in which it was recorded, it can enter the present-present only by virtue of some *thing*, here, a tape recorder. The supposed "immediacy" of the present of the tape recordings is really just a mediated-immediacy, signaling it from the start as a non-immediacy. In fact, even what one would normally call the "present" in this play—the action of Krapp listening to and making recordings—is not a "present" at all. As the very first words of this play tell us, what happens on stage takes place on a late evening "in the future." Be that as it may, this is something the spectators would know only if they had previously read the text or if the director chose to highlight this significant detail in the production.

Although Krapp himself never articulates it as such, he is not ignorant of the effects of the passage of time. While his taped voice manages to stay fixed in the moment in which it was taped, he recognizes that he himself has changed dramatically since the taping and scarcely resembles or even remembers the "stupid bastard [he] took [himself] for thirty years ago."[41] The difference between the two versions of himself is evident in the many parts of the play when the older, more cantankerous Krapp attempts to interact and identify with the voice of the more youthful, confident, and "resolute" person he used to be:

The voice! Jesus! And the aspirations! [Brief laugh in which Krapp joins.] And the resolutions! [Brief laugh in which Krapp joins.] To drink less in particular. [Brief laugh of Krapp alone.] (218)

Try as he might to fully correspond fully to his younger self, and thus to repeat a present long past, difference—in the form of time—has already entered the equation, rendering the retrieval of that moment impossible.

Krapp's memory, or lack thereof, is another confirmation of this impossibility of ever fully recovering the past. Frequently, the older, less mentally agile Krapp has difficulty remembering aspects of what he evidently once knew so well. The business about "the black ball" that he wrote of in his ledger is now as lost to him as the not so-memorable "memorable equinox":

Hm...The black ball...[he raises his head, stares blankly front. Puzzled.] Black ball?...[He peers again at ledger, reads.] The dark nurse... [He raises his head, broods, peers again at ledger, reads.] [...] Hm...Memorable...what? [He peers closer.] Equinox, memorable equinox. [He raises his head, stares blankly front. Puzzled.] Memorable equinox?

Hearing the sounds of his voice describing these past feelings and events does little to jog his failing memory. The word "viduity" that he used in reference to his mother and that is repeated on the recording year after year, through time has become somehow "different" and is now as foreign to him as if it had been in another language:

...there is of course the house on the canal where mother lay a-dying, in the late autumn, after her long viduity [KRAPP gives a start.] and the -[KRAPP switches off, winds back tape a little, bends his ear closer to machine, switches on.]—a-dying, after her long viduity, and the–[KRAPP switches off, raises his head, stares blankly before him. His lips move in the syllables of 'viduity.' No sound...]. (219)

The only way he is able to regain at least the semblance of what the younger Krapp once meant by "viduity" is by referring to a text:

[...He gets up, goes backstage into darkness, comes back with an enormous dictionary, lays it on the table, sits down and looks up the word.] KRAPP: [Reading from dictionary.] State—or condition—of being—or remaining—a widow—or widower [...].

Yet, even while he is able to find the definition of "viduity" in a text, and thus seems to have found the means with which to regain a past present, in the end the dictionary—because it offers too many possibilities—is just as incapable of recovering the present as the recorded voice had been:

> [*Pause. He peers again at dictionary. Reading.*] Deep weeds of viduity....Also of an animal, especially a bird...the vidua or weaver-bird...Black plumage of male...[*He looks up. With relish.*] The vidua-bird!

To reinforce the proximity of writing and speech, Beckett shows how similar the recorded voice is to the written text of the ledger. He treats the spoken recorded word it as if it were transcribed on paper: material, manipulatable, and subject to the breaks in the flow of meaning involved in reading. For example, when Krapp stops in the middle of a word to turn the page of his ledger he obscures the signification of what is being read in the process. With his oft-cited "Adieu à l'a...(*il tourne la page*)...mour," meaning hangs precariously, if only for an instant, between "goodbye to....death" on one hand, and "goodbye to....love" on the other. These breaks in the flow of discourse that are a fact of the very material act of reading are paralleled by the ceaseless hesitations in the spoken discourse captured on the tape recording: "The face she had! The eyes! Like... [*hesitates*] ...chrysolite! [*Pause.*] Ah well... [*Pause.*]" (220). This, coupled with the maniacally obsessive rewinding and fast-forwarding of the tape also allows Krapp to manipulate the spoken discourse in much the same way as he controls the flow, and thus the meaning, of the written discourse by turning the pages of his ledger back and forth at will.

Sharing many of the qualities traditionally assigned to writing, speech can no longer lay claim to being the bearer of presence, at least no more so than writing. This is particularly so in a play like *Krapp's Last Tape* in which there is no pure present of which to speak. But even those plays that appear to stage sheer presence reveal with time and with close attention to detail that there is no presence—whether in the form of the body on stage or the spoken word—that is not already tainted by time, consciousness, and mediation. Beckett's rumored turn to the theatre is not indicative of a belief in and desire for a pure presence. Instead, Beckett anticipates what philosophers like Jacques Derrida will later theorize as the unsettling of the speech/writing hierarchy and presents the reader with the very undecidabilty that lies at the heart of all binary oppositions. Indeed, Samuel Beckett's dramatic texts stage presence, but ultimately it is to expose the notions of presence of being and present time as little more than theoretical impossibilities.

"The Aborted Cogito": Writing, Presence, and the Subject

Along with the tendency of Beckett scholars to theorize a pure present in Beckett's work, there is also a predisposition of critics to equate his work with his life. Beckett himself encourages this type of reading by peppering his work with supposed childhood memories, references to his Irish background (Irish towns, foods, street names, and so forth), and by allowing both his English and French language texts to be colored by Irish colloquialisms. Despite the many references in his texts that seem to beg for autobiographical interpretation, I would suggest that Beckett's work is less an example of autobiography than an illustration of what H. Porter Abbott refers to as "auto-graphy."[42] Rather than attempting to define or give shape to his own life—to make *himself* present to himself through writing—his work explores the notion of *the* Self, the subject, and its relation to the written word. Beckett's work thus again dialogues with so-called postmodern thinkers like Deleuze and Derrida who, like Beckett, evoke elements of traditional narrative and readings of the Self in order to ultimately problematize any beliefs we might have about the writing/written subject.

As previously mentioned, *Of Grammatology* is Derrida's major work on the history and status of writing in Western civilization where he challenges the long held speech/writing power structure. An offshoot of this hierarchy is the question of how presence relates (or does not relate) to both writing and to our conceptualization of the Self. Focusing primarily on Rousseau's work as the object of his inquiry, Derrida examines the role that presence has historically played in the construction of the stable, authoritative, Cartesian subject. According to this equally well-known model, the self is determined by applying systematic doubt to everything about which the mind cannot be absolutely certain. The Cartesian self is therefore what remains after everything external to the mind, and everything that could be potentially deceptive, has been eliminated. This subject then is arrived at by making the self as "present" to the mind as possible, by a process of self-reflexive mediation.

The question many scholars have asked themselves is whether or not self-presence is even possible. If it is not possible, what happens to the subject? Similar to Derrida, Jean Starobinski examines this predicament as it relates to Rousseau, primarily because he lauded both the healing properties of the present time, saying "The great remedy to the miseries of this world is the absorption into the present moment" ("Le grand remède aux misères de ce monde, c'est l'absorption dans l'instant présent")[43] and the related, but certainly not identical idea, of presence of being.[44] Rousseau also based his abstraction of the self on this notion of presence. Yet, as Starobinski notes, in order to show himself for what he really is—to reveal his "true self" to both himself and to the world—Rousseau does not himself cultivate presence at all:

> I would love society as much as any other man, where I not sure of showing myself there not only to my disadvantage but quite *other than I really am*. My decision to write and *to hide myself* was perfectly suited to me. *With me present, no one would ever have known what I was worth*.[45]

As Starobinski argues, paradoxically Rousseau must hide "in order to make himself more visible."[46] He must be absent in order to be present.

In *Difference and Repetition*, Deleuze makes a similar argument about the relationship between the self and self-presence. He begins by asserting that Descartes was correct in stating that one can only come to an idea of the self through contemplation. However, Deleuze, like Paul de Man, does not believe that the self, as a subject, can ever be contemplated by itself, for in order to contemplate itself, the subject must cease to be the *subject* that contemplates and become instead the *object* of contemplation.[47] In other words, the self can *never* be present to itself as itself as a subject. As Deleuze affirms, "we must always contemplate *something else* in order to be filled with an image of ourselves."[48]

Deleuze actually attributes this new and improved version of the cogito—one he qualifies as a "cogito for the dissolved self" or the "aborted cogito" (110)—to Immanuel Kant. He claims that the moment Kant called rational theology into question, in the same stroke "he introduce[d] a kind of disequilibrium, a fissure or crack in the pure self of the 'I think.'" It is this "open[ing] of Being directly on to difference" that exposes the "schizophrenic" makeup of the subject: "*Underneath the self* which acts *are little selves* which contemplate and which render possible both the action and the active subject" (75). From this point on, there is no denying that the subject can "represent its own spontaneity only as an Other" (58), only live itself "like an Other within itself." "I," Deleuze writes, "is an Other" (86). The self has become the equivalent of "the unequal in itself" (90).

"Let's Just Say You're Not Quite There": Self Presence and the Beckettian Subject

As suggested in chapter two, though many scholars have noted Beckett's continual allusions to Descartes' method of forming the subject,[49] the results that Beckett's characters get after using this method are radically different from those of Descartes. Where Descartes ultimately is able to give form to the subject through self-reflection, Beckett's characters never achieve that same stability. Billy Whitelaw, one of Beckett's favorite actresses, became acutely aware of the ambiguous status of being in Beckett's work while preparing for a production of *Footfalls*. Whitelaw was set to play the ephemeral "May": a character who converses with the many voices in her "poor mind" and denies being where other characters claim to have seen her. Unsure of the relative nature of her character, Whitelaw asked Beckett whether May was even alive. His response has become a favorite of Beckett scholars: "Let's just say *you're not quite there*."[50]

This is the status of the majority of Beckett's characters: if they *are*, what they *are* is *not quite there*. This lack of pure presence in the subject comes in a variety of forms. Some of his characters are literally absent in one way or another. "Auditor" in *Not I* can, for example, be seen but not heard. Others, like "V," the offstage voice in *Footfalls*, can be heard but not seen. Some characters, like Ada in *Embers*, cannot be called "present" simply because they are not alive. They are instead ghosts. Others, such as the barely visible, scarcely audible Willy in *Happy Days*, are merely ghost-like, not entirely absent, but not present either. Malone of *Malone Dies*—a text Beckett had initially entitled *The Absent (One)*—is described as visible, audible, and alive, yet he is from the start, as the title suggests, always in the process of expiring.

The first narrator of *The Unnamable* questions the idea of an authoritative, whole subject as early as the first words of the text: "Where now? Who now? When now? Unquestioning. I, say I. Unbelieving" ("Où maintenant ? Quand maintenant ? Qui maintenant ? Sans me le demander. Dire je. Sans le penser"). The "characters" of this text, if one could call them that, are also continuously rendered suspect. According to one of the narrators, there is nothing "truthful" or "real" about Basil and his gang. They are, he informs us, "[i]nexistent, invented to explain I forget what" ("inexistants, inventés pour expliquer je ne sais plus quoi"). What is more, they were invented, this narrator admits, "by me alone," just like "God and man, nature and the light of day, the heart's outpourings and the means of understanding."[51] There are some references to characters—many who appeared in Beckett's earlier novels—who seem to correspond more to the traditional subject in that they are endowed with a name and a familiar, human physical form. However, these identities do not remain stable long. Murphy, Mercier, Camier, Watt, Molloy, Moran, and Malone are all brought back to life again by the narrator of this text only to be instantly waved away, rendering their status as subjects questionable: "Let them be gone now, them and all the others, those I have used and those I have not used [...]. There, now there is no one here but me" (304). The narrators themselves have difficulty comprehending their own limits, exclaiming more than once, "I don't know where I end." When trying to define himself, one of the narrators begins by describing his head as "a great smooth ball [he] carr[ies] on [his] shoulders." Soon though he describes his entire being as nothing more than a head, "a big talking ball" (305). But this portrait does not last long, for he later states that it is not just that he *has* a head, or *is* a head, but that he is only *inside* a head. Over the course of a few pages, he has recoiled into something that no longer has a form or is a form, but now exists within a form: within the confines of what we can only assume is a skull.

"Virtual Subjects": Beckett's Subjects and Deleuze's Virtual Objects

Perhaps, as the narrator of *The Unnamable* proposes, just who or what the subject is in Beckett's work in the end "doesn't matter," because, in the end, "there is none" (360). Although Beckett's subjects seem to have little in common with those imagined by Descartes, they greatly resemble what Deleuze calls the "virtual object": an entity that escapes determination, and in particular humanization. It should be noted that Deleuze's use of the word "virtual" to describe this "object" does not mean that it has no place in the "real." In fact, paradoxical as it may sound, it is what all metaphysically imagined subjects and objects "really" are, underneath. They are, like Ada, May, V, and Willy never *quite there*. Never fully present, they are also never entirely absent. They have the property of "being *and* not being where they are, wherever they go."[52]

For Deleuze, the most salient quality of the virtual object is that it "lacks its own identity" (101). This is primarily because it can never, like "Mouth" and "Auditor" of *Not I*, be anything more than a "fragment of itself." It is at any time but a "shred or remainder" of what it ought to be (102). This is the very condition for its possibility. Born of a split within itself that causes it to be forever "displaced in relation to itself" (105), the virtual object is the embodiment of self-estrangement. The Beckettian character shares this fundamental characteristic. It too is split apart on the inside and is often unrecognizable even to itself. Molloy is exemplary of this schizophrenic subject. He refers to himself alternately in the first person and the third person, consistently forgets his own name, and admits to "strut[ting]" before himself "like a stranger."[53] Even his relationship to objects and to language is characterized by a split or separation: the separation between an object and its function, a word and its meaning. Constantly signaling his inability to comprehend "regular," ordinary, discourse—often more attuned to that of birds—Molloy describes his relationship to language in the following way: "The words I heard were heard [...] as pure sounds, free of all meaning" (50). His relationship with language could thus be characterized by the French word *délire*. In the most immediately available sense of the word, the relationship is *delirious* in that it does not correspond to the way in which we imagine that we experience language. But it is also a relationship that is constitutive of a general *dé-lire* (un-reading), or more specifically by a *dé-lier*—an un-linking, or a separation of the signifier from the signified. Despite the negative connotations created by the negative prefix of the words "un-linking" and "un-reading," the split that occurs within the virtual object is in no way a hindrance to its wellbeing. On the contrary, the virtual object is only actualized in "splitting up and being divided." As Maurice Blanchot argues, this is also the condition of possibility for all writing.

In *The Book to Come* Blanchot lays the foundations for what he calls the fate of all writers: "The work demands that the man who writes it sacrifice himself for the work, become other [...]."[54] In order for words to spill out onto a blank page—for any text to be written—the writing subject must splinter apart and become a stranger to himself. This description of the subject's need to separate from itself is not at all uncommon in contemporary theory. Blanchot's writer's sacrifice of self is also strikingly reminiscent of Lacan's "mirror stage," the foundation of subjectivity, as well as Heidegger's conception of the forward and outward projection of the self: "l'être-pour-la-mort."[55] All three theorize not only the benefit of the subject perceiving itself as Other, but also the inevitability of this separation. The fragmentation of the subject is a consequence of being born into language.

Of all of Beckett's works, the one that is most illustrative of the splintering and self-estrangement of the writing subject is *Malone Dies*. Malone, who remains unnamed for the first eighty pages of this text, spends his bedridden time alternately thinking about what he owns and the stories he creates in an attempt to both solidify an image of himself and to forget it. However, writing and stable, solidly unchanging, identities do not go hand in hand. Caught up as he is in the act of writing, Malone is unable to resist the split that occurs within: "They are *not mine*, but I say *my pots*, as I say *my bed, my window*, as I say *me*" (252). Malone is often not simply conscious of the need for this dispossession of self, he even goes so far as to cultivate his own alterity: "I began again, to try and live, cause to live, *be another, in myself, in another*."[56] He willingly strives for self-abandon (255) so as to reach the point of finally being able to feel behind his closed eyes, "other eyes close" (195).[57] He finds himself not only forgetting his own being (224), and unconscious of his own actions (234), but also on the verge of "vanishing" (195) or "go[ing] liquid" (225). Indeed, it is in this tenuous place where the self is nearly entirely dispossessed that he accomplishes this endeavor: "On the threshold of being no more," says Malone, "I succeed in being another" (194).[58] This projection away from and outside of the self is facilitated by Malone's recounting of "stories," those micro-narratives into which we are drawn and from which we are incessantly ejected. But while Malone claims to resort to telling himself stories so as to take the focus off himself ("I shall not watch myself die [...] Have I watched myself live?" (179)),[59] these fictions often lead right back to the teller. By inventing characters in his proper likeness (Sapo / MacMann), by endowing them with qualities or actions that recall his own,[60] and finally by confusing himself altogether with the characters,[61] the reader learns that even when speaking of others Malone is still, and always, speaking of himself. Rather than observing his own self-diminishment in the course of recounting his tales, Malone finds himself at times "swelling, in spite of [his] stories" (257). Yet, while this increased self-awareness might lead one to believe that Malone does not succeed in making himself Other, this is not at all the case. He is, in fact, all throughout this work, wavering between subject and object: at once on the threshold of holding his own and on the verge of becoming no one at all.

In other texts by Beckett, the subject does not split into just two parts or hover between only two states of being. In *Molloy, The Unnamable,* and *Company,* the subject splinters off into a myriad simulacrum. Constantly in the process of morphing into something new, these subjects embody what Deleuze refers to as the only real form of Being: the "being of-becoming." Just as there is no way to contain the split within the virtual object from breaking off and splitting indefinitely, there is no way to stop the proliferation of the Beckettian subject once it starts—and it has already started. Moran is acutely aware of this, but especially where it concerns the object of his quest, Molloy:

> The fact was there were three, no, four Molloys. He that inhabited me, my caricature of same, Gaber's and the man of flesh and blood somewhere awaiting me. To these I would add Youdi's were it not for Gaber's corpse fidelity to the letter of his messages [...]. I will therefore add a fifth Molloy, that of Youdi [...]. There were others too, of course. But let us leave it at that, if you don't mind, the party is big enough. (115)

> Il y avait en somme trois, non, quatre Molloy. Celui de mes entrailles,—la caricature que j'en faisais, celui de Gaber et celui qui, en chair et en os, m'attendait quelque part. J'y ajouterais celui de Youdi, n'était l'exactitude prodigieuse de Gaber pour tout ce qui touchait à ces commissions. [...] J'ajouterai donc un cinquième Molloy, celui de Youdi. [...] Il y en avait d'autres évidemment. Mais restons-en là, si vous voulez bien, dans notre petit cercle d'initiés. (156)

This proliferation of identities within one subject is also reflected in the multiple names conferred upon certain characters. As formerly stated, in *Molloy*, "Mrs. Loy" changes to "Lousse," only to be later baptized as "Sophie." "Ruth" mutates into "Edith," and finally "Rose." In *The Unnamable*, this splintering sometimes manifests itself as a mingling of several formerly distinct identities. The narrator claims, for example, that while Basil simply "usurp[ed] [his] name" (298), Mahood and others before him went so far as to "take themselves" for him (315). The narrator himself is not immune to such confusions, admitting that "more than once, I took myself for the other" (316). As the following excerpt demonstrates, "more than once" turns out to be something of an understatement:

> Decidedly Basil is becoming important, I'll call him Mahood instead, I prefer that, I'm queer. It was he who told me stories about me, lived in my stead, issued forth from me, came back to me, entered back into me, heaped stories on my head. I don't know how it was done [...]. It is his voice that has often, always, mingled with mine, and sometimes drowned it completely. Until he left me for good, or refused to leave me any more. I don't know. (309)

> Décidément Basile prend de l'importance. Je vais donc l'appeler Mahood plutôt, j'aime mieux ça, je suis bizarre. C'est lui qui me racontait des histoires sur moi, vivait pour moi, sortait de moi, revenait vers moi, rentrait dans moi, m'agonissait d'histoires. Je ne sais pas comment ça se faisait. [...] C'est sa voix qui s'est souvent, toujours, mêlée à la mienne, au point quelquefois de la couvrir tout à fait, jusqu'au jour où il m'a quitté pour de bon, ou n'a plus voulu me quitter, je ne sais pas.[62]

Basil(e), otherwise referred to as Mahood, is at first distinguished from the narrator; he lives in his "stead" and tells him stories about himself. Next, he becomes the narrator's product, then a part of him, and eventually even overcomes him. Finally, in a decidedly indefinite move, Basil(e)/Mahood separates definitively from the narrator ("he left me for good") *or* decides never to do so ("or refused to leave me any more"). But one of the most extreme examples of identity shifting occurs several pages later when the narrator attempts to relate the conclusion of one of his stories, only to stumble clumsily over the referents:

> According to Mahood, *I* never reached them [...]. But not so fast, otherwise *we'll* never arrive. It's no longer *I* in any case. *He'll* never reach us if *he* doesn't get a move on. *He* looks as if *he* had slowed own, since last year. Oh the last laps won't take *him* long. *My* missing leg didn't seem to affect them. (318, my emphasis)

> D'après Mahood *je* ne suis jamais arrivé [...]. Mais n'anticipons pas, sinon *nous* n'arriverons jamais. D'ailleurs ce n'est plus *moi*. Qui sait s'*il* arrivera jamais, du train où *il* va. *Il* a ralenti, on dirait, depuis l'année dernière. Oh les derniers tours, ça va vite. *Ma* jambe en moins leur était indifférente. (53, my emphasis)

In this example, Mahood, once referred to by the narrator as Basil(e), "my master," and even "me," informs the narrator that "I" never reached his family. But this "I" quickly transforms into "we," then "he" and finally "my." Given the incessant amount of splintering within each subject and shifting between each of them, one cannot help asking—just as one of the narrators does—"what then is a subject?" If one takes the example illustrated in *The Unnamable*, one can only respond—indeed, just as this narrator does—"Bah, any old pronoun will do" (343).

"Any Old Pronoun Will Do": Attempts to Stabilize the Subject

What the subject must submit to in *The Unnamable* is nothing less than an amputation of all recognizable body parts. There is, in other words, a general dis-*articulation* of the subject. Subjects mutate, divide, and multiply to the point where they become completely unrecognizable as subjects. Worm is a case in point. He is an amorphous creature with almost nothing that would link him to what one would traditionally conceive of as a subject, nothing save one lidless and endlessly tearing eye. However, one must not assume that just because many of Beckett's "characters" do not resemble traditional subjects that no attempt was ever made to make them so. "Basil(e) and the gang" try desperately to "humanize" (360) Worm by conferring upon him feelings and the ability to hear. But it is not until Worm is given physical shape in the form of a face that he becomes a satisfactory subject in the eyes of "the committee":

> A face, how encouraging that would be [...] passing from unmixed joy to the sullen fixity of marble, via the most characteristic shades of disenchantment, how pleasant that would be [...]. It might even pause, open its mouth, raise its eyebrows, bless its soul, stutter, mutter, howl, groan and finally shut up, the chaps clenched to cracking point, or fallen, to let the dribble out. (362)

> Un visage, comme se serait encourageant [...] changeant méthodiquement d'expression, [...] depuis la joie sans mélange jusqu'à la morne fixité du marbre, en passant par les nuances les plus caractéristiques du désenchantement, comme se serait agréable [...]. Il pourrait même s'arrêter, ouvrir la bouche, jubiler, s'étonner, tiens tiens, balbutier, marmotter, hurler, gémir et finalement la fermer, les mâchoires serrées à se rompre, ou ballantes, pour laisser passer l'écume. (126)

Finally, with feelings and a face to match, Worm would have what the committee so desperately wants him to have: "A presence at last" (362). Only then could others (Basil(e), the committee, the narrator and the reader) really relate to Worm, and speak of him using the same clichéd terms one would use for any cliché of a subject: "Look at old Worm," the others yearn to say, "waiting for his sweetheart" (363).[63] But despite their effort, Basil(e) and the others do not succeed in making Worm a human subject. As the narrator concedes, while Worm's humanization would certainly be "worth seeing," it is really just a "dream." It is just a "fairy-tale, yet another," like all of the others, with their "heads, trunks, arms, legs, and all that follows" (307). "For here," the narrator informs us, "there is no face, nor anything resembling one, nothing to reflect the joy of living and succedanea" (367).

The attempt to solidify the subject takes the form of a parody of the psychoanalytic endeavor in Beckett's *Not I* and *Company*, with however, the same limited success as in *The Unnamable*. *Not I* is structured like a nightmarish therapy session in which only the most rudimentary elements of the doctor/patient pairing remain. There is a Mouth that attempts to establish itself as a subject by taking control verbally of the pronoun "I/me." There is also an Auditor that presumably listens to the mouth, but in actuality does little more than effect "the simple sideways raising of arms from sides and their falling back, in a gesture of helpless compassion." Dipping in and out of the past, Mouth recounts what appears to be a story—fragmented though it is—that will eventually lead "her" to say "I/me":

> [...]...a few steps then stop...stare into space...then on...a few more...step and stare again...soon drifting around...when suddenly...gradually all went out...all that early April morning light...and she found herself in the—what? who?...not ...she![64]

Yet although it appears that Mouth is on the verge of affirming her selfhood by uttering "I"—even if it is only to deny herself by saying "I" after the word "not"—she never does. Mouth attempts this five times during the play—repeating the pattern "what? who? no..." verbatim—only to wind up at the same place: the third person singular "she." For Deleuze, this is the only place in which one can end up: "it is always a third person who says 'me.'"[65]

Less has been written about Beckett's short prose text *Company*, but it too highlights the impossibility of ever forming a whole subject. Like *Not I*, *Company* also starts out with what seems to be two subjects engaged in a pseudo-psychotherapy session, but here the roles of the speaker and the listener are reversed. In *Company*, the speaker is not trying to lay claim to the "I" as much as it is trying to help the auditor—or the "hearer"—to do so.

In his introduction to *Nohow On*, S.E. Gontarski describes this work as a dance: it is a "fugue" between "he" and an external voice which addresses the hearer as "you," "in which the former tries to provide the latter with a history and so a life."[66] As the title suggests, this is all done in order to create "company." The narrator presents this desire for company as a primordial need "to temper" the "nothingness"[67] in which we exist, to populate the darkness in which we are, as we "always were," "alone" (46). As the text progresses, this need for company becomes for the "hearer" a matter of desperation akin to an addiction. For although the narrator speaks of a certain relief in the thought of the "voice" becoming silent, the "craving" for company always inevitably "revives." Little by little the "need" to hear that voice again becomes overwhelming, even if it were only to repeat what it has already said one too many times before: the constant reminder that "You, are on your back in the dark" (40).

While "the voice alone is company," it is not enough: "Company apart this effect," explains the narrator, "is clearly necessary" (11). What is really being sought is the "I." The voice's objective then is to aid the hearer in the formation of his own being: "to have the hearer have a past and acknowledge it" (24). To accomplish this goal, the "voice" uses a method that greatly resembles hypnosis. The hearer, lying "on his back in the dark," is exposed to an incessantly repetitive internal cinema of so-called memories and pressed to take them on as representative of his proper past. Repeating these often pathetic tales, "with only minor variants, as if willing him by this dint to make them his [own]," the voice seeks to prod the hearer into taking on the first person singular pronoun, into finally uttering, "Yes I remember," twice (10).[68]

However, in spite of the voice's constant prodding for the hearer to become one with the "I," this never happens. The few times that the pronoun "I" is actually uttered it is always the "voice" that articulates it, and never even in relation to itself. The "I" is left floating somewhere between the voice and the hearer, never belonging to either one, thus never, like the voice, speaking and, one can logically assume, never hearing either. What we witness instead of a condensation of the subject is an apparent accumulation of distinct subjects. The text begins with only two subjects; the "one" who lies on his back in the dark and the "voice" that comes to him. But it is not long before the vast space in which they are initially presented as occupying alone is teaming with various "devised" and "divided" voices (the "voice," the "you," the "he," the "I," and the narrator), all "devising it all" for "company."

Beckett reveals in this work the subject's position in language, a position in which one can never be simply alone, nor simply "one." As Deleuze writes, the subject can speak of the self "only by virtue of these thousands of little witnesses which contemplate within us."[69] From the moment the subject enters into language it is multiple: "devised" and "divided." Like a multi-talented musician, one is one's own company, one accompanies oneself. "Subject" is just a name for the constant mingling and separating of various pronouns. It is only "natural" then that the subject automatically "speaks of himself as of another"[70] and asks, "whose voice asking this? Who asks, Whose voice asking this?" only to respond to himself: "The unthinkable... Unnamable. Last person. I" (17).[71]

Beckett continuously reminds us that being a subject *in* language entails being *subject to* language: to internal division and to the transitory character of pronouns, the shifters of language. This idea of the subjugated subject is one that also haunts the pages of the trilogy. For the characters of all three texts it manifests itself initially as physical subjugation. Although Molloy and Moran of *Molloy* are capable at one point of walking and riding a bike, they both eventually need to rely on crutches or sticks to support themselves and end up unable to leave their beds. Malone of *Malone Dies* is bedridden from the beginning of his narration. The narrators of *The Unnamable* remain motionless throughout the entire work. But these three texts highlight more than just the physical subjugation of their subjects. This is especially true of *Malone Dies* and *The Unnamable* which not only underscore how we are born into language and are henceforth subjected to language, they also suggest that we as subjects—especially as writing subjects—are perhaps nothing more than language itself.

"A Man of Letters": Language and the Self in *Malone Dies* and *The Unnamable*

Let us recall that Blanchot claims that in order to write there must be some form of self-estrangement. But he suggests that just being Other within the self, or even Others within the self, is not enough to produce writing. In order for writing to take place, the writing subject must in some sense cease to be:

> The work demands [...] that the man who writes it sacrifice himself for the work become [...] *not other* than the living man he was, the writer with his duties, his satisfactions, and his interests, *but he must become no one* [...].[72]

> L'œuvre demande [...] que l'homme qui l'écrit se sacrifie pour l'œuvre, [...] devienne *non pas un autre*, non pas, du vivant qu'il était, l'écrivain avec ses devoirs, ses satisfactions et ses intérêts, *mais plutôt personne* [...].[73]

The work demands of the author a transformation not into someone different, but into "no one," into "the empty and animated space where the call of the work resounds" (216). Blanchot describes this evacuation of self in ominous terms as a "threat" to which the author has no choice but to "give in" (215). The expression employed by Blanchot to communicate this notion of "giving in" is "s'y livrer," which suggests the notion of giving in to, or giving over to, but which also includes the French word for book: "livre." In giving himself over to this demand, the author gives himself over to the work, gives in to it, even becomes the work in the process.

In *Malone Dies*, Malone often seems to desire this self-erasure. "What I sought," he explains, "was the rapture of vertigo, the letting go, the fall, the gulf, the relapse to darkness, to nothingness...." (195).[74] Yet, this is not accomplished without some trepidation on his part. For although there is a "rapture" to be enjoyed in the vertigo of self-loss, there is also an evident distress in the possibility of self-erasure. The anxiety of the narrative "I" when faced with a progressive dispossession of the self manifests itself in the narrator's obsession with his objects. Thus, while he claims to invent stories so as not to "watch" himself, his description of what he calls his "present state" (significantly referred to as time set aside to take inventory of his "possessions") is meant to do just the opposite. His subjective assessment of the existence of his objects[75] serves to temporarily reinforce his own sense of being when faced with the threat of self-dispossession.

Given this link between possessions and self-possession, it is not surprising that the narrator/writer is ceaselessly compelled to reassess the objects that surround him and to interrupt his own stories in order to reestablish what is progressively lost both of himself and his objects which keep disappearing. Yet if the objects in his possession are indeed constitutive of his being, what is to be said of his subject when he himself admits that nothing is his anymore ("plus rien n'est à moi..." (135)), except his exercise-book and a French pencil, "assuming it really exists" (255).[76] The association of his identity with "nothing more"[77] than those objects involved in writing is further reinforced later in the text when Malone equates his life with his "child's exercise-book" (274).

Although Malone does, from time to time, defy total dispossession of the self by effecting a continuous "coming and going" between descriptions of his "present state" and the telling of his stories, towards the end of the narration he loses more and more control of himself. The progressive diminishing of what he officially classifies as his possessions, once indicative of his own self-possession and self-definition, reduces the narrative subject to the level of his many disposable "characters": "the Murphys, Merciers, Molloys, Morans and Malones" (236). With an existence and self-definition that is entirely dependent upon the material tools of language, "Malone"—the text seems to suggest—is but a word.

Beckett's portrait of the self as a linguistic construct anticipates what many structuralist and post-structuralist thinkers—in particular Barthes, Lacan, Derrida, and Deleuze—would later theorize about subjectivity. We cannot come to an idea of the self by way of an exploration of self-reflection, precisely because there is no self outside of language. In "Self (Pygmalion)" Paul de Man likewise contends that the self is in fact nothing if not "a structure of tropes" (186). Beckett's illustration of this concept, while apparent in *Malone Dies*, becomes much more explicit in *The Unnamable*. Similar to *Malone Dies*, the narrator of *The Unnamable* also justifies his existence by cataloguing what he refers to as "my little heap of my possessions," which includes but is not limited to his "system of nutrition and elimination." He soon admits though that these "possessions" that were the guarantee of his Being are perhaps nothing but "*vers*." In other words, his existence is predicated upon the "worms," for which all life eventually becomes fodder, and/or, on "verses," words, language itself. Soon after making this claim, the narrator plays down the identification of himself with living creatures ("worms" or even Worm) and instead emphasizes his relationship with the second meaning of the word "vers":

> [...] I'm in words, made of words, other's words [...] I'm all these words, all these strangers, this dust of words, with no ground for their settling, no sky for their dispersing, coming together to say, fleeing one another to say, that I am they, all of them, those that merge, those that part, those that never meet, and nothing else [...].[78]

> [...] je suis en mots, je suis fait de mots, des mots des autres [...] je suis tous ces mots, tous ces étrangers, cette poussière de verbe, sans fond où se poser, sans ciel où se dissiper, se rencontrant pour dire, se fuyant pour dire, que je les suis tous, ceux qui s'unissent, ceux qui se quittent, ceux qui s'ignorent, et pas autre chose [...].[79]

If the subject *is* anything, it is a textual object. Like everything else that seems to *be*, it too is made of, produced by, and exists only as language. As the narrator puts it, "It all boils down to a question of words" (335).[80] Words in Beckett's œuvre are increasingly divorced from any human container. Where the "human subjects"—the Malones, Morans, and Molloys—lose progressively more and more of their ability to move, the words of these texts come to life. Hence, the logic of Malone's proclamation towards the end of *Malone Dies* that he will never really disappear: "My story ended I'll be living yet" (283).[81]

In his essay "Dante...Bruno. Vico...Joyce," Beckett characterizes James Joyce's writing in a similar fashion, describing it as if the words themselves had a life of their own separate from the events they describe. For any Beckett scholar, this description of Joyce rings more like a characterization of his own work:

> Here form "is" content, content "is" form. You complain that this stuff is not written in English. It is not written at all. It is not to be read—or rather it is not only to be read. It is to be looked at and listened to. His writing is not "about" something; it is that something itself.

Thus, Beckett continues, "when the sense is sleep, the words go to sleep. When the sense is dancing, the words dance [...]." Light years from "the polite contortions of 20th century printer's ink," the words in Joyce's works are "alive": "They elbow their way on to the page, and glow and blaze and fade and disappear."[82]

Given the ambiguous, even delicate status of the subject in Beckett's work, it makes little sense to dwell on the question of who, finally, is speaking. For the response to such a question is that no one speaks—no being and no "body." It is rather, as Barthes said, "ça" or "it" that speaks: the text, the words, Blanchot's *"rumeur"* of language that lives inside of us from the moment of our birth. Indeed, Beckett's works often seem to be generated by words themselves that combine and multiply in order to create text. In *Company*, these words are sometimes even produced by letters, in French *"lettres"*—such as those articulated by the "characters" M and W created to fill the empty space—as opposed to by "beings," or in the French singular *"l'être"*—a word that is phonetically identical to "lettres" and therefore only shows its difference in writing.

But to equate the Beckettian subject with language alone is naïve, despite the fact that we are invited to do so several times by *The Unnamable*'s narrator. For, although this narrator claims to be words, "made of words" and "nothing else," he quickly follows that up with a denial of this declaration:

> [...] yes, something else, that I'm *something quite different*, a *quite different thing*, a *wordless thing* in an empty place, a hard shut dry cold black place, where nothing stirs, nothing speaks [...]. (386)

> [...] si, tout autre chose, que je suis tout autre chose, une chose muette, dans un endroit dur, vide, clos, sec, net, noir, où rien ne bouge, rien ne parle [...]. (166)

The narrating subject is comprised exclusively of words, yet it is also "wordless." It is present, but only to the extent that it is absent. It claims to both participate in its stories and remain outside of them ("I'll have said it inside me, then in the same breath, outside of me..."). Neither one thing nor the other, it remains unidentifiable, virtually unnamable. The only possible "name" that one could give it, it gives itself. Appropriately enough, it is a name that represents the impossibility of determination and thus nomination:

> perhaps [...] I am the thing that divides the world in two [...] thin as foil, I'm neither one side nor the other, I'm in the middle, I'm the partition, I've two surfaces and no thickness, [...]I'm the tympanum [...]. (383)

> [...] c'est peut-être ça que je suis, la chose qui divise le monde en deux, [...] mince comme une lame, je ne suis ni d'un côté ni de l'autre, je suis au milieu, je suis la cloison, j'ai deux faces et pas d'épaisseur [...] je suis le tympan [...]. (160)

As Derrida argues in his essay of (almost) the same name ("Tympan"), the "tympanum" is the ultimate representative of *différance*. Denoting on one hand the ear drum and on the other a term associated with the printing press, it symbolizes all that is between: between speech and writing, inside and outside, origins and copies. In plain English, the tympanum represents everything that is outside the grasp of representation as we know it. As the narrator of *The Unnamable* asserts, to expect this of a subject is, to say the least, somewhat unfair: "It's a lot to expect of one creature, it's a lot to ask, that he should first behave as if he were, then as if he were not [...] to be borne to the end." But it is by presenting the subject as an entity that is indefinite, that hovers between the polarities of being and nothingness, presence and absence, subject and object, that Beckett is able to gesture to what lies outside traditional Western thought and representation: to that place where the subject "neither is, nor is not, and where the language dies that permits of such expressions." According to Deleuze, this is the *pensum par excellence*. In avoiding the temptation to explain away the unknown, and instead attempting to articulate the unknown as such, we permit writing to go on. Beckett's unexplainable subject is, paradoxically, the concrete manifestation of the unimaginable in general. It names, as it were, the place and a subject that exists outside the metaphysical margins, and thus allows for the continual exploration of the ever "unthinkable unspeakable" beyond (334-335).

‡ Conclusion

"Art is and remains for us, on the side of its highest possibilities, a thing of the past."
—Hegel, *Philosophy of Fine Art.*

Hegel and the End of the Narrative

I would like to return to one of the primary concerns outlined in the introduction: that of limits. This time the discussion will focus less on inaugural boundaries than on conclusions, and not simply because it is a matter of protocol; introductions are for beginnings, conclusions for concluding (often in exhaustion). The subject of ending merits reflection at this point because this is where we find ourselves after having read repetition in the works of Deleuze, Beckett, and Derrida, at that place where we might ask if we have reached an end. If we accept that repetition reveals the intrinsic instability of classificatory terms—temporal, discursive, phenomenological—then we must consequently consider the possibility that the idea that we can know anything with certainty is illusory: that anything that can be said to be true is only provisionally so. Definitions, categories, and boundaries are simple constructs that we make in order to see and think clearly. Repetition and difference suggests that we never truly do. If we acknowledge statements such as these to be, in their own paradoxical way, "true," we find ourselves at something of an end, for where can we go from here? To invoke again the words of Derrida, perhaps there is simply "not much *left* to do." So, what then is left to say?

It would be easy to conclude by repeating and simply expanding upon the findings of Chapters 2 and 4: to say, for example, that this lack of definitive knowledge of any kind is what allows discourse to "go on." As Deleuze writes, it is precisely there, on "the frontiers of our knowledge," that one has "something to say." One writes thinking that one is explaining, imagining that one is able to do so because one has defined, classified, solved, and known. But in reality, one's writing, the fact that one is writing, only proves the opposite. One is writing because these things do not exist. One cannot conclude, cannot come to a definition, and so on. To write is not to explain away the unknown, but rather to articulate the unknown as such. By making us acutely aware of all that one does not, and cannot, ever know, by explicitly pointing to all that slips through our grasp—and let's assume for now that all slips through our grasp—repetition and difference gives rise to writing.

It would be easy to stop here, but it would not be satisfactory. Conclusions like those above—although admittedly a little neat—do remain faithful to the boundlessness that is at the heart of repetition with difference by giving us a reason not to see this as an end; that of writing, for example. Yet, by intimating that all claims are threatened in advance by the equally possible "truthfulness" of their counter claims, it makes it difficult to write in any other way than against oneself and one's own writing. So the question may be less "what is left to say," for there are an infinite amount of things to still say, than "why bother saying anything at all?"

There is another more compelling reason to not simply end here. The main focus of this text until this point has been repetition and difference as it has manifested itself in philosophy and literature in the mid-twentieth century, and specifically how it was developed and exploited in various ways by Derrida, Beckett, and Deleuze. However, despite this long pause to linger over what I consider to be a decisive moment in repetition theory and practice, if we take the whole of this text into consideration it presents something of a *history* of repetition. In other words, antithetical though it may be to the tenants of repetition and difference, this work is nonetheless a linear narrative of repetition as a concept and how it has evolved over time. Stopping now without reference to anything beyond repetition with difference—without naming anyone beyond Beckett, Derrida, or Deleuze for that matter—would be to suggest that that is where that history ends. In a way, this is what I mean to imply, but only in the sense that it is here that the history perhaps *begins* to end.

In order to explain this, I will once again look briefly to Hegel. Of interest at this juncture is not his insistence on a beginning (or several) as it was in the introduction, but on ending. As we can see in the epigraph that heads this conclusion, Hegel makes the radical sounding claim that art has somehow reached its apex and, consequently, its end. Which is not to say that there are no longer artists producing creative works or that these works are not worthy of the title "art"; but rather that there was, for some time, a *narrative* of art that has come to its logical conclusion. This narrative, as with most narratives, had a goal towards which it strove. When it reached the goal, art had simply become a "thing of the past."

Arthur Danto is perhaps the most well-known scholar to have interpreted and expanded upon Hegel's thesis of art "as a thing of the past." First expressed in his essay "The End of Art," then further developed in *Encounters and Reflections*, *The State of the Art*, and *After the End of Art*, Danto positions his reading of the end of art in line with Hegel's historicist and aesthetic theories. In brief, Hegel imagines both art and history to be determined by their own "master narratives" that progress in a linear fashion towards some end point. In *After the End of Art*,[1] Danto compares the structure of such narratives to the German *Bildungsroman* where "a story is told of the stages through which the hero or heroine progresses on the way to self-awareness" (4). Once self-awareness is attained, the story ends. This is the moment when art and history, which have run parallel to each other for some time, definitively diverge and although art may continue thereafter, "its existence carries no historical significance whatever."[2]

Arthur Danto's Age(s) of Representation

There are certain similarities between Hegel's conceptualization of the narrative of art and its conclusion, Danto's interpretation of this story, and the narrative of repetition theory and practice as I have endeavored to describe it in this work. Danto defines the various stages in the narrative of art according to their relation to mimetic representation. The first stage of the story—when the idea of "art" began to be an important component of its production—first came into being in approximately 1400 AD with primitive and aboriginal art that was oftentimes used to guide and keep in check social behavior.[3] Following this initial stage were the eras of "imitation," "ideology," and finally—the period in which we now find ourselves, *outside* of the margins of the master narrative—the "post-historical era."

The longest stage thus far has been the era of imitation which lasted from approximately 1300 AD until the late 1800's. During this time, art was measured according to its proximity to reality. Accordingly, "painters set about representing the world the way it presented itself, painting people and landscapes and historical events just as they would present themselves to the eye." In contrast, the era of ideology, also referred to as the era of modernity, lasted less than one century, dating from the late 1800's until the sometime during the 1960's. During this period, it was less a question of representing a reality that became the determinant for art, than representing the means of representation: "With modernism, the conditions of representation themselves became central, so that art in a way becomes its own subject."[4] The break from the era of imitation coincided with the appearance of impressionism on the art scene. Although the impressionists were still depicting "real" things—places, people, events—they were not attempting to disguise the means with which they were doing so. Clement Greenberg, in his seminal essay "Modernist Painting," too describes the impressionists as the forerunners of the modernist period because they left "the eye under no doubt as to the fact that the colors they used were made of paint that came from tubes or pots" (7). Visible brushstrokes, a reduction of dimension, a disfigured perspective and other "non-mimetic" elements steered the focus from the object depicted to the means of depiction.

Danto argues that philosophy followed an analogous narrative comprised of several distinct historical stages which also had some relation to mimesis: ancient, medieval, and modern. Prior to the modern period, philosophy—like mimetic art—set out to "describe the world" in an imagined objective fashion. Descartes is the philosopher who is commonly thought of as the first modern philosopher because of his move away from attempting to describe things as they are—"how things really are"—and towards describing them how we perceive them to be—"how someone whose mind is structured in a certain way is obliged to think they are."[5] For Greenberg, it is Kant who marks the split between the medieval and the modern, because, in his words, Kant—as the title of his *Critique of Pure Reason* suggests—"was the first to criticize the means itself of criticism." Regardless of which philosopher is posited as the pioneer of this modern period, in both cases modern philosophy is thought to have come into being when thinkers began to use philosophy in order to question the nature of philosophy itself. Perhaps this is also where we might position the respective works of Derrida and Deleuze for in both authors' œuvres—to borrow Danto's reading of Kant—it is less a question of "adding to our knowledge [...] as answering the question of how knowledge [is] possible" (7). As with Descartes and Kant, here it is no longer the question "what is this *type* of philosophy," that directs their philosophical inquiries, but rather—to borrow now from Deleuze—*What is Philosophy?*

With respect to literature, as suggested in the introduction, the ways of conceiving of modernism are often varied and conflicting. If we examine literature in light of Danto's reading of modernism, the modern period would be characterized by a decreased emphasis on the thing or person reproduced and an increased concentration on the process and tools of reproduction. While it is not my aim to pinpoint any precise moment as the actual beginning of this age or any particular author as its forerunner, there are several writers who would undoubtedly fall into this category, among them Joyce, Kafka, and Brecht. Beckett's œuvre would seem to conform readily to this category as well, since he takes pains to remind us that what we hold in our hands is not some "reassuring narrative" (4) but rather a stack of paper on which there is text. To paraphrase *The Unnamable*'s narrator, any and all stories are comprised of words, "and nothing else."

This emphasis not simply on the non-mimetic elements of representation in art or philosophy—which serve to distinguish the respective modernist periods from the pre-modernist periods—but rather on the nature of art itself is what triggers the beginning of the conclusion of many of these so-called master narratives of the West. It is art's increased self-awareness and self-absorption— its turning back upon itself, when it becomes "vaporized in a dazzle of pure thought about itself" remaining "solely as the object of its own theoretical consciousness,"[6]—that eventually sets in motion the infamous "end of art" theorized by Hegel, Danto, and others.[7] This is not to say that the narratives of literature or philosophy have also concluded. They have, however, perhaps begun to conclude with the advent of modernism. Nor, does the claim that "art has ended" mean that art really "ends" once and for all. Again, it is not that "art"—the production of artistic works or even good artistic works—ceases, but rather that the "story" or direction of art is over. Art would still be produced but "whatever art there was to be would be made without benefit of a reassuring sort of narrative in which it was seen as the appropriate next stage in the story." The narrative would end, but the "subject of the narrative" would not. As Danto expresses it, "life really begins when the story comes to an end, as in the story every couple relishes of how they found one another and 'lived happily ever after'" (4). Or, to paraphrase Beckett, the end brings forth its (new) beginning.

The conclusion of modernism gave way to an inauguration of the "post-historical" or "contemporary" age. Although there are some styles (such as post-modernism[8]) and some artistic concepts associated with it (the use of electronic media, pluralism, multiculturalism, etc.), Danto describes this age as essentially ahistorical. Because there is no longer any "stylistic unity" or any clear path where one style dominates and leads the way to another, there is no longer the possibility of "periods." This is the age of "information disorder" where "everything is permitted" at any one time (13).

Interesting, particularly within the context of this study, is the fact that two of the major artistic gestures of the post-historical age are the recycling of styles and image appropriation. While this would seem to link the post-historic to the narrative that preceded it, the distinction between these activities and the mimetic activity associated with the narrative of art is immense. During the various ages of the narrative of reproduction, mimesis circulated around the idea of a "real" on which copies could be based, whether in order to reinforce this real as primary in relation to its copies or to displace it as secondary. In the post-historic, the idea of the real is of little consequence. Danto cites Warhol's reproductions of everyday objects as an example of how there was no longer any "special way" a work of art had to look in relation to the so-called "real" object, stating that "nothing need mark the difference between Warhol's Brillo Box and those in the market" (13). Like the narrative of art, the concept of the real had become a "thing of the past," historically bound and thus no longer relevant. Some, like Jean Baudrillard, have claimed that there came a point not long thereafter when the real became more than negligible; it became impossible. After the end of the age(s) of reproduction, came the "precession of simulacra," announcing the "age of simulation,"[9] otherwise known as the age of the "hyperreal."

Jean Baudrillard's Age of Simulation

> "The simulacrum is never that which conceals the truth—it is the truth which conceals that there is none. The simulacrum is true."
>
> —Ecclesiastes

Although more concerned with social theory than aesthetics, Baudrillard, like Danto, understands Western thought as though it were determined by various degrees of the relationship between a representation and a "real." What he refers to as the "successive phases of the image" basically correspond to those which Danto designates for the narrative of art. There is the addition, however, of a final stage in which—as the above citation, which also heads Baudrillard's "Simulacra and Simulations," intimates—the real is no longer part of the equation. The stages are the following:

1. The image attempts to tell the "truth" of a reality by reflecting it
2. The image attempts to "mask" and thus "pervert" that reality
3. The image tries to hide the fact that there is no reality

4. The image is no longer engaged in any relationship whatsoever with a "real" because the real itself has ceased to exist (173)

As a condensed illustration of the progression from one stage to the next, Baudrillard offers the very short, one paragraph long, story by Jorge Luis Borges entitled "Del rigor en la ciencia" ("Of Exactitude in Science"). The tale describes the relationship between a real—a particular territory—and its simulacra—a map. In this tale, an already oversized map of an empire, large enough to cover a whole Province, is found to be insufficient in its lack of detail. As a result, its size is increased to the point where it corresponds in scale exactly to the territory it defines, point by point. At the end of the story, the simulacrum has taken over the real.

While it accounts for some transitions of the "phases of the image," Borges' tale proves to be an unsatisfactory allegory for Baudrillard's stages of simulacra because it ends too soon, thus leaving the map to be a mere "second-order simulacra" (169). Baudrillard explains how far this example is from our present-day situation by stating that today simulacra can no longer be related to maps, even to those which cover and consequently consume their territories. Now, the idea that there was ever a territory—or a real—prior to the map is in question. Derrida, Beckett, and Deleuze all, in one way or another, signaled and even activated this eventual erasure of the real; which is why, even though they do not explicitly theorize this next, perhaps last, step of the narrative of repetition, they are pivotal players in bringing about an end.

Examining social and political structures, Baudrillard comes to see that once we allow signs to take the first steps towards replacing the real—such as one sees in capitalist societies when the use-value of a product is replaced by its exchange-value—the real, undergoes a "liquidation" (170). The gesture, whether related to art, philosophy, politics, or any cultural phenomena, passes from being one of dissimulation—where one "feigns not to have what one has" and thus "leaves the reality principal intact"—to becoming one of simulation—where one "feigns to have what one hasn't" and so "threaten[s] the difference between "true" and "false," between "real" and "imaginary" (170-171).

What was once considered to be real is now "hyperreal," and with this transformation comes the passing of metaphysics: "No more mirror of being and appearances, of the real and its concept; no more imaginary coextensivity [...]" (170). Gone is the age of reproduction where some real thing—a territory, the value of materials, our actual needs, the real Los Angeles—is able to engender copies of itself. Now, it is the map, the stock market, advertisements, and Disneyland that precede the territory. If a "real" exists, it can only be one that lacks the very quality of the real because it is now a real that is produced by models, which themselves are "without origin or reality" (169).

Contemporary popular culture has taken to extending this idea to apocalyptic proportions; robot warriors who exceeded the limitations of their creators and then set out to destroy them were the forerunners who paved the way for matrices and matrix-produced "beings." These beings presented themselves as "real," but in fact concealed only the absence of any actual reality. Likewise, Baudrillard's language makes it clear that what he describes is also not innocuous in nature. The real is "liquidated" (170), the unmasking "dangerous" (172), the sign, "like the bomb" (178), "murderous" and is even a "death sentence" (173) for its reference. But he also reminds us, recalling Derrida's and Beckett's readings of supplements, that simulation or even reproduction has always been fraught with risk. This "murderous capacity" of images was something of which even the Iconoclasts were acutely aware:

> [The Iconoclasts'] rage to destroy images rose precisely because they sensed this omnipotence of simulacra, this facility they have of erasing God from the consciousnesses of the people, and the overwhelming, destructive truth which they suggest; that ultimately there has never been any God; that only simulacra exist. (172)

"Diabolical in its very essence" reproduction, whatever the form, has always entailed "manipulation," "control," and, now more than ever, "death" (185). The reaction to this inevitable danger of losing the real—a danger which Baudrillard claims has, in our age, already reached its own apex—is one of denial, nostalgia, and panic:

> When the real is no longer what it used to be, nostalgia assumes its full meaning. There is a proliferation of myths of origin and signs of reality; of second-hand truth, objectivity and authenticity. There is an escalation of the true, of the lived experience; a resurrection of the figurative where the object and substance have disappeared. And there is a panic-stricken production of the real and the referential. (174)

When faced with the loss of concepts that were once a guarantee of meaning, truth, knowledge, originality, and the like, Baudrillard argues that the common reaction is to attempt to reestablish origins, re-imagine the "real," and to fortify structures. Danto's statement regarding the fallout that ensued in the 1960's after artists tested one boundary after another only to find that "the boundaries all gave way," suggests that he would agree with Baudrillard on this point. The collapsing of boundaries, like the disappearance of the real, makes us understandably uncomfortable. As Danto says, it is "not the easiest kind of world to live in." The result is what he calls the "political reality of the present" which he describes as consisting in "drawing and defining boundaries wherever possible."[10] The reaction is to begin again, to reestablish what was lost.[11]

The question remains as to whether or not the effacement of the real signals the end of the narrative or history of repetition theory. Clearly, I do not mean to suggest that repetition theory—particularly that of simulation—has nothing more to teach us. There is still much to be written about repetition and its relation to human experience, certainly with respect to cultural studies and identity studies. However, it seems reasonable to assume that with the age of simulation, repetition theory itself has reached its logical conclusion. Repetition was conceived of first as consisting of two objects or ideas, one of which had priority as the original, and the other secondary status as the copy. Next, the priority of the original—the originality of the original—was called into question and the hierarchy of the two terms became unstable. Then, one of the two terms was taken out of the equation altogether. We must ask ourselves if there can be repetition when only one term remains, and although this term is able to produce of itself again and again, the only "real" it is able to re-produce is one that is unreal, since it is engendered by a model for which there is no prior real. Is there anything that can follow simulation in the narrative of repetition theory? Is there any other possible direction to go in besides going backwards, beginning again, and retracing erased boundaries? If there is nothing else that can succeed simulation, if simulation represents the conclusion of this narrative, we might ask ourselves what lies outside the margins of the narrative? I would like to say that I have the answers to these questions, but that is not the case, and I have not yet found someone who has. It is likely that these answers will reveal themselves—like many other ends—in the future; as a *fait accompli*, only understood for what they were belatedly.

‡Notes

Introduction

[handwritten margin note: " that is not my desire / Is it desire for fulfilment? / climax?]

1 Bruce Kawin suggests as much in *Telling It Again and Again: Repetition in Literature and Film* (Ithaca: Cornell University Press, 1972), p. 141.

2 Evidently, this present text is not the only work to examine repetition in Beckett's work. I would suggest, however, that the uncontrollable desire to seek out the Same that conditions the way in which we perceive the physical world also seems to be the motivating force behind much of the research on Beckett and repetition. Many studies do not explore the differences that invariably insert themselves between the so-called original event or expression and its copy. Of those studies that do acknowledge difference amongst different types of repetition and within each repetition, few are more than archival in nature, doing little more than cataloguing and giving names to the various occurrences of repetition in his work. Ruby Cohn, for example, has systematically recorded much of the repetition that takes place in Beckett's drama, and in one essay even invented names for the apparently formerly unnamed species of verbal repetition that dominates his plays. However, she generally forgoes theorizing repetition and the differences produced by it, instead favoring thematic analysis. See, for example, Cohn's *Back to Beckett* (Princeton: Princeton University Press, 1974). Here, Cohn describes repetition as "thematic" in *Fin de partie* ("the old questions, the old answers repeating themselves unto death [...]," p. 142). With regards to *Endgame*, she describes repetition's function as limited to the creation of "dramatic tension" (p. 153). In other words, although her frequent references to the repetitive aspects of Beckett's œuvre attest to the importance she places on repetition in his work, repetition for Cohn becomes little more than the "foundation" for Beckett's thematically dominated "moribund stage world," "appropriately" colored gray to reflect upon this "sameness" (p. 155, my emphasis). This is in no way to imply that her work is without merit. Cohn's research on Beckett unquestioningly represents some of the most valuable secondary scholarship on repetition in Beckett's œuvre, and I would imagine that anyone who has written on repetition in Beckett has engaged with her work. But her critical orientation, as she has stated directly on several occasions, is not greatly influenced by theory. In the introduction to *Back to Beckett*, for example, Cohn expresses a wish to simply "get back to Beckett," without recourse to philosophy or theory, to get back to "the words of the works, which penetrate the width and depth of human experience." Likewise, in "The Churn of Stale Words," Cohn distances herself from some of the major theorists of repetition—notably Deleuze, Freud, Frye, and Kierkegaard—claiming to find them "too distant from Beckett's basic verbal practice [...]" (p. 96).

There are readers who both theorize repetition and concede difference—Pilling, Rabinowitz, and Kawin, for example—but, as Steven Connor notes, many of these scholars conclude by imagining repetition to be governed by some "centering" or "unifying" principle. Repetition becomes associated with synthesis, and is thus responsible for bringing together the jumbled and chaotic elements of the work, forming in the end a neat and complete œuvre. For example, Connor asserts that Rabinowitz's *The Development of Samuel Beckett's Fiction* suggests that the ultimate goal of repetition is to permit the discrete elements of Beckett's texts to reveal "their beauty" by "coalesce[ing] into a unified pattern" (Chicago: University of Illinois Press, 1984, p. 71). Similarly, Connor describes Cohn's treatment of repetition as a means for insisting on the eventual synthesis of diversion, stating that for Cohn "repetition is above all intensification and magnification of a centre, so that, in the end it is a metaphorical device which collapses art and life into unity" (p. 12). Kawin—whose work *Telling it Again and Again,* on one hand elegantly theorizes the complexities of repetition by dividing it into diverse types and by theorizing each (habitual repetition, destructive repletion, repetition and time, and emphasis)—nonetheless also views repetition and difference as something that strives for an amalgamation of diversity—here, in the hope of reaching *a* or even *the* "truth." For example, of *Watt*, Kawin states that "Every possible variation of a statement is given in the hope that one of the formulations may happen to correspond to the truth" (Denver: University Press of Colorado, 1972, p. 131).

To my knowledge, Steven Connor is the only writer to have written a book-length text on repetition in Beckett's work. He is also the only author of whom I am aware who has written on these subjects without leveling difference or compromising its significance in Beckett's textual practice. This present text expands upon Connor's parameters both in content and in method.

3 In the first chapter, I will argue that repetition and difference can be traced back to Eastern conceptualizations of duration and imitation.

4 I say "mislabeled" because, as I will address in the first chapter, the idea of an idealized and identical duplication can be found in the work of Pythagoras and his disciples, specifically with respect to cyclical theorizations of time.

5 This is particularly true of Beckett scholarship. Even those writers wishing to extricate themselves from the Beckett industry by pulling away from this orientation often wind up writing philosophically inspired analyses, without labeling them as such. Ruby Cohn's *Back to Beckett* (Princeton: Princeton University Press, 1974) is a case in point. Cohen acknowledges the value of philosophically influenced scholarship, but expresses a wish to "get back to Beckett"—without recourse to philosophy or theory—to get back to "the words of the works, which penetrate the width and depth of human experience" (p. 96). However, by focusing on "the cry of human mortality," which Cohn sees as the center of the Beckettian experience, Cohn is still describing philosophical notions, without directly referencing the ideas as such or the associated philosophers.

6 In his *From Postmodernism to Postmodernity: The Local/Global Context* (online essay, http://www.ihabhassan.com/postmodernism_to_postmodernity.htm), Ihab Hassan traces the term "postmodernism" back to the 1870's when John Watkins Chapman used it in reference to painting. In the 1930's, Hassan locates the term in the work of Federico de Onís, this time in relation to poetry, and in the 1940's, Bernard Smith employed it again in reference to painting. Expanding on Hassan's history of the term, John McGowan claims that the term first came into use in 1947 to describe changes that were taking place in architecture (*The Johns Hopkins Guide to Literary Theory and Criticism.* Michael Groden

and Martin Kreiswirth, eds. Baltimore: The Johns Hopkins University Press, 1994). Finally, in *After the Great Divide: Modernism, Mass Culture, Postmodernism* (Bloomington: Indiana University Press, 1986), Andreas Huyssen signals that the word first appeared in the field of literary criticism in the 1950's in the works of Irving Howe and Harry Levin (p. 184).

[7] S.E. Gontarski, David Cunningham, Stephen Watt, Richard Begam, David Wheatley, H. Porter Abbott, John Fletcher, Andreas Huyssen, and Ewa Plonowska Ziarek suggest that Beckett's œuvre is illustrative of a modernist aesthetic. On the side of postmodernism, one finds Brian Richardson, Jeanette R. Malkin, Lance Olsen, Donald Perret, Paul Bové, Nicholas Zurbrugg, Jeffrey Nealon, Ihab Hassan, and Brian Finney. Some, like Karen Laughlin, Leslie Hill, Jonathan Boulter, and Olga Taxidou, hedge their theoretical bets by placing his work on both sides of the fence. Laughlin refers to Beckett's subjects as potentially embodying both modernist and postmodernist principles by tucking the "post" in parenthesis, as in "(post)modern." In a similar gesture, Hill, in *Beckett's Fiction: In Different Words* (Cambridge: Cambridge University Press, 1990)—by way of Blanchot—states that a knowledge of Beckett's trilogy is vital for an understanding of what he calls neither "modern" nor "postmodern" texts, but rather "modern (or postmodern)" texts. Boulter describes Beckett's texts as containing "the central expression of the modernist and postmodernist experience" (*Interpreting Narrative in the Novels of Samuel Beckett*, Gainesville: University Press of Florida, 2001). Finally, Taxidou dispenses altogether with combining the terms and instead cleaves Beckett's theatre in two, referring to his dramatic writing as espousing a modern aesthetic, while labeling his performance as postmodernist.

[8] In the three decades that followed the first critical uses of the term, the terrain of the postmodern widened to embrace the domains of literature, architecture, dance, music, film, sociology, and fashion.

[9] Huyssen, *After the Great Divide* (Bloomington: Indiana University Press, 1986), p. 203.

[10] Jean-François Lyotard, *La Condition Postmoderne* (Paris: Editions de Minuit, 1979).

[11] Huyssen states that these competing cultures were of primary importance from the end of the 19th century to the first years of the 20th century, and then again for several decades following World War II (*After the Great Divide*, p. viii).

[12] Gianni Vattimo, *The End of Modernity* (Jon R. Snyder, trans. Cambridge: Polity Press, 1988).

[13] Richard Begam, *Samuel Beckett and the End of Modernity* (Stanford: Stanford University Press, 1996), p. 26.

[14] Roland Barthes, in his description of *Waiting for Godot*, manages to do both at once. "Le Théâtre français d'avant-garde" and "Godot adulte" both question the status of *Waiting for Godot* as an avant-garde play. With a décor that has been stripped bare and a virtual "absence" of reference to space and time, *Godot* clearly has some of the qualities of avant-garde theatre, a theatre which can be characterized, like Beckett himself, as having transformed its "pauvreté économique" into a "style volontaire." However, despite having some of the traits of the "paupérisme" of avant-garde dramatic works and in spite of having been first staged in small avant-garde theatres, Barthes argues that the widespread success of Beckett's *Godot* amongst the masses and its resultant appropriation by the general public deprive it of its original avant-garde designation ("Le Théâtre français d'avant-garde," in

Œuvres complètes, Paris: Seuil, 1993, p. 917). Having abandoned the place of avant-garde "hermétisme" where the critics—or, as Barthes refers to them, the "guardians" of "la pureté des genres"— wanted to hold it, *Godot* nonetheless lost none of its original character. Aesthetically still avant-garde, it could no longer be considered "sociologically" so ("Godot adulte," *Œuvres Complètes*. Paris: Seuil, 1993, pp. 413-415).

15 Georg Lukács, *The Meaning of Contemporary Realism*. (John and Necke Mander, trans. London: Merlin Press, 1963), p. 31. Both Bataille and Lukács comment on how Beckett's language contributes to the ultimate lack of humanity of his characters.

16 Julia Kristeva references the language in *Not I* as illustrative of the role of narcissism in the development of the Ego in "Freud and Love: Treatment and its Discontents," *Tales of Love (Histoires d'amour)* (Leon S. Roudiez, trans. New York: Columbia University Press, 1983), pp. 238-71.

17 In the last essay of *Lectures d'enfance* (Paris: Galilée, 1991), Lyotard compares the "mute perseverance" of the voice of the unconscious in Freud's work to the stuttering voice just below the surface of language in Beckett's trilogy.

18 Philippe Sollers, "Le Reflexe de réduction," *Théorie d'ensemble*. (Paris: Seuil, 1968), and *La Guerre du goût* (Paris: Gallimard, 1996).

19 Michel Foucault, "Archéologie d'une passion" and "Le Style de l'histoire," in *Dits et écrits : IV* (Paris: Gallimard, 1994). Foucault's decision to begin several lectures by quoting Beckett's work attests to the impact that it had on his thinking. In his 1969 address to the Société Française de la Philosophie entitled "What is an author?" Foucault opened with the words of Beckett's *The Unnamable*: "What does it matter who speaks, someone said, what does it matter who speaks." Several years later in his inaugural lecture at the Collège de France, Foucault again began with Beckett's words: "Behind me I should have liked to hear, behind me, a voice speaking thus: 'I must go on, I can't go on. I must go on, I must say words as long as there are words, I must say them until they find me, until they say me—heavy burden, heavy sin. I must go on; maybe its been done already, maybe they've already said me; maybe they've already borne me to the threshold of my story, right to the door opening onto my story...I'd be surprised if it opened." On both occasions, Foucault offers up Beckett's words as typifying the condition of writing of his time. It is in these words, Foucault contends—in the assertions and questions of Beckett's work, or rather in the *indifference* expressed in those assertions and questions—that "the most fundamental principles of contemporary writing" are asserted). Quoted from Didier Eribon, *Foucault* (Boston: Harvard University Press, 1991), p. 210.

20 "Littérature et Signification," "A l'avant-garde de quel théâtre," "Godot adulte," "Comment s'en passer," "Littérature objective," "Œuvre de masse et explication de textes," "Le Théâtre français d'avant-garde," in Barthes, *Œuvres Complètes* (Paris : Seuil, 1993).

21 Adorno, Theodor. "Trying to Understand Endgame." *New German Critique*, no. 26, Critical Theory and Modernity (Spring-Summer, 1982): 119-150. "Versuch, das Endspiel zu verstehen" was first published in *Noten zur Literatur II* (Frankfurt am Main, 1961).

22 Huyssen, *After the Great Divide*, p. 207. For Huyssen, this is particularly true in the work of French poststructuralist theorists who rarely examined the postmodern, stating that "Lyotard's *La Condition Postmoderne*, we must remember, is the exception not the rule. What

French intellectuals explicitly analyze and reflect upon is *le texte moderne* and *la modernité*. Where they talk about the postmodern at all, as in the cases of Lyotard and Kristeva, the question seems to have been prompted by American friends, and the discussion almost immediately and invariably turns back to problems of the modernist aesthetic" (p. 214).

23 As one example of a not so favorable critique of Beckett, Leslie Hill brings up Philippe Sollers who, in *Théorie d'ensemble* (Paris: Seuil, 1968), referred to Beckett's work as an example of writing that "may be apparently subversive and yet conceal a naturalist mode of writing," p. 396. Twenty some-odd years later, Sollers' changes his tune, classifying Beckett now as one of the two "greatest poets of the 20th century" (*La Guerre du gout*. Paris: Gallimard, 1996, p. 499). I would however, respectfully disagree with Hill's claim that Barthes' criticism of the apolitical character of Beckett's work colored his appreciation of its importance at the time of its production. Although Barthes did condemn the lack of political engagement of the content of *Godot*, for example, the great majority of his comments about Beckett applaud the revolutionary nature of his language and the sweeping opposition it offered to traditional ways of reading and understanding.

24 Kristeva, who characterized Beckett as "the best example" of postmodern writing, is however, an exception ("Postmodernism?" *Bucknell Review* 25 (1980): 136–41, p. 141).

25 Among these readers, one might reference Richard Begam, Steven Connor, Leslie Hill, Thomas Trezise, and Anthony Uhlmann.

26 Dearlove, Perloff, and Critchley, for example.

Chapter 1: The Unthinkable

1 Samuel Beckett, *Molloy* (New York: Grove Press, 1955).

2 Whether these calendars were as primitive as markings on bones over 20,000 years old detailing the phases of the moon, or as sophisticated as the first Egyptian calendars measuring the rising and falling of the Nile, cyclic calendars were the time keeping devices of many early civilizations, including the Aztecs, Mayans, Babylonians, and the ancient Chinese.

3 In the early Vedic period from 1600-500 BC, the notion of reincarnation was actively theorized in the Hindu religion, as is evidenced in the following passage from the *Bhagavad gita*, or "Song of God": "Just as a man discards worn out clothes and puts on new clothes, the soul discards worn out bodies and wears new ones" (2.22).

4 "What has been will be again, what has been done will be done again; there is nothing new under the sun" (*Ecclesiastes* 1:9–14, NIV).

5 See the *Timaeus* and the *Politicus*.

6 Although here there is no suggestion of a destruction and regeneration of the cosmos, there is the idea of beginning again in the description of a multi-directional planetary movement, where the astral bodies perpetually fulfill a cycle in one direction, then change to complete the cycle in reverse.

7 Mircea Eliade, *The Myth of the Eternal Return* (New York: Pantheon Books, 1954), p. 90.

8 As his *Confessions* suggest, St. Augustine was aware of many of the cyclical motifs at work in these very same texts, such as the repetitive patterns of nature in *Ecclesiastes* 3.1–8. He

was also cognizant of the repetitive nature of employing the life of Christ as a model for Christian believers (*De Civitate Dei* XXII.5). However, despite these references to circularity, Augustine insists—and Peter 3:18, the *Epistle to the Hebrews* (chapter 9), Romans 6:10, and *Hebrews* 9:12 26 seem to confirm—that the major events in Christian scripture are unique, homogenous, and unrepeatable events, establishing the primacy of a linear account of history: "Christ died only once because of our sins and since having risen from the dead he does not die again...". St. Augustine, *De Civitate Dei*, Book Xii, Ch. XIV.

9   Eliade identifies St. Thomas, Joachim of Floris, Francis Bacon, Isaac Newton, Marquis de Condorcet, Auguste Comte, and Georg Wilhem Friedrich Hegel, among others, as perpetuators of linear views of duration. For the cyclical interpretations, he signals the work of Clement of Alexandria, Minucius Felix, Arnobius of Sicca, Theodoret of Cyrrhus, Sir Thomas Browne, and Giambattista Vico.

10   The formerly mentioned Hindu notion of time as comprised of continuously spiraling units (*Kalpas*) is an example of the merging of cyclical and linear ways of understanding duration.

11   Søren Kierkegaard, *Fear and Trembling and Repetition*. (Howard V. and Edna H. Hong, eds. and trans. Princeton: Princeton University Press, 1983), p. 131.

12   Plato, *Phaedrus, Phaedo*, and *Meno*.

13   Merleau-Ponty relies on such a theory of knowledge in order to describe the pleasure we receive before certain texts. According to Merleau-Ponty, we are less apt to respond to those texts or philosophies that offer us something new than we are to appreciate texts which continue to provide us with what we have always known: "La question n'est donc pas tant de compter les citations que de fixer et d'objectiver cette *phénoménologie pour nous* qui fait qu'en lisant Husserl ou Heidegger plusieurs de nos contemporains ont eu le sentiment bien moins de rencontrer une philosophie nouvelle que de reconnaître ce qu'ils attendaient." *Phénoménologie de la perception* (Paris: Gallimard, 1945), p. 11.

14   Kierkegaard, *Fear and Trembling and Repetition* (Howard V. and Edna H. Hong, eds. and trans. Princeton: Princeton University Press, 1983), p. 149.

15   Heine, *Last Poems and Thoughts*. As quoted in Kaufmann's "Translator's Introduction" of *The Gay Science*. (Walter Kaufmann, trans. New York: Random House, 1974), p. 16.

16   Written between 1883 and 1885.

17   Nietzsche, "The Convalescent," from *Thus Spoke Zarathustra* in *The Collected Works of Friedrich Nietzsche* (Oscar Levy, ed. London: Foulis Press, 1909), pp. 269–271.

18   It should be noted that the material from *The Will to Power* comes from a notebook that Nietzsche himself never submitted for publication.

19   Friedrich Nietzsche, *The Will to Power* (Kaufmann, W. & Hollingdale, R.J, trans. New York: Random House, 1968), sec. 1066.

20   Nietzsche, *The Gay Science* (Kaufmann, W. trans. New York: Random House, 1974), p. 341.

21   Nietzsche, *The Will to Power* (Kaufmann, W. & Hollingdale, R.J, trans. New York: Vintage, 1967), p. 35.

22   "infiniment supérieure" to the "influence du milieu et des causes extérieures." My translation. Nietzsche, *Fragments posthumes (Automne 1885-Automne 1887)* (Colli/Montinari, ed.

OPC 12, Paris : Gallimard, 1978), p. 154.

[23] "Un nombre incalculable d'individus de niveau supérieur est maintenant en train de périr: mais celui qui en réchappe est fort comme le diable." My translation. Nietzsche, *Fragments posthumes (Printemps 1884-Automne 1884)* (Colli/Montinari, ed. OPC 10, Paris: Gallimard, 1982), p. 281.

[24] Deleuze, *Difference and Repetition* (New York: Columbia University Press, 1994), p. 27.

[25] "...la circulation infinie de l'identique à travers la négativité," Deleuze, *Différence et répétition*, (Paris: Presses Universitaires de France, 1968), p. 71.

[26] Deleuze, Gilles. *Difference and Repetition*, p. 55 ("Ceux qui portent le négatif ne savent pas ce qu'ils font: ils prennent l'ombre pour la réalité, ils nourrissent les fantômes, ils coupent la conséquence des prémisses, ils donnent à l'épiphénomène la valeur du phénomène et de l'essence," *Différence et répétition*, p. 74).

[27] For Nietzsche, this would be particularly relevant in the Darwinian inspired version of the Eternal Return, where only the most divergent are permitted to return.

[28] It is perhaps not surprising that the spiral is also considered by many societies to be the quintessential expression of all life. T.A. Cook, who devoted five-hundred pages to cataloguing these "curves of life" in biology, botany, architecture, mathematics and astronomy, argues that the spiral is both the foundation of all life and it is also the principle for the "objective" recognition of all beauty. Regardless of whether or not such claims can be considered to be "truths," Cook's exhaustive study is valuable for its highlighting of the high incidence of this shape in both nature and art. It is part of animals as small as protozoa and as large as elephants, and is found in the bones, intestine, umbilical cords, and ears of humans and animals alike. The shape of specific universes, and Archimedes' famous curve, the spiral is a dominant form in astronomy and mathematics.

[29] Eliade offers as a prime example of this doubling of the world the Iranian Zarvanitic tradition where there is a division between the terrestrial world (*gētīk*) and the celestial world (*mēnōk*). Eliade, *The Myth of the Eternal Return*, pp. 6-7.

[30] Ibid, p. 34. It should, however, be noted that while imitation allows religious societies to approach the divine, they are never meant to overtake it. Though such gestures allow men to approximate the sacred, complete conflation between men and gods, between the terrestrial and the celestial, is not encouraged. To paraphrase Kipling, east is east and west is west and never the two *should* meet.

[31] Koller, Else, and Sörbom trace all three terms as far back as the 4th and 5th century B.C., without ever signaling any one precise origin. Hermann Koller, *Die Mimesis in der Antike. Nachahmung, Darstellung, Ausdruck* (Dissertationes Bernenses, Ser. 1, 5. Bern, 1954). Gerald F. Else, "Imitation in the Fifth Century," *Classical Philology* vol. LIII, 2. (1958): pp. 73-90. Göran Sörbom, *Mimesis and Art: Studies in the Origin and Early Development of an Aesthetic Vocabulary* (Bonniers: Scandinavian University Books, 1966).

[32] As Vincent Descombes, Marvin Carlson, Steven Connor, and Art Berman, among others, do.

[33] Perhaps more troubling than historical inaccuracy for those who have an appreciation for repetition and difference is the question of "origin" that is problematized here. For if

repetition with difference renders the notion of "an" origin suspect, than we can assume that there can be no one origin for the term itself.

34   In *Theories of Mimesis* (Cambridge: Cambridge University Press, 1995), Arne Melberg argues that the word "*mimesis*" is itself ambiguous enough in Plato's work to be referred to as a "floating" term. He suggests that while the most common translation of this word in his texts is "imitation" (*μιμηση*, transliterated as *mimisi*) there are at least ten "divergent meanings or directions" of the family *mimos / mimeisthai / mimetikous / mimesis*" at work. Plato himself hints to a certain ambiguity at the heart of this word by first referring to it in *The Republic* as "play," then by associating it later in this same text with another word in which there is considerable "play": *pharmakon* (382C), which signifies both its conventional meaning ("poison") and its opposite ("antidote").

    Given the ambiguity that even Plato, the philosopher credited with establishing a Western logic of limits and classification, attributes to the word *mimesis*, it is not surprising that many writers and philosophers fail to clearly define this term. Nor is it surprising that many of these same writers (even those such as Sörbom and Melberg who claim this as the primary objective of their work) do not make any clear distinction between *mimesis* and the related terms of representation and repetition. The possibility that there may be no clear-cut distinction to make is likewise never addressed.

35   Plato, *Cratylus/Plato* (Dorothea Frede, trans. Indianapolis: Hackett Publishing Co., 1993).

36   *μιμηση*, transliterated from the Greek as "*mimēsē.*"

37   Plato, *The Republic of Plato* (Allan Bloom, trans. New York: Basic Books, 1968).

38   Plato, *The Republic*, Book X.

39   Ibid.

40   Aristotle. *Poetics, IV,* (Colden, Leon, trans. Englewood Cliffs: Prentice Hall, 1968).

41   Ibid.

42   Ibid., Book XXV, my emphasis.

43   Among the means of reproduction, Benjamin lists—in order of historical appearance—founding and stamping, woodcut graphics, the printing press, lithography, photography, and the technical reproduction of sound and sight in film.

44   Walter Benjamin, "The Work of Art in Mechanical Reproduction," *The Nineteenth-Century Visual Culture Reader* (Vanessa R. Schwartz and Jeannene M. Przyblyski, eds. New York: Routledge, 2004), p. 64.

45   This is something that museumization by definition means to protect: the aura of the original.

46   In keeping with this tradition, Descombes, along with the author of the preface Alan Montefiore, subjects *Le même et l'autre* to its own doubling. This is a text that is, from the start, simultaneously itself and Other. In the first of the two prefaces to this text, Alan Montefiore not only addresses his own alterity as potentially perceived by the reader, but also any future objection to his presence in a book that, by virtue of his native language and nationality, seem to have "always already" excluded him: "On s'étonnera peut-être de ce que la préface d'un livre écrit en français par un philosophe français, et dont le sujet est la philosophie française, soit signée par un philosophe britannique." Born and raised in Great Britain, with English as his maternal language, Montefiore does seem justified, in

the context of this work, in identifying himself as the "other" in relation to Descombes' French-defined "Same." This text is not however "one," and Montefiore does not wait long to expose the transitory, exceedingly fragile nature of labeling something as exclusively "Same" or "other." While he may well be the "other" and Descombes "the Same" with respect to Le même et l'autre (i.e., the text as it first appeared in French), the eventual translation of the text into English (mentioned in his preface), and its subsequent incorporation into a collection of European philosophies edited by a British press, soon reverses these roles. As representative of both the country producing the collection and of the language in which the entire work will be transcribed, Montefiore is destined to remain the "other" for only a short period of time. Moreover, since it was a British press that instigated the writing of the French text in the first place and was thus the condition for its existence, one could even argue that Descombes himself was from the start already the "other," even while appearing in the French text to be representative of the "Same."

This doubling of the "Same" and the "other" is even passed on to the reader. By informing the reader of the French "version" of this text that this book is also, simultaneously, addressing itself to Anglophone readers, Montefiore manages to place the French reader in the precarious position that both he and Descombes share. Reading this text, the French language reader is likely to be confronted by his own alterity, even while acknowledging his "sameness." Curiously, even in the French text, the only reader Descombes ever considers is the one that he "supposes, by hypothesis" (11) to be as exterior as possible to the tradition of the French ways of philosophizing. The intended reader of this text written in French is thus English. He too is at once "other" and the "Same."

47 Vincent Descombes, Le même et l'autre (Paris: Editions de Minuit, 1979), p. 13. For more on this score, see Michel Foucault's article "Nietzsche, Marx, Freud," in Gayle Ormiston & Alan Schrift, eds., Transforming the Hermeneutic Context (Albany: SUNY Press, 1990), pp. 59-68.

48 Repetition and recollection on one hand, cosmological and Darwinian conceptualizations on the other.

49 Christopher Norris, Deconstruction: Theory and Practice (New York: Methuen, 1982).

50 Jacques Derrida, "La structure, le signe et le jeu dans le discours des sciences humaines," L'écriture et la différence (Paris: Seuil, 1967).

51 Derrida, "La scène de l'écriture," L'écriture et la différance (Paris: Seuil, 1967), pp. 301 and 302.

52 Descombes, Modern French Philosophy (Cambridge: Cambridge University Press, 1980), p. 145. Although this extension of Derrida's "retard originaire" does not appear until more than halfway through Le même et l'autre, (on page one hundred and seventy of this two hundred and twenty-one page text), an illustration of this theory is actually present from the very start of the book. By deferring his own "beginning," like the narrator of Beckett's Molloy,—by exploiting both definitions of the verb "différer" ("to differ" and "to defer"), like Derrida—Descombes not only describes but also gives a powerful example of repetition with a difference before the text proper ever starts. The book initially appears to "begin" like any other. The book's half-title page is preceded by a blank verso. The verso of the next page lists the author's previous works, while the recto is the title page, listing the full

title of the book, the name of the author, and the name of the publishing house. It is not until the following page that the front matter of this book distinguishes itself from many others. What follows the title page is not a preface (as one might find in either a French or English edition), but rather another title page on which the author's name, the title of the book, the subtitle, and the press all appear again. This title page is, in other words, exactly the same as the previous title page. But lest the reader mistake this doubled page for simple negligence on the part of the binders, Descombes adds to it an "avertissement au lecteur":

"Cette page reproduit la précédente. *Autre*, elle est la *même*. Mais pour éviter que le lecteur ne *compte pour rien* cette seconde première page, en l'attribuant par exemple à un erreur de reliure, j'ai dû y inscrire cet avertissement, qui ne figure pas sur la première page. Pour être *même*, il faut qu'elle soit *autre*."

In this "avertissement," Descombes demonstrates, both visually and linguistically, Derrida and Deleuze's conceptualization of "true" repetition: that in order for something to be recognized as the "Same" (i.e., repeated, duplicated) it must indeed be "Other." It is only through difference that we are able to conceive of something as being the Same. In other words, "it is only the strange that is familiar, and only difference which is repeated."

53   Descombes, *Le même et l'autre* (Paris: Editions de Minuit, 1979), pp. 170-171.

54   "C'est le non-origine qui est originaire." Derrida, "La scène de l'écriture," *L'écriture et la différance* (Paris: Seuil, 1967), p. 303.

55   Jacques Derrida, *Positions* (Alan Bass, trans. Chicago: University of Chicago Press, 1981), p. 28.

56   Jacques Derrida, *Margins of Philosophy* (Bass, Alan, trans. Chicago: University of Chicago Press, 1982), p. 65.

57   Jacques Derrida, *Marges de la philosophie* (Paris: Editions de Minuit, 1972), p. 75.

58   Jacques Derrida, "La structure le signe et le jeu dans le discours des sciences humaines," *L'écriture et la différence* (Paris: Editions de Seuil, 1967), p. 410.

59   Jacques Derrida, "The Double Session," *Dissemination* (Chicago: Chicago University Press, 1981), p. 191.

60   Stéphane Mallarmé, "Mimique," *Œuvres complètes: Stéphane Mallarmé; texte établi et annoté par Henri Mondor et G. Jean-Aubry* (Paris: Gallimard, *Pléiade* edition, 1961), p. 310.

61   Ibid. "Le mime doit seulement s'écrire sur une page blanche qu'il est," p. 225.

62   Derrida, "The Double Session," p. 200.

63   Derrida, "La structure le signe et le jeu dans le discours des sciences humaines," p. 416.

64   Derrida, "La Différence," *Marges de la philosophie*.

65   Derrida, *La voix et le phénomène*, p. 95.

66   Derrida, *L'écriture et la différence* (Paris: Editions du Seuil, 1967). Here Derrida is referring specifically to Levinas' critique of Hegel, which, according to Derrida (because Levinas uses Hegel's terminology), resulted in his confirmation of Hegel. "Dès qu'il parle contre Hegel, Levinas [...] l'a déjà confirmé" (p. 279).

67   Descombes, *Modern French Philosophy* (Cambridge: Cambridge University Press, 1980), p. 139. As we will see in chapter two, this will be an important component in an argument

for why one should continue to write literary theory about the work of Samuel Beckett despite—or perhaps because of—its resistance to such efforts.

[68]   "[...] *différance* has no name in our language. But we "already know" that if it is unnamable, it is not provisionally so, not because our language has not yet found or received this *name*, or because we would have to seek it in another language [...] It is rather because there is no *name* for it at all [...]." Derrida, *Margins of Philosophy*, p. 26.

[69]   Derek Attridge, ed., *Jacques Derrida: Acts of Literature* (New York: Routledge, 1992).

[70]   Samuel Beckett, *Waiting for Godot* in *Samuel Beckett: The Complete Dramatic Works* (London: Faber and Faber, 1982), p. 82. The French reads, "elles accouchent à cheval sur une tombe," *En Attendant Godot* (Paris: Editions de Minuit, 1952), p. 126.

[71]   In his interview with Attridge, Derrida points to Beckett's use of a "particular French" that is very foreign to Derrida and is therefore difficult for him to identify with.

[72]   Deleuze dedicates a short analysis—about two pages of text—to Beckett's one cinematographic attempt, *Film*. Only once did he write an essay devoted exclusively to Beckett's work: a short *hommage* published by Minuit as an afterward for Beckett's teleplay "Quad" entitled *L'épuisé* (Beckett, "*Quad*" *et autres pièces pour la télévision, suivi par "L'épuisé" par Gilles Deleuze.* Paris: Editions de Minuit, 1992).

[73]   Gilles Deleuze, "Le langage nomme le possible," *L'épuisé*, p. 65.

[74]   Ibid. "Appelons *langue I*, chez Beckett, cette langue atomique, disjonctive, coupée, hachée [...]," p. 66.

[75]   Ibid. "tarir le flux [...]," p. 78.

[76]   Ibid. "... trouve dans la télévision le secret de son assemblage [...]," p. 74.

[77]   Samuel Beckett, *Disjecta: Miscellaneous Writings and a Dramatic Fragment* (Ruby Cohn, ed. London: John Calder, 1983), p. 172.

[78]   Deleuze, *L'épuisé*, p. 103.

[79]   Beckett, *Disjecta*, p.172.

[80]   Deleuze, *L'épuisé*, p. 103.

[81]   Samuel Beckett, *The Unnamable* (New York: Grove Press, 1958), p. 66.

Chapter 2: A Critical Reader

[1]   Michele Aina Barale and Rubin Rabinowitz, *A KWIC Concordance to Samuel Beckett's Trilogy: Molloy, Malone Dies and The Unnamable* (New York: Garland Publishing, 1988).

[2]   There are approximately one hundred and sixteen instances of the word "end," "ending," "ends," or "ended" in *The Unnamable*, in comparison with thirty-nine in *Malone Dies* and fifty-four in *Molloy*.

[3]   As opposed to only fifty-six instances of the word "beginnings" (or some derivative of it) in *Malone Dies*.

[4]   Samuel Beckett, *Three Novels: Molloy, Malone Dies, The Unnamable* (New York: Grove Press, 1955), p. 390.

[5]   Readers who are familiar with Kant may see here a subtle allusion to his "*Zweckmäßigkeit ohne Zweck*" from the *Critique of Judgment* (§§ 10-17). However, since the most generally accepted English translation of this phrase is "purposiveness without a purpose," Beckett's

rendering of it—and he was responsible for the English wording—as "finality without end" turns out to be one among many false leads.

6   Jacques Derrida, "The Law of Genre" *Glyph: Textual Studies* (Baltimore, MD 1980, 7), pp. 176–201, (Eng. tr., pp. 202–32), p. 217.

7   Beckett, *Three Novels*, p. 179.

8   Deleuze, *Difference and Repetition* (Paul Patton, trans. New York: Columbia University Press, 1994), p. xix.

9   Descombes, *Le même et l'autre*, p. 217.

10   Samuel Beckett, *Mercier and Camier* (New York: Grove Press, 1974), p. 9.

11   Jürgen Habermas, *The Philosophical Discourse of Modernity: Twelve Lectures* (Frederick Lawrence, trans. Cambridge: Polity Press, 1987), pp. 185–210.

12   Deleuze, *Difference and Repetition*, p. xx.

13   Habermas focuses specifically on the *Envoi* section of this piece.

14   "[Derrida] holistically levels these complicated relations *in order to* equate philosophy with literature and criticism." My emphasis. Habermas, *The Philosophical Discourse of Modernity*, p. 207. Habermas is not entirely correct in stating that it was Derrida's *intent* to contaminate one discourse with another. In his interview with Attridge, Derrida voices a desire to go even further than simply writing something *between* philosophy and literature. He dreams, as he says "more desperately than ever," of a writing that would be *neither* philosophy *nor* literature "nor even contaminated by one or the other," but that would retain "the memory of philosophy and literature" (Derrida, *Acts Of Literature*, Derek Attridge, ed. New York: Routledge, 1992, p. 73).

15   Richard Rorty, "Philosophy as a Kind of Writing: An Essay on Derrida," *Consequences of Pragmatism*. Minneapolis: University of Minnesota Press, 1982), pp. 89–109.

16   Habermas, *The Philosophical Discourse of Modernity*, p. 209.

17   Derrida, "La Loi du genre/The Law of Genre," *Glyph: Textual Studies* 7 (Baltimore, MD 1980, pp. 176–201, Eng. tr., 202–32), p. 228.

18   Derek Attridge, in his introduction to "The Law of Genre," *Acts of Literature*, p. 221.

19   Derrida, "The Law of Genre," p. 208.

20   Ibid, 205. Here, Derrida is re-citing the words of Philippe Lacoue-Labarthe.

21   Derrida, "The Law of Genre," p. 207.

22   J.E. Dearlove. "The Weaving of Penelope's Tapestry: Genre in the Works of Beckett" *Journal of Beckett Studies* 11–12 (1989): pp. 123–129.

23   For more on reader-reception theory and criticism, see also Stanley Fish, *Is There a Text in This Class? The Authority of Interpretive Communities* (Cambridge: Harvard University Press, 1982), Umberto Eco, *The Role of the Reader: Explorations in the Semiotics of Texts* (Bloomington: Indiana University Press, 1979), Michael Riffaterre, *Semiotics of Poetry* (Bloomington: Indiana University Press, 1978), Hans Robert Jauss, *Toward an Aesthetic of Reception* (trans. Timothy Bahti, Minneapolis: University of Minnesota Press, 1982), Jane Tompkins, ed., *Reader Response Criticism: From Formalism to Post-Structuralism* (Baltimore: The Johns Hopkins University Press, 1980), Susan Suleiman and Inge Crosman, eds, *The Reader in the Text: Essays on Audience and Interpretation* (Princeton: Princeton University Press, 1980), and Rubin Rabinowitz, *Before Reading: Narrative Conventions and the Politics of Interpretation* (Ithaca:

Cornell University Press, 1987).

24   Riffaterre, Michael. *Semiotics of Poetry*. Bloomington: Indiana University Press, 1978, p. 116.

25   In a letter to Barney Rosset, Beckett expressed his desire to adhere to generic conventions—and thus perhaps to oblige the reader to do so also—by stating that "if we can't keep our genres more or less distinct, or extricate them from the confusion that has them where they are, we might as well go home and lie down." Quoted from Linda Ben-Zvi's "Samuel Beckett's Media Plays," *Modern Drama* 28:1 (March, 1985): p. 24.

26   Derrida, *Acts of Literature*, p. 319.

27   This seems to be consistent with the Minuit, Faber and Faber, and Calder editions, regardless of the language in which the texts were written.

28   Tom Bishop, *From the Left Bank: Reflections on the Modern French Theater and Novel* (New York: New York University Press, 1977). Martin Esslin, "Mrozek, Beckett, and the Theatre of the Absurd" *New Theatre Quarterly* 10:40 (Nov 1994): pp. 377–81, "The Theatre of the Absurd" *Tulane Drama Review* 4:4 (1960): pp. 3–15, and "Beckett and the 'Theatre of the Absurd,'" *Approaches to Teaching Beckett's Waiting for Godot*, Enoch Brater, (ed.) (New York: Mod. Language Association of America, 1991). Bob Mayberry, *Theatre of Discord: Dissonance in Beckett, Albee, and Pinter* (Rutherford: Fairleigh Dickinson University Press, 1989). Saloua Beji, "Approche du théâtre de l'absurde: Adamov, Beckett, Al Hakim, Ionesco" (*Th. 3e cycle: Littérature comparée* Toulouse 2: 1988).

29   The dominant novelistic genre chosen to describe his work is by far that of the quest. Among the many readings of this type, one finds the following: Laura Barge, "Beckett's Questing Hero: Mystic or Pseudomystic" *Cithara: essays in the Judaeo-Christian Tradition* 24:2 (May 1985): pp. 49–58 and "God, the Quest, the Hero: Thematic Structures in Beckett's fiction" (*Chapel Hill: Dept. of Romance Languages, Univ. of North Carolina*, 1988). Charles Bernheimer, "Watt's in The Castle: the Aporetic Quest in Kafka and Beckett" *Newsletter of the Kafka Society of America* 6:1–2 (June-December 1982): pp. 19–24. Julie Campbell, "Pilgrim's Progress/Regress/Stasis: Some Thoughts on the Treatment of the Quest in Bunyan's *Pilgrim's Progress* and Beckett's *Mercier and Camier*, *Comparative Literature Studies* 30:2 (1993): pp. 137–52.

30   Hornung, Alfred. "Fantasies of the Autobiographical Self: Thomas Bernhard, Raymond Federman, Samuel Beckett" *Journal of Beckett Studies* 11–12 (1989): pp. 91–107. Catanzaro, Mary. Michael J. Meyer, "Whose Story is it? Samuel Beckett's *Malone Dies* and the Voice of Self-Invention," *Literature and the Writer* (Amsterdam: Rodopi, 2004), pp. 119–134. Park Ilhyung, "Beckett's Autobiographical Drama, Allography or Thanatography: Not I and That Time" *Journal of Modern British and American Drama* 17:2 (Aug 2004): pp. 49–73. Aspasia Velissariou, "Not I: An Aborted Autobiography" *Journal of Dramatic Theory and Criticism* 8:1 (Fall 1993): pp. 45–59. James Olney, *Memory & Narrative: The Weave of Life-writing* (Chicago: University of Chicago Press, 1998).

31   Beckett, *Three Novels*, p. 115.

32   Beckett, *The Complete Dramatic Works* (London: Faber and Faber, 1956, pp. 89–134), p. 93.

33   Ibid. Nagg continues, but his continuation does not help to bridge the rift in communica-

tion: "It's true if it hadn't been me it would have been someone else. But that's no excuse. [*Pause*] Turkish Delight, for example, which no longer exists [...]," p. 119.

34   I attended a performance of *Endgame* in 1999 at Madison Wisconsin's "Bravehart Theater" where I saw this happen. Due to the lack of meaningful correspondence from one line to the next, the actors not only spoke lines out of turn, they even ended by repeating lines from the opening. They ended by beginning again.

35   J.E. Dearlove, "The Weaving of Penelope's Tapestry: Genre in the Works of Samuel Beckett" *Journal of Beckett Studies* Tallahassee, FL (1989): p. 123.

36   Beckett, *Three Novels*, p. 176.

37   Richard Begam, *Samuel Beckett and the End of Modernity* (Stanford: Stanford University Press, 1996), p. 37. This quote was excerpted from Rubin Rabinowitz's *The Development of Samuel Beckett's Fiction* (Urbana: University of Illinois Press, 1984), p. 20.

38   Samuel Beckett, *Dream to Fair to Middling Women* (Eoin O'Brien and Edith Fournier, eds. New York: Arcade Publishing, 1993), pp. 12-13.

39   Jean-Paul Sartre, *Qu'est-ce que la littérature* (Paris: Gallimard, 1948 / Gallimard, Idées, 1972), pp. 38/25.

40   Ibid. pp. 342/211, my emphasis.

41   It begins with scenic directions, then continues with the characters names, followed by punctuation indicating that direct discourse will be expressed, and so on.

42   "Beckett's genius: the concentration and the absolutely controlled simplicity of language, the easy movement between the colloquial and the allusive, the interplay between wit, compassion, and despair...," A. Alvarez, "Poet Waiting for Pegasus," Review of *Poems in English. The Observer* 31 (December 1961): p. 21.

43   James Knowlson, *Damned to Fame: The Life of Samuel Beckett* (London: Bloomsbury Publishing, 1996).

44   Sameul Beckett, *Echo's Bones and Other Precipitates* (Paris: Europa Press, 1935).

45   Knowlson states that Beckett wrote to the publisher of this collection of poems because he wished to change the title from *Poems* to *Echo's Bones, and Other Precipitates*, claiming that this change was necessary because his poems were "Not poems after all." Knowlson, *Damned to Fame*, p. 221.

46   Apart from the sometimes enthusiastic *thematic* interpretations of poems such as *Whoroscope*, Beckett's poems were not generally well-received critically. For more on the reception of Beckett's poetry, see Lawrence Harvey's *Samuel Beckett: Poet and Critic* (New Jersey: Princeton University Press, 1970).

47   Harvey, *Samuel Beckett: Poet and Critic*, p. x.

48   Johannes Hedberg, "Some Thoughts on Three Poems by Samuel Beckett" *Moderna Språk* Vol. LXVIII, No. 1, pp. 11-18.

49   Marjorie Perloff, "Between Verse and Prose: Beckett and the New Poetry" *Critical-Inquiry* 9:2 (Dec 1982): pp. 415-433.

50   Northrop Frye, *The Well-Tempered Critic* (Bloomington; Indiana University Press, 1963), p. 18.

51   Frye actually locates this rhythm first in Beckett's *The Unnamable*.

52   Samuel Beckett, *Nohow On, Company, Ill Seen Ill Said, Worstward Ho* (New York: Grove

Press, 1980), pp. 6-7.

53   Frye, p. 21. This poetry/prose confusion in *Company* is perhaps also the reason why this text was not included in Gontarski's collection of Beckett's prose texts, entitled *Samuel Beckett: The Complete Short Prose* (New York: Grove Press, 1995).

54   Beckett, *Three Novels*, p. 233.

55   Anthony Uhlmann, "Towards an Ethics: Spinoza, Deleuze and Guattari and Beckett" *Beckett and Poststructuralism* (Cambridge: Cambridge University Press, 1999), pp. 107-136. David Berman, *Berkeley and Irish Philosophy* (London; Continuum, 2005). James Acheson, "Beckett's Film, Berkeley, and Schopenhauer" *Beckett and Beyond* (Bruce Stewart, ed. New York: Oxford University Press, 1999), pp. 10-15. *Alain Badiou: Philosophy and its Conditions* (Gabriel Riera, ed. Albany: State University of New York Press, 2005). Lance St. John Butler, "Hegel's *Phenomenology of Mind* and Beckett's The Unnamable" *Samuel Beckett and the Meaning of Being* (London: MacMillan Press, 1984), pp. 114-149. Phillip Tew, "Philosophical Adjacency: Beckett's Prose Fragments via Jürgen Habermas" *Beckett and Philosophy* (Richard Lane, ed. New York: Palgrave, 2002), pp. 140-153. Steve Barfield, "Beckett and Heidegger: A Critical Survey" *Beckett and Philosophy*, pp. 154-165. Also, see Lance St. John Butler's "Heidegger's *Being and Time* and Beckett" *Samuel Beckett and the Meaning of Being*, pp. 7-73. Maude Ulrika, "The Body of Memory: Beckett and Merleau-Ponty" *Beckett and Philosophy*. Lance St. John Butler, "Sartre's *Being and Nothingness* and Beckett" *Samuel Beckett and the Meaning of Being*, pp. 74-113. Anthony Uhlmann, "Language, Between Violence and Justice: Beckett, Levinas and Derrida" *Beckett and Poststructuralism* (Cambridge: Cambridge University Press, 1999), pp. 156-186. Thomas Hunkeler, "The Role of the Dead Man in the Game of Writing: Beckett and Foucault." *Beckett and Philosophy*, pp. 68-79. Hans H. Rudnick, "Joyless Laughter: Sophocles - Hesse - Beckett" *Enjoyment: from Laughter to Delight in Philosophy, Literature, the Fine Arts, and Aesthetics.* (Tymieniecka, Anna-Teresa ed. Boston: Kluwer Academic, 1998), pp. 257-265. James Martin Harding, *Adorno and a Writing of the Ruins: Essays on Modern Aesthetics and Anglo-American Literature and Culture* *Albany: State University of New York Press, 1997). Dave Cunningham, "Trying (Not) to Understand: Adorno and the Work of Beckett" *Beckett and Philosophy*, pp. 125-139.

56   Among the existentialist readings of Beckett's work, one finds the following: Paul B. Kelley, "Correspondence with the Void: Negativity and Narrativity in Sartre's *La Nausée* and Samuel Beckett's *Malone meurt*" *Dalhousie French Studies* 59 (2002): pp. 76-82. Livio Dobrez, "Beckett, Sartre and Camus: The Darkness and the Light" *Southern Review* 7 (1974): pp. 51-64. Marguerite Tassi, "Shakespeare and Beckett Revisited: A Phenomenology of Theater" *Comparative Drama* Vol. 31, iss. 2 (Summer 1997): pp. 248-276. Tassi characterizes Beckett's *Endgame*, for example, as a "stunning example of the physical and spiritual depletion of humankind [...]," which exposes "the profound truths of Beckett's pained vision of life as an interminable waiting to be endured and a crouching towards death" (p. 254).

57   Barker, "Waiting for Godot" *Plays and Players* (September 1955): pp. 18-19. For Clurman, Harvey, and Duckworth on *Godot*, see the following examples: Harold Clurman, "Thea-

tre" *The Nation* 5 May (1956): pp. 487–90. Lawrence E Harvey, "Art and the Existential" *PMLA* 75.1,
(Mar.1960): pp. 137–146. Colin Duckworth, *Angels of Darkness: Dramatic Effect in Samuel Beckett with Special Reference to Eugène Ionesco* (London: George Allen & Unwin Ltd., 1972).

[58]   Clurman, "Theatre" *The Nation* 5 May (1956): pp. 487–90.

[59]   Duckworth, *Angels of Darkness* (London: George Allen & Unwin Ltd., 1972), p. 22.

[60]   Hugh Kenner, Simon Critchley, Thomas Trezise to name a few.

[61]   Thomas Trezise, *Into the Breach: Samuel Beckett and the Ends of Literature* (Princeton: Princeton University Press, 1990), p. ix.

[62]   Beckett, *Three Novels*, p. 297.

[63]   Samuel Beckett, *Nohow On, Company, Ill Seen Ill Said, Worstward Ho* (New York: Grove Press, 1980), pp. 6–7

[64]   Trezise, *Into the Breach*, p. 5.

[65]   Simon Critchley, *Very Little...Almost Nothing: Death, Philosophy, Literature* (New York: Routledge, 1997), p. 176.

[66]   Critchley defines the "sub-Heideggerian interpretation" in the following manner: it is where one imagines that Beckett "[...] strives to attain 'the existential authenticity of being prior to language or of being as language [...]'" (p. 142). As for the "sub-Pascalian absurdist interpretation," Critchley states that this is where the reader identifies in Beckett "the quintessential and pessimistic tragic fate of modern man [...]" (p. 142).

[67]   Jacques Derrida, *Glas* (J.P. Leavey Jr. and R. Rand, trans. Lincoln: Nebraska University Press, 1986), p. 205. Quoted from Critchley, *Very Little...Almost Nothing*, p. 146.

[68]   Beckett, *Disjecta*, p. 19.

[69]   Critchley, *Very Little...Almost Nothing*, p. 143. *The Unnamable*'s narrator also refers to his own use of the first person "I" as "too red a herring," *Three Novels*, p. 342.

[70]   Beckett, *Three Novels*, p. 217.

[71]   The reference in *Malone Dies* was taken from the preface to Francis Bacon's *Instauratio Magna*: "De nobis ipsis silemus: De re autem, quae agitur, petimus: ut homines eam non Opinionem, sed Opus esse cogitent; ac pro certo habeant, non Sectae nos alicuius, aut Placiti, sed utilitatis et amplitudinis humanae fundamenta moliri. Deinde ut suis commodis aequi . . . in commune consulant . . . et ipsi in partem veniant. Praeterea ut bene sperent, neque Instaurationem nostram ut quiddam infinitum et ultra mortale fingant, et animo concipiant; quum revera sit infiniti erroris finis et terminus legitimus."
The Great Instauration: Preface: "Of our own person we will say nothing. But as to the subject matter with which we are concerned, we ask that men think of it not as an opinion but as a work; and consider it erected not for any sect of ours, or for our good pleasure, but as the foundation of human utility and dignity. Each individual equally, then, may reflect on it himself . . . for his own part . . . in the common interest. Further, each may well hope from our instauration that it claims nothing infinite, and nothing beyond what is mortal; for in truth it prescribes only the end of infinite errors, and this is a legitimate end."

[72]   Beckett, *Three Novels*, p. 329.

73 Leibniz adapts the expression to suit his own purposes by adding "praeter intellectum" to "Nihil est in intellectu quod prius non fuerit in sensu."

74 Beckett, *Three Novels*, p. 218.

75 Ibid, pp. 8–9. The uncertainty is further emphasized by the excessive repetitions of the words "apparently," and "perhaps," that riddle the opening pages.

76 Samuel Beckett, *Whoroscope* (Paris: The Hours Press, 1930), verse 73.

77 Samuel Beckett, "Three Dialogues Beckett's with Georges Duthuit" *A Samuel Beckett Reader*, John Calder, ed. *Transition* 1949), p. 103.

78 Theodor Adorno, *Trying to Understand Endgame*, Jones, Michael T. trans. *New German Critique: An Interdisciplinary Journal of German Studies* 26 (Spring-Summer 1982): pp. 119-50, p. 120.

79 Critchley, *Very Little...Almost Nothing*, p. 160. In the end, Critchley concedes that Beckett manages to render even a philosopher as "subtle and intelligent" as Adorno "slightly maladroit and flat-footed […]."

80 Nelly Furman, "Textual Feminism" *Women and Language in Literature and Society* (Nelly Furman, Sally McConnell-Ginet, and Ruth Borker, eds. New York: Praeger Publishers, 1980), pp. 45-54, p. 49.

81 Furman, "Textual Feminism," p. 51.

82 I have chosen to examine the definitions in the *Robert* because the French highlights the ideas of "clarity" and "obscurity" that are crucial for an understanding of what is involved in philosophical interpretation.

83 Ronald Barker, "Waiting for Godot," pp. 18-19. My emphasis.

84 Duckworth, *Angels of Darkness*, p. 14.

85 Clurman, "Theatre," and *The Critical response to Samuel Beckett* (Cathleen Culotta Andonian, ed. Connecticut: Greenwood Press, 1998), p. 93.

86 Roland Barthes, "The Structuralist Activity" *Contemporary Literary Criticism* (Robert Con Davis and Ronald Schleifer, eds. New York: Longman, 1989), pp. 170-174.

87 Maurice Blanchot, *Le Livre à venir*. Paris: Gallimard, 1959), p. 290.

88 Beckett, *Three Novels*, p. 233.

89 Derrida, "The Law of Genre," p. 215.

90 Critchley, *Very Little...Almost Nothing*, p. 512. My emphasis.

91 Attridge, *Acts of* Literature, p. 61.

92 Critchley, *Very Little...Almost Nothing*, p. 152. My emphasis.

93 Levy, Shimon. *Samuel Beckett's Self Referential Drama: The Three I's* (New York: St. Martin's Press, 1990), p. 2.

94 Beckett, *Three Novels*, p. 299.

95 Beckett, *Three Novels*, p. 338.

Chapter 3: "This Text Which is Not One"

1 Deleuze, *Difference and Repetition* (New York: Columbia University Press, 1994), p. 195.

2 Cited from an interview with Henri Ronse. Derrida, *Positions* (Alan Bass, trans. Chicago: University of Chicago Press, 1981), pp. 3-4.

[3]   *Genesis*, 1:4–1:18.

[4]   Ibid, 1:26.

[5]   Jacques Derrida, "Ellipsis" *Writing and Difference* (Alan Bass, trans. Chicago: University of Chicago Press, 1978), p. 296.

[6]   Jacques Derrida, *Of Grammatology* (Gayatri Chakravorty Spivak, trans. Baltimore: Johns Hopkins University Press, 1974), p. 18.

[7]   Jacques Derrida, *De la grammatologie* (Paris : Minuit, 1967), pp. 30–31.

[8]   "Comment penser le dehors d'un texte? Plus ou moins que sa propre marge? Par exemple, l'autre de la métaphysique occidentale?" Derrida, "La différance" *Marges de la philosophie* (Paris: Minuit, 1972), p. 27.

[9]   Derrida, *Of Grammatology*, p. 18.

[10] Derrida, *Positions*, pp. 3–4.

[11] Derrida, *Of Grammatology*, p. 18. The French reads "L'idée du livre [...] est profondément étrangère au sens de l'écriture," p. 30.

[12] In Greek, *palímpsestos* is defined as "rubbed again," *pálin* being the equivalent of "again" and *psestós* of "scraped" or "rubbed."

[13] I say "so-called trilogy" because although these texts are generally referred to as the trilogy and are often published together as a trilogy, Ruby Cohn notes that Beckett himself did not originally conceive of these works as such. *Back to Beckett* (Princeton: Princeton University Press, 1974), p. 112.

[14] Ian Watt, *The Rise of the Novel: Studies in Defoe, Richardson, and Fielding* (Harmondsworth: Penguin Books, 1963).

[15] Beckett, *Three Novels*, p. 7.

[16] Beckett, *Molloy* (Paris: Editions de Minuit, 1951), p. 7.

[17] Beckett, *Three Novels*, p. 64.

[18] Deleuze, *Difference and Repetition* (Paul Patton, trans. New York: Columbia University Press, 1994).

[19] Ibid, p. xxi. In French, "Comment faire pour écrire autrement que sur ce qu'on ne sait pas, ou ce qu'on sait mal?" *Différence et répétition* (Paris: Presses Universitaires de France, 1968), p. 4.

[20] Derrida, "La Loi du genre / The Law of Genre." *Glyph: Textual Studies*, 7 (1980): pp. 176–201, (Eng. tr., pp. 202–32). "Au bord de la littérature," p. 201.

[21] Deleuze, *Difference and Repetition*, p. xxi. The French reads: "à la pointe de son savoir, à cette point extrême qui sépare notre savoir et notre ignorance, *et qui fait passer l'un dans l'autre*," *Différence et répétition*, p. 4.

[22] Ibid, p. xxi. In French, "Combler l'ignorance, c'est remettre l'écriture à demain, ou plutôt la rendre impossible," *Différence et répétition*, p. 4.

[23] Samuel Beckett, *Three Dialogues With Georges Duthuit* (London: John Calder, 1965), p. 103.

[24] Beckett, *Three Novels*, p. 28. The French reads: "Ne pas vouloir dire, ne pas savoir ce qu'on veut dire, ne pas pouvoir dire ce qu'on croit qu'on veut dire, et toujours dire ou Presque, voilà ce qu'il importe de ne pas perdre de vue [...]," *Molloy* (Paris: Minuit, 1951), p. 36.

[25] "What I need now is stories, it took me a long time to know that, and I'm not sure of it," Beckett, *Three Novels*, p. 13.

26 *Molloy*, p. 10, my emphasis.

27 Beckett, *Three Novels*, p. 322.

28 "j'y parachève mes gyrations, en piétinant les restes méconnaissables, des miens, à qui le visage, à qui le ventre, selon le hasard de leur distribution, et en y enfonçant les bouts de mes béquilles, à l'arrivée comme au départ," *L'Innommable* (Paris: Minuit, 1953), p. 61.

29 "Mais laissons tout ça. Je n'ai jamais été ailleurs qu'ici, personne ne m'a jamais sorti d'ici," *L'Innommable*, p. 62.

30 "comment procéder? Par pure aporie [...]."

31 Begam, *Samuel Beckett and the End of Modernity*, p. 158.

32 Ibid, p. 215, n.23.

33 Beckett, *Three Novels*, p. 88.

34 Beckett, *Molloy*, p. 118.

35 In the French, "Je m'excuse de ces détails," *Molloy*, p. 84.

36 The French reads, "Mais je ne pouvais pas ! Quoi? M'appuyer dessus. [...] Mais je ne le pouvais pas ! Quoi ? La plier," *Molloy*, p. 104.

37 In French, "Non, ça ne va pas," *Malone meurt*, p. 24.

38 Self-criticism such as this and "quelle misère" are continuously repeated in *Malone Dies/Malone meurt* (see, for example, p. 27 in the French, and in the English, p. 191). In the French *Molloy*, the narrator exclaims, "Cette phrase n'est pas claire, elle ne dit pas ce que j'espérais," p. 224, and in the English version on page p. 165. See also, "This story is no good," p. 330.

39 The French reads, "Quel ennui," *Malone meurt* (Paris: Minuit, 1953), pp. 20 and 23.

40 "Sapo loved nature, took an interest _____." Ibid, p. 191.

41 The last five pages of *The Unnamable* are one sole phrase, pp. 409–415.

42 The entire first half of *Molloy* is one paragraph.

43 Derrida, *Writing and Difference*, p. 296. My emphasis.

44 Leslie Hill, *Beckett's Fiction: In Different Words* (Cambridge: Cambridge University Press, 1990), p. 58.

45 Derrida, *Writing and Difference*, p. 296.

46 As described in chapter one.

47 Deleuze, *Difference and Repetition*, p. 90. In French, "nous ne produisons quelque chose de nouveau qu'à condition de répéter [...] l'absolument nouveau lui-même n'est rien d'autre à son tour que [...] l'éternel retour," *Différence et répétition*, pp. 121–122.

48 Michel Foucault, *Theatrum Philosophicum*. Review of *Différence et Répétition*. *Language, Counter-Memory, Practice: Selected Essays and Interviews* (Donald F. Bouchard, ed., Donald F. Bouchard and Sherry Simon, trans. Oxford: Basil Blackwell, 1977), p. 184.

49 Deleuze, *Difference and Repetition*, pp. 5 and 19. In French, "si l'on meurt de la répétition, c'est elle aussi qui sauve et qui guérit [...] si la répétition nous rend malades, c'est elle aussi qui nous guérit; si elle nous enchaîne et nous détruit, c'est elle encore qui nous libère," *Différence et répétition*, pp. 15 and 30.

50 Steven Connor, *Samuel Beckett: Repetition, Theory, and Text* (New York: Basil Blackwell, 1988), p. 11.

51 Beckett, *Company*: "So as to plod on from nought anew," p. 27, and "Then sooner or later

on from nought anew," p. 36, "Halting now and then with bowed head to fix the score. Then on from nought anew," p. 45.

52 Beckett, *Nohow On: Company, Ill Seen Ill Said, Worstward Ho.* (Gontarski, S.E. ed. New York: Grove Press, 1980), p. xvii.

53 Beckett, *Company*, p. 10.

54 "[…] le sentiment bien moins de rencontrer une philosophie nouvelle que de reconnaître ce [que l'on] attendait," Descombes, *Le même et l'autre*, p. 15.

55 Deleuze also participated in collaborative ventures with Claire Parnet, André Cresson, and Carmelo Bene.

56 Jean-Jacques Lecercle, "Speaking Is Dirty, Writing Is Clean': The Rules of Dialogue" *Comparative Criticism: An Annual Journal* 2RU (CCAJ) 20 (1998): pp. 17-32.

57 Interestingly, the words "come and go" do not, however, figure in the play which they actually name.

58 Beckett, *Three Dialogues with Georges Duthuit*, p. 33.

59 Beckett, *Three Novels*, p. 7, my emphasis.

60 Beckett, *Molloy*, p. 7, my emphasis.

61 Beckett, *Malone meurt*, pp. 13-14, my emphasis.

62 *Genesis*, 1:1, 11:1.

63 "L'intervalle entre la chose même et sa reproduction […] n'est parcouru que par une traduction […] l'imagination, elle, permit la représentation d'un objet à partir d'un signe, son simple nom […] C'est le péché originel," Derrida, *Signature, événement, contexte*, p. 400.

64 Derrida, *Positions*, p. 20.

65 Derrida, "Les Tours de Babel" *Difference in Translation* (Graham, Joseph F., ed. Ithaca: Cornell UP, 1985), pp. 165-248, p. 184.

66 Avital Ronell, "Why I Write Such Good Translator's Notes" *Glyph: Textual Studies* 7 (1980): p. 230.

67 Derrida, Jacques. "Différance" *Margins of Philosophy* (Alan Bass, trans. Chicago: University of Chicago Press, 1982), p. 14. The French reads, "une sorte de déplacement à la fois infime et radical," *Marges de la philosophie*, p. 15.

68 Philip E. Lewis, "The Measure of Translation Effects" *Difference in Translation* (Gramm, Joseph F., ed. Ithaca: Cornell University Press, 1985), p. 41.

69 "ce pas impossible," means both "this impossible step" and "this not impossible."

70 Derrida, "Shibboleth" *Acts of Literature* (New York: Routledge, 1992), p. 408. My emphasis.

71 Derrida, "Ulysses Gramophone," *Acts of Literature* (New York: Routledge, 1992), p. 256.

72 Beckett, *Three Novels*, p. 200.

73 Beckett, *More Pricks Than Kicks* (London: Calder and Boyars, 1966), p. 182.

74 Tom Bishop, "Samuel Beckett: Working Multi-Lingually" *Centerpoint: A Journal of Interdisciplinary Studies* 4:2 (Fall, 1980): pp. 140-142, p. 142.

75 Deirdre Bair, *Samuel Beckett: A Biography* (London: Jonathan Cape, 1978), p. 485.

76 Leslie Hill, *Beckett's Fiction: In Different Words* (New York: Cambridge University Press, 1990), p. 172, note 9.

77 See Connor, *Samuel Beckett: Repetition, Theory, and Text*, p. 88, for example.

78 Rabinowitz, "Samuel Beckett, Revisionist Translator" *Review*, Charlottesville, VA 13 (1991): pp. 273-281.

79 Connor, *Samuel Beckett: Repetition, Theory and Text*, p. 90.

80 Brian Fitch, *Beckett and Babel* (Toronto: University of Toronto Press, 1988).

81 Samuel Beckett, *Premier amour* (Paris: Minuit, 1970), p. 25. *First Love. Collected Shorter Prose 1945-1980*. (London: John Calder, 1984), p. 8.

82 Fitch, *Beckett and Babel*, p. 77.

83 For other alterations of this sort in the translations of *Waiting for Godot* see Duckworth's "Introduction of *En attendant Godot* (London: Harrap, 1966).

84 Bair, *Samuel Beckett : A Biography*, p. 438.

85 "Dire que l'écrivain va du réel au livre, et le traducteur d'un livre à un autre livre, c'[est] méconnaître ce qu'on sait aujourd'hui, qu'il a y toujours déjà eu des livres entre l'expérience et le livre," *Pour la poétique II* (Paris: Gallimard, 1970). My translation.

86 Ronell, *"Why I Write Such Good Translator's Notes" Glyph: Textual Studies* 7 (Baltimore, MD, 1980): pp. 176-201, p. 231.

87 Beckett, *Three Novels*, p. 280.

88 Beckett, *Molloy*, p. 23.

89 Hill, *Beckett's Fiction: In Different Words*, p. 41.

90 Beckett, *Molloy*, p. 37.

91 Beckett, *Mercier et Camier*, p. 201.

92 Walter Benjamin, "The Task of the Translator" *Illuminations* (Zohn, Harry, trans. Arendt, Hannah, ed. London: Collins, 1973), pp. 69-82, p. 75.

93 Beckett, *Three Novels*, p. 176.

94 Ibid, p. 236.

95 Deleuze, *Difference and Repetition*, p. 105.

96 Derrida, *Of Grammatology*, p. 304. "On veut remonter du supplément à la source; on doit reconnaître qu'il y du supplément à la source," *De la grammatologie*, p. 429.

97 "Au commencement, la répétition," from Derrida's *La voix et le phénomène* (Paris: PUF, 1967), p. 64.

Chapter 4 : "The Ether of Metaphysics"

1 From Rousseau's *Les Solitaires*, quoted in Derrida's "Du Supplément à la source," in *De la grammatologie*, p. 436.

2 Israel Schenker, "Moody Man of Letters" *New York Times* 6 (May 1956), part two, p. 3.

3 In *Telling It Again and Again*, Kawin describes Beckett's "turn" to the theatre for "pure present" as the next logical step after beginning with "prolonged presents" and proceeding to "continuous presents." This insistence on Beckett's desire for a presence of the theatre is often also justified by citing the self-referential quality of his plays. See, for example, Enoch Brater's "Light, Sound, Movement, and Action in Beckett's *Rockaby*" *Modern Drama*, 25:3 (September, 1982): pp. 342-348, Ruby Cohn's *Just Play: Beckett's Theater* (Princeton: Princeton University Press, 1980), pp. 27-33, William Worthen's "Beckett's Actor" *Modern Drama* 26:4 (December 1983): pp. 415-424. See also Shimon Levy's *Samuel Beck-*

ett's Selfreferential Drama (New York: St. Martin's Press, 1990), and Sidney Homan's *Beckett's Theaters: Interpretations for Performance* (London: Associated University Presses, 1984).

4   Michael Robinson, *The Long Sonata of the Dead: A Study of Samuel Beckett* (New York: Grove Press, 1969), p. 230.

5   Bruce Kawin, *Telling It Again and Again: Repetition in Literature and Film* (Ithaca: Cornell University Press, 1972), p. 146.

6   My translation. The word "Erholung" also has a health related connotation, meaning "recovery," or "recuperation." From Michael Haerdter, *Materialien zu Becketts Endspiel* (Frankfurt: Suhrkamp Verlag, 1968), p. 88.

7   My translation.

8   Marvin Carlson, *Theories of the Theatre: A Historical and Critical Survey, from the Greeks to the Present* (Ithaca: Cornell University Press, 1984), p. 503.

9   Herbert Blau, "Notes from the Underground: "Waiting for Godot" and "Endgame" *On Beckett* (Gontarski, S.E., ed. New York: Grove Press, 1986), p. 269.

10   Derrida, Jacques. "The Theater of Cruelty and the Closure of Representation." *Writing and Difference* (Alan Bass, trans. Chicago: University of Chicago Press, 1978), p. 236.

11   In this idealized "non-representational theatre" there would be nothing re-presented at all. There would be only "presentation." Here, the distinction between the audience and the actor would become ambiguous. Derrida notes the resemblance between Rousseau's "theatre" and Artaud's "festival" in which there would not be "anything to see" and where the spectators themselves would become actors." Derrida, "The Theater of Cruelty," p. 245.

12   Ibid, 234.

13   Alain Robbe-Grillet, "Samuel Beckett, or Presence on the Stage" *Snapshots and Towards A New Novel* (Barbara Wright, trans. London: Calder & Boyars, 1965), p. 119.

14   Sydney Homan, *Beckett's Theaters: Interpretations for Performance* (Lewisburg: Bucknell University Press, 1984), p. 17. Homan is quoting from Beckett's *How It Is.*

15   Robbe-Grillet, "Samuel Beckett, or Presence on the Stage," p. 119.

16   Derrida, *Of Grammatology*, p. 12. In French, "présence de la chose au regard comme *eidos*, présence comme substance/essence/existence (*ousia*), présence temporelle comme pointe (*stigmè*) du maintenant ou de l'instant (*nun*), présence à soi du cogito, conscience, subjectivité, co-présence de l'autre et de soi, intersubjectivité comme phénomène intentionnel de l'ego, etc.," *De la Grammatologie*, p. 23.

17   Ibid, p. 16.

18   In a conversation with Lois Oppenheim, later published in *Directing Beckett* (Ann Arbor: University of Michigan Press, 1994, p. 55), Herbert Blau distinguishes his manner of directing Beckett's work from that of Alan Schneider by referring to the latter as one of Beckett's favorite directors because he was always "very dutiful." As for himself, Blau asserts that he was in "no way influenced by [Beckett's] productions," and was generally "not taken with productions that, when you read a text, seem pretty much the way you'd do it if you did it straight." Of course, according to Gerry McCarthy, "playing it straight" is exactly what Beckett expects of and wants from his directors, and "any strain between directors and Beckett is the result of a feeling that they must 'do it his way.'" ("Emptying the

Theater: On Directing the Plays of Samuel Beckett," also in *Directing Beckett*, p. 250). In a letter 1953 to Roger Blin, Beckett as much as reprimands Blin for precisely this type of transgression, asking him to "just be kind enough to restore [the scene] as indicated in the text, and as [they] had agreed upon in rehearsal, and have the trousers fall completely around his ankles" (*Directing Beckett*, p. 297).

[19] Beckett, *Happy Days*, p. 146.

[20] Beckett, *Footfalls*, p. 399.

[21] This thought was echoed—*avant la lettre*—by Harold Hobson, drama critic for *The Sunday Times* from 1947–76, in a review published on August 7, 1955, of *Godot*. In a review published on the same date, Kenneth Tynan, drama critic of *The Observer*, labels *Godot* a "dramatic vacuum," in which one can find "no plot, no climax, no dénouement; no beginning, no middle, and no end."

[22] Vivian Mercier, "The Uneventful Event." *Irish Times* 18 February 1956, p. 6.

[23] Cohn, *Back to Beckett*, p. 132.

[24] Martin Esslin, "A Theatre of Stasis—Beckett's Late Plays" *Critical Essays on Samuel Beckett* (Boston: G.K. Hall & Co., 1986), p. 194.

[25] Cohn, *Back to Beckett*, p. 135. In *Just Play* (Princeton: Princeton University Press, 1980), Cohn characterizes Beckett's dramatic speech—with its hesitations, and contradictions—as indicative of a general mistrust of language, and in its place a privileging of physical action, adding that "Gesture is apparently keener and cleaner than phrase," p. 6.

[26] Cohn, "At This Moment in Time" *Just Play*, pp. 36, 46, 49, 50.

[27] Cohn, *Back to Beckett*, p. 156.

[28] Herbert Blau, "Notes from the Underground : 'Waiting for Godot' and 'Endgame'" *On Beckett: Essays and Criticism* (New York: Grove Press, 1986), p. 261.

[29] Enoch Brater, "A Footnote to *Footfalls*: Footsteps of Infinity on Beckett's Narrow Space" *Critical Essays On Samuel Beckett* (Patrick A. McCarthy, ed., Boston: C.K. Hall & Co, 1986), p. 212.

[30] Derrida considers Artaud's theatre of cruelty itself—and not simply the desire for pure presence—an impossibility because the concepts behind it speak less to the theatre than to metaphysics. He describes *The Theater and Its Double* as "more a system of critiques shaking the entirety of occidental history than a treatise on theatrical practice." From "The Theater of Cruelty and the Closure of Representation," p. 235.

[31] Derrida, "The Theater of Cruelty or the Closure of Representation," p. 249.

[32] Vincent Descombes, *Modern French Philosophy* (trans. L. Scott-Fox and J.M. Harding. Cambridge: Cambridge University Press, 1986), p. 145. In French, "Il y a histoire, parce que dès l'origine, le présent est comme en retard sur lui-même," Vincent Descombes, *Le même et l'autre : quarante-cinq ans de philosophie Française (1933-1978)* (Paris : Minuit, 1979), p. 170.

[33] Beckett, *Three Novels*, p. 17.

[34] Derrida, *Of Grammatology*, 3.

[35] "Ne sait-on pas que les statues et les tableaux n'offensent les yeux que quand un mélange de vêtements rend les nudités obscènes?" Rousseau, "Lettre à M. d'Alembert," p. 232, from *De la Grammatologie*, p. 436, and *Of Grammatology*, p. 309.

36   Jacques Derrida, "Signature Event Context" *Margins of Philosophy* (Bass, Alan, trans. Brighton: Harvestor Press, 1982), p. 320.

37   Derrida, "Signature événement contexte" *Marges de la philosophie* (Paris: Minuit, 1972), p. 381.

38   Derrida, *Margins of Philosophy*, p. 318.

39   For references to this "turn" to the theatre, see Ruby Cohn, *Back to Beckett*, p. 129, and Steven Connor, *Samuel Beckett: Repetition, Theory and Text*, p. 115. See also Bruce Kawin, *Telling It Again and Again: Repetition in Literature and Film*, p. 146.

40   Ruby Cohn, "Waiting" *Critical Essays on Samuel Beckett* (Boston: G.K Hall & Co, 1986), p. 153.

41   Samuel Beckett, "Krapp's Last Tape," *Complete Dramatic Works*, p. 222.

42   H. Porter Abbott, *Beckett Writing Beckett: The Author in the Autograph* (Ithaca: Cornell University Press, 1996), pp. 35-46.

43   Quoted in Derrida's "From/Of the Supplement to the Source," p. 309, and "Du Supplément à la source," p. 436.

44   I am working off of Derrida's definition of the present as one of the many subdeterminations that are produced from the association of Being with Presence which was quoted earlier in this chapter: "presence of the thing to the sight as eidos, presence as substance/essence/existence [ousia], temporal presence as point [stigma] of the now or of the moment [nun], the self-presence of the cogito, consciousness, subjectivity, the co-presence of the other and of the self, intersubjectivity as the intentional phenomenon of the ego, and so forth," *From/Of Grammatology*, p. 12.

45   Rousseau, p. 116, my emphasis.

46   Jean Starobinski, *Jean-Jacques Rousseau: Transparency and Obstruction* (Arthur Goldhammer, trans. Chicago: University of Chicago Press, 1988), p. 125.

47   Paul De Man, "Self (Pygmalion)" *Allegories of Reading* (New Haven: Yale University Press, 1979), pp. 160-187, p. 168.

48   Deleuze, *Difference and Repetition*, p. 74.

49   See, for example, Connor, Begam, Kenner, and Harvey.

50   "Rockaby Baby," interview with John Connor for *City Limits* (January, 1986): pp. 24-30, quoted from Connor, *Samuel Beckett: Repetition, Theory and Text*, p. 212, n.13. My emphasis.

51   Beckett, *Three Novels*, p. 304, and *L'Innommable*, p. 29.

52   Deleuze, *Difference and Repetition*, p. 102. The French reads, "[la] propriété d'être *et* de ne pas être là où il est, où qu'il aille," p. 135.

53   Beckett, *Three Novels*, p. 42.

54   Maurice Blanchot, *The Book to Come* (Mandell, Charlotte, trans. Stanford, Calif.: Stanford University Press, 2003), pp. 215-216. In French, "L'œuvre demande [...]que l'homme qui l'écrit se sacrifie pour l'œuvre, devienne autre..." *Le Livre à venir* (Paris: Gallimard, 1959), p. 294.

55   Malone is in fact Heidegger's "l'être-pour-la-mort" par excellence. His very first utterances of this text "I shall soon be quite dead at last," (p. 179) remind us that we are indeed born astride a grave (*Godot*, p. 126).

56   Beckett, *Three Novels*, p. 195, my emphasis. The French reads, "je recommençais, à vouloir vivre, faire vivre, être autrui, en moi, en autrui," *Malone meurt*, p. 34.

57   In French, "derrière mes yeux fermés, se fermer d'autres yeux," *Malone meurt*, p. 35.

58   "Et à la veille de ne plus être j'arrive à être un autre," *Malone meurt*, p. 32.

59   "Je ne me regarderai pas mourir [...] Me suis-je regardé vivre ?" *Malone meurt*, 8.

60   One example of this is Sapo's lack of knowledge with respect to the "art of thinking": that he did not know to "put the index on the subject and the little finger on the verb," *Three Novels*, p. 193, *Malone meurt*, p. 30. Not long after Malone makes this description, he mentions his own inability to control the subject and the verb while sleeping: that when dozing off and continuing to write, the "subject falls far from the verb," *Three Novels*, p. 234. *Malone meurt*, p. 100.

61   "Je me demande si ce n'est pas encore de moi qu'il s'agit, malgré mes précautions," *Malone meurt*, p. 23. And in the English version: "I wonder if I am not talking yet again about myself," *Three Novels*, p. 189. Several pages following this statement, however, he takes back this assertion, stating that "rien ne me ressemble moins que ce gamin raisonnable et patient [...]," *Malone meurt*, p. 31. In the English, "Nothing is less like me than this patient, reasonable child," *Three Novels*, p. 193.

62   Beckett, *L'Innommable*, p. 37.

63   "Regarde-moi ce vieux Worm qui attend sa belle," *L'Innommable*, p. 127.

64   Samuel Beckett, *Not I, The Complete Dramatic Works* (London: Faber and Faber, 1956), p. 37.

65   Deleuze, *Difference and Repetition*, p. 75. "C'est toujours un tiers qui dit moi," p. 103.

66   Beckett, *Nohow On: Company, Ill Seen Ill Said, Worstword Ho*, p. xxi.

67   Beckett, *Company* in *Nohow On*, p. 32.

68   It is interesting to note that the French version does not, however, repeat "je me rappelle."

69   Deleuze, *Difference and Repetition*, p. 75. "que par ces mille témoins qui contemplent en nous," p. 103.

70   Beckett, *Company*, p. 18. "parle de soi comme d'un autre," *Compagnie* (Paris : Minuit, 1985), p. 33.

71   "L'impensable ultime. Innommable. Toute dernière personne. Je," *Compagnie*, p. 31.

72   Blanchot, *The Book to Come*, pp. 215–216, my emphasis.

73   Blanchot, *Le Livre à venir*, p. 293, my emphasis.

74   "Ce à quoi je voulais arriver [...] c'était aux extases du vertige, du lâchage, de la chute, de l'engouffrement, du retour au noir, au rien," *Malone meurt*, p. 34.

75   See, for example, his description of his stick (p. 255). Seeing only a part of it, "as of all one sees," he is still able to recognize it as not just any stick but the one that belongs to him.

76   "à supposer qu'il existe réellement," *Malone meurt*, p. 135.

77   This is compounded at the end when the text closes with these very words "plus rien."

78   Beckett, *Three Novels*, p. 386.

79   Beckett, *L'Innommable*, p. 166.

80   "Il ne faut pas oublier, quelquefois je l'oublie, que tout est une question de voix. Ce qui se passe ce sont des mots," *L'Innommable*, p. 98.

81   "Mon histoire arrêtée je vivrai encore," *Malone meurt*, p. 183.

82   Samuel Beckett, "Dante...Bruno...Joyce" *Disjecta: Miscellaneous Writings and a Dramatic Fragment* (Ruby Cohn, ed. London: John Calder, 1983), pp. 27–28.

Conclusion

1   Arthur Danto, *After the End of Art: Contemporary Art and the Pale of History* (Princeton: Princeton University Press, 1997).

2   Danto, "The End of Art" *The Philosophical Disenfranchisement of Art* (New York: Columbia, 1986), p. 84.

3   Although he does give approximate dates for each age, Danto is careful not to posit any exact dates for art's beginning or ending, stating that the "era of art did not begin abruptly in 1400, nor did it end sharply either, sometime before the mid-1980's" (*After The End of Art*, p. 4). He also insists that these stages in the narrative—although presented as corresponding to particular moments along a historical timeline—are not temporally determined. Not every work of art produced from the 1880's to the 1960's can be considered modern, and not every piece created just prior to the 1880's is indicative of the "era of imitation."

4   Danto, *After the End of Art*, p. 7.

5   Danto reminds us that Descartes was not the first to explore the nature of the "self." However, it was only with Descartes' *Discours de la méthode* that the idea of the self came to determine "the entire activity of philosophy," *After the End of Art*, p. 6.

6   "The End of Art," p. 111. In *After the End of Art*, Danto signals the cataclysmic "paroxysm of styles" of the 1960's, which all focused on the philosophical question "what is art", as that which precipitated the end of the narrative of the visual arts (p. 13).

7   Clement Greenberg and Hans Belting, for example.

8   Danto makes a distinction between "post-modern" which he considers to be a style with easily appreciable characteristics (it is hybrid, ambiguous, etc.) and "post-historic," which is the period in which there are no longer any stylistic rules (*After the End of Art*, pp. 11–12).

9   Jean Baudrillard, "Simulacra and Simulation" *Jean Baudrillard, Selected Writings* (Mark Poster, ed., Stanford; Stanford University Press, 2001), pp. 169–187, pp. 1–2.

10   Danto, *After the End of Art*, p. 14.

11   Often the reaction is also accompanied by an attempt to neutralize the effects of such ideas with aggressive and dismissive language. See, for example, Jorn K. Bramann's critique of Danto's work. Bramann associates Danto's idea of art after the end of art with deconstruction, which he refers to as a "fad" that is "winding down" and the theorists of such ideas as perpetuators of a "dogmatic relativism" that is nothing more than the "other side of the coin of Absolutism" or "the habit of seeing no construction as arbitrary." I do not take issue with the notion that the idea that all constructs are arbitrary is the flip side of the idea that no constructs are arbitrary. I am interested rather in the way that this fact— along with the use of words such as "fad," "habit" and "dogmatic" to describe deconstruction—is offered as a reason to dismiss such theories as irrelevant. Bramann's reading of Danto is also something of a misreading. While Danto does claim that the idea of boundaries was called into question at the end of the narrative of art and thereafter, it is

not this lack of boundaries that characterizes the post-historic but rather an apparent lack of direction or continuity from one movement to another.

‡ Bibliography

Abbott, H. Porter. *Beckett Writing Beckett: The Author in the Autograph*. Ithaca: Cornell University Press, 1996.

Acheson, James. "Beckett's Film, Berkeley, and Schopenhauer." *Beckett and Beyond*. Bruce Stewart, ed. New York: Oxford University Press, 1999, 10-15.

Adorno, Theodor. "Trying to Understand Endgame." *New German Critique*, 26, *Critical Theory and Modernity* (Spring-Summer, 1982).

———. "Versuch, das Endspiel zu verstehen." *Noten zur Literatur II*. Frankfurt am Main, 1961.

Alvarez, A. "Poet Waiting for Pegasus." Review of *Poems in English*. *The Observer*, 31 December, 1961.

Aristotle. *Poetics*. Leon Colden, trans. Englewood Cliffs: Prentice Hall, 1968.

Artaud, Antonin. "Production and Metaphysics." *The Theatre and its Double*. Mary Caroline Richards, trans. New York: Grove, 1958.

Attridge, Derek, ed. *Jacques Derrida: Acts of Literature*. New York: Routledge, 1992.

Bacon, Francis. *Instauratio Magna*. Electronic resource. London: Printed by John Haviland for William Lee, and Humphrey Mosley, 1638.

Bair, Deirdre. *Samuel Beckett: A Biography*. London: Jonathan Cape, 1978.

Barale, Michele Aina and Rubin Rabinowitz. *A KWIC Concordance to Samuel Beckett's Trilogy: Molloy, Malone Dies, and The Unnamable*. New York: Garland Publishing, 1988.

Barfield, Steve. "Beckett and Heidegger: A Critical Survey." *Beckett and Philosophy*. Richard Lane, ed. New York: Palgrave, 2002.

Barge, Laura. "Beckett's Questing Hero: Mystic or Pseudomystic." *Cithara: Essays in the Judaeo-Christian Tradition* 24:2 (May, 1985).

———. "God, the Quest, the Hero: Thematic Structures in Beckett's fiction." *Chapel Hill: Dept. of Romance Languages, Univ. of North Carolina*, 1988.

Barker, Ronald. "Waiting for Godot." *Plays and Players*. (September, 1955) 18-19.

Barthes, Roland. "A l'avant-garde de quel théâtre." *Œuvres Complètes*. Paris: Seuil, 1993, 1224-1226.

———. "Comment s'en passer. " *Œuvres Complètes*. Paris: Seuil, 1993, 432-434.

———. "Godot adulte." *Œuvres Complètes*. Paris: Seuil, 1993, 413-416.

———. "Littérature objective." *Œuvres Complètes*. Paris: Seuil, 1993, 1185-1193.

———. "Littérature et signification."*Œuvres Complètes*. Paris: Seuil, 1993, 1362-1375.

———. "Œuvre de masse et explication de textes."*Œuvres Complètes*. Paris: Seuil, 1993, 1109-1110.

———. "The Structuralist Activity." Robert Con Davies and Roland Schleifer, eds. *Contemporary Literary Criticism*. New York: Longman, 1989, 170-174.

———. "Le Théâtre français de l'avant-garde." *Œuvres Complètes*. Paris: Seuil, 1993, 915-921.

Baudrillard, Jean. *Jean Baudrillard: Selected Writings*. Mark Poster, ed. Stanford: Stanford University Press, 2001.

Beckett, Samuel. *Compagnie*. Paris: Minuit, 1985.

————. *The Complete Dramatic Works*. London: Faber and Faber, 1956.

————. *The Complete Short Prose: 1929-1989*. S.E. Gontarski, ed. New York: Grove Press, 1995.

————. "Dante...Bruno...Joyce." *Disjecta: Miscellaneous Writings and a Dramatic Fragment*. Ruby Cohn, ed. London: John Calder, 1983.

————. *Disjecta: Miscellaneous Writings and a Dramatic Fragment*. Ruby Cohn, ed. London: John Calder, 1983.

————. *Dream of Fair to Middling Women*. Eoin O'Brien and Edith Fournier, eds. New York: Arcade Publishing, 1993.

————. *Echo's Bones and Other Precipitates*. Paris: Europa Press, 1935.

————. *En Attendant Godot*. Paris: Editions de Minuit, 1952.

————. *First Love* in *Collected Shorter Prose 1945-1980*. London: John Calder, 1984.

————. *Footfalls*. *The Complete Dramatic Works*. London: Faber and Faber, 1956.

————. *Happy Days*. *The Complete Dramatic Works*. London: Faber and Faber, 1956.

————. *L'Innommable*. Paris: Editions de Minuit, 1953.

————. *Krapp's Last Tape*. *The Complete Dramatic Works*. London: Faber and Faber, 1956.

————. *Malone Dies*. New York; Grove Press, 1956.

————. *Malone meurt*. Paris: Editions de Minuit, 1951.

————. *Mercier and Camier*. New York: Grove Press, 1974.

————. *Mercier et Camier*. Paris: Les Editions de minuit, 1970.

————. *Molloy*. Paris: Editions de Minuit, 1951.

————. *Molloy*. New York: Grove Press, 1955.

————. *More Pricks Than Kicks*. London: Calder and Boyars, 1966, c1934.

————. *Not I*. *The Complete Dramatic Works*. London: Faber and Faber, 1956.

————. *Nohow On: Company, Ill Seen Ill Said, Worstward Ho*. New York: Grove Press, 1980.

————. *Premier amour*. Paris: Minuit, 1970.

————. *Proust and Three Dialogues with Georges Duthuit*. London: John Calder, 1965.

————. *"Quad" et autres pièces pour la télévision, suivi par "L'épuisé" par Gilles Deleuze*. Paris: Editions de Minuit, 1992.

————. "Three Dialogues with Georges Duthuit." *Transition* 48 (1949): 97–103.

————. *Three Novels: Molloy, Malone Dies, The Unnamable*. New York: Grove Press, 1955.

————. *The Unnamable*. New York: Grove Press, 1958.

————. *Waiting for Godot*, in *Samuel Beckett: The Complete Dramatic Works*. London: Faber and Faber, 1982.

————. *Whoroscope*. Paris: The Hours Press, 1930.

Begam, Richard. *Samuel Beckett and the End of Modernity*. Stanford: Stanford University Press, 1996.

Beji, Saloua. "Approche du théâtre de l'absurde: Adamov, Beckett, Al Hakim, Ionesco." *Th. 3e cycle: Littérature comparée* Toulouse 2 (1988).

Benjamin, Walter. "On the Mimetic Faculty." *Reflections: Essays, Aphorisms, Autobiographical Writings*. Peter Demetz, ed. New York: Schocken, 1986.

————. "The Task of the Translator." *Illuminations*. Harry Zohn, trans and Hannah Arendt, ed. London: Collins, 1973, 69-82.

————. "The Work of Art in Mechanical Reproduction." *The Nineteenth-Century Visual Culture Reader.* Vanessa R. Schwartz and Jeannene M. Przyblyski, eds. New York: Routledge, 2004, 63–70.

Ben-Zvi, Linda. "Samuel Beckett's Media Plays." *Modern Drama* 28 (March, 1985): 22–37.

Berman, Art. *From the New Criticism to Deconstruction: The Reception of Structuralism and Post-Structuralism.* Urbana: University of Illinois Press, 1988.

Berman, David. *Berkeley and Irish Philosophy.* London; Continuum, 2005.

Bernheimer, Charles. "Watt's in The Castle: the Aporetic Quest in Kafka and Beckett." *Newsletter of the Kafka Society of America* 6:1–2 (June-Dec 1982): 19–24.

Bishop, Tom. *From the Left Bank: Reflections on the Modern French Theater and Novel.* New York: New York University Press, 1977.

————. "Samuel Beckett: Working Multi-Lingually." *Centerpoint: A Journal of Interdisciplinary Studies,* 4:2, (Fall, 1980): 140–142.

Blanchot, Maurice. *The Book to Come.* Charlotte Mandell, trans. Stanford, Calif.: Stanford University Press, 2003.

————. *Le Livre à venir.* Paris: Gallimard, 1959.

Blau, Herbert. "Notes from the Underground: "Waiting for Godot" and "Endgame." *On Beckett.* S.E. Gontarski, ed. New York: Grove Press, 1986, 255–279.

Brater, Enoch. "A Footnote to *Footfalls*: Footsteps of Infinity on Beckett's Narrow Space." *Critical Essays On Samuel Beckett.* McCarthy, Patrick A., ed. Boston: C.K. Hall & Co, 1986.

————. "Light, Sound, Movement, and Action in Beckett's *Rockaby*," *Modern Drama,* 25:3 (September, 1982): 342–348.

Boulter, Jonathan. *Interpreting Narrative in the Novels of Samuel Beckett.* Gainesville: University Press of Florida, 2001.

Carlson, Marvin. *Theories of the Theatre: A Historical and Critical Survey, From the Greeks to the Present.* New York: Cornell University Press, 1993.

Campbell, Julie. "Pilgrim's Progress/Regress/Stasis: Some Thoughts on the Treatment of the Quest in Bunyan's *Pilgrim's Progress* and Beckett's *Mercier and Camier*." *Comparative Literature Studies* 30:2 (1993): 137–152.

Catanzaro, Mary. "Whose Story is it? Samuel Beckett's *Malone Dies* and the Voice of Self-Invention." Michael J. Meyer, Michael. *Literature and the Writer.* Amsterdam: Rodopi, 2004.

Clurman, Harold. "Theatre." *The Nation,* 5 May 1956, 487–90.

Cohn, Ruby. *Back to Beckett.* Princeton: Princeton University Press, 1974.

————. *Just Play: Beckett's Theater.* Princeton: Princeton University Press, 1980.

————. *Samuel Beckett: The Comic Gamut.* New Brunswick: Rutgers University Press, 1962.

Connor, John. "Rockaby Baby." *City Limits,* 1986, 24–30.

Connor, Steven. *Samuel Beckett: Repetition, Theory and Text.* Oxford: Basil Blackwell Press, 1988.

Cook, Theodore Andreas. *The Curves of Life; Being an Account of Spiral Formations and their Application to Growth in Nature, to Science and to Art.* London: Constable Press, 1914.

Critchley, Simon. *Very Little...Almost Nothing: Death, Philosophy, Literature.* New York: Routledge, 1997.

Cunningham, Dave. "Trying (Not) to Understand: Adorno and the Work of Beckett." *Beckett and Philosophy.* Richard Lane, ed. New York: Palgrave, 2002, 125–139.

Danto, Arthur. *After the End of Art: Contemporary Art and the Pale of History*. Princeton: Princeton University Press, 1997.

———. "The End of Art." *The Philosophical Disenfranchisement of Art*. New York: Columbia, 1986, 81–115.

Deleuze, Gilles. *Difference and Repetition*. New York: Columbia University Press, 1994.

———. *Différence et répétition*. Paris: Presses Universitaires de France, 1968.

———. "L'épuisé." Samuel Beckett. *"Quad" et autres pièces pour la télévision, suivi par "L'épuisé" par Gilles Deleuze*. Paris: Editions de Minuit, 1992.

———. *Nietzsche et la philosophie*. Paris: Editions de Minuit, 1972.

Dearlove, J.E. "The Weaving of Penelope's Tapestry: Genre in the Works of Samuel Beckett." *Journal of Beckett Studies*, Tallahassee, FL. (1989): 123–129.

De Man, Paul. "Self (Pygmalion)." *Allegories of Reading*. New Haven: Yale University Press, 1979, 160–187.

Derrida, Jacques. "La différance." *Marges de la philosophie*. Paris: Editions de Minuit, 1972.

———. "La double séance." *La Dissémination*. Paris: Seuil, 1972.

———. "The Double Session." *Dissemination*. Chicago: Chicago University Press, 1981.

———. *L'écriture et la différence*. Paris: Seuil, 1967.

———. *De la grammatologie*. Paris: Minuit, 1967.

———. *Glas*, trans. J.P. Leavey Jr. and R. Rand. Lincoln: Nebraska University Press, 1986.

———. "The Law of Genre." *Glyph: Textual Studies*, Baltimore, MD, 1980, 7, pp. 202-232.

———. *Positions*. Chicago: University of Chicago Press, 1981.

———. "La scène de l'écriture." *L'Ecriture et la différance*. Paris: Seuil, 1967.

———. "Shibboleth." *Acts of Literature*, Derek Attridge, ed. New York: Routledge, 1992.

———. "Signature, Event, Context." *Margins of Philosophy*. Alan Bass, trans. Chicago: University of Chicago Press, 1982.

———. "Signature, événement, contexte." *Marges de la philosophie*. Paris: Minuit, 1972.

———. "La structure, le signe et le jeu dans le discours des sciences humaines." *L'Ecriture et la différence*. Paris: Seuil, 1967.

———. "Structure, Sign and Play." *Writing and Difference*. Trans. Alan Bass, Chicago: University of Chicago Press, 1978.

———. "Du supplément à la source." *De la grammatologie*. Paris: Minuit, 1967.

———. "Of/From the Supplement to the Source." *Of Grammatology*, Gayatri Chakravorty Spivak, trans. Baltimore: Johns Hopkins University Press, 1984.

———. "The Theater of Cruelty or the Closure of Representation." *Writing and Difference*, Alan Bass, trans. London: Routledge and Kegan Paul, 1978.

———. "Les tours de Babel." *Difference in Translation*. Graham, Joseph F., ed., Ithaca: Cornell University Press, 1985.

———. "Tympan." *Marges de la philosophie*. Paris: Minuit, 1972.

———. "Tympan." *Margins of Philosophy*. Alan Bass, trans. Chicago: University of Chicago Press, 1982.

———. "Ulysses Gramophone." *Acts of Literature*. Derek Attridge, ed. New York: Routledge, 1992.

———. *La voix et le phénomène*. Paris: Presses Universitaires de France, 1967.

———. *Writing and Difference*. Alan Bass, trans. London: Routledge and Kegan Paul, 1978.

Descartes. *Discours de la méthode*. Bruxelles: Didier, 1971.

Descombes, Vincent. *Le même et l'autre*. Paris: Editions de Minuit, 1979.

————. *Modern French Philosophy*. Cambridge: Cambridge University Press, 1980.

Dobrez, Livio. "Beckett, Sartre and Camus: The Darkness and the Light." *Southern Review* 7 (1974): 51-63.

Duckworth, Colin. *Angels of Darkness: Dramatic Effect in Samuel Beckett with Special Reference to Eugène Ionesco*. London: George Allen & Unwin Ltd., 1972.

Eco, Umberto. *The Role of the Reader: Explorations in the Semiotics of Texts*. Bloomington: Indiana University Press, 1979.

Egebak, Niels. *L'écriture de Samuel Beckett*. Copenhagen: Akademisk Forlag, 1973.

Eliade, Mircea. *The Myth of the Eternal Return*. New York: Pantheon Books, 1954.

Else, Gerald F. "Imitation in the Fifth Century," in *Classical Philology*, vol. LIII (1958) 73-90.

Eribon, Didier. *Foucault*. Boston: Harvard University Press, 1991.

Esslin, Martin. "Beckett and the 'Theatre of the Absurd.'" *Approaches to Teaching Beckett's Waiting for Godot*. Enoch Brater and June Schlueter, eds. New York: Mod. Language Association of America, 1991.

————. "Mrozek, Beckett, and the Theatre of the Absurd." *New Theatre Quarterly* 10:40 (Nov 1994): 377-381.

————. "The Theatre of the Absurd." *Tulane Drama Review* 4:4 (1960): 3-15.

————. "A Theatre of Stasis—Beckett's Late Plays." *Critical Essays on Samuel Beckett*. Boston: G.K. Hall & Co., 1986, 192-198.

Fish, Stanley. *Is There a Text in this Class? The Authority of Interpretive Communities*. Cambridge: Harvard University Press, 1982.

Fitch, Brian. *Beckett and Babel*. Toronto : University of Toronto Press, 1988.

Foucault, Michel. "Archéologie d'une passion." *Dits et écrits : IV*. Paris: Gallimard, 1994, 599-609.

————. "Nietzsche, Marx, Freud." *Transforming the Hermeneutic Context*. Gayle Ormiston and Alan Schrift, eds. Albany: SUNY Press, 1990, 55-67.

————. "Le Style de l'histoire." *Dits et écrits : IV*. Paris: Gallimard, 1994.

————. "Theatrum Philosophicum," in *Language, Counter-Memory, Practice: Selected Essays and Interviews*, ed. Donald F. Bouchard, trans. Donald F. Bouchard and Sherry Simon. Oxford: Basil Blackwell, 1977.

Frye, Northrop. *The Well-Tempered Critic*. Bloomington: Indiana University Press, 1963.

Furman, Nelly. "Textual Feminism." *Women and Language in Literature and Society*. Nelly Furman, Sally McConnell-Ginet, and Ruth Borker, eds. New York: Praeger Publishers, 1980, 45-54.

Gontarski. *Samuel Beckett: The Complete Short Prose: 1029-1989*. New York: Grove Press, 1995.

Groden, Michael and Martin Kreiswirth, eds. *The Johns Hopkins Guide to Literary Theory and Criticism*. Baltimore: The Johns Hopkins University Press, 1994.

Habermas, Jürgen. *The Philosophical Discourse of Modernity: Twelve Lectures*, Frederick Lawrence, trans. Cambridge: Polity Press, 1987.

Haerdter, Michael. *Materialien zu Becketts Endspiel*. Frankfurt: Suhrkamp Verlag, 1968.

Harding, James Martin. *Adorno and a "Writing of the Ruins": Essays on Modern Aesthetics and Anglo-American Literature and Culture*. Albany: State University of New York Press, 1997.

Harvey, Lawrence. "Art and the Existential in *Waiting for Godot*." *PMLA Publications of the MLA: Publications of the Modern Language Association of America* 75:1 (1960): 137-146.

————. *Samuel Beckett: Poet and Critic*. New Jersey: Princeton University Press, 1970.

Hassan, Ihab. "From Postmodernism to Postmodernity: The Local/Global Context." Online essay: http://www.ihabhassan.com/postmodernism_to_postmodernity.htm.

Hedberg, Johannes. "Some Thoughts on Three Poems by Samuel Beckett." *Moderna Språk*, Vol. LXVIII No. 1 (1974): 11-18.

Hegel, Georg Wilhelm Friedrich. *Encyklopädie der philosophischen Wissenschaften im Grundrisse*. Heidelberg: A. Oswald, 1827.

Hill, Leslie. *Beckett's Fiction: In Different Words*. Cambridge: Cambridge University Press, 1990.

Homan, Sidney. *Beckett's Theaters: Interpretations for Performance*. London: Associated University Presses, 1984.

Hornung, Alfred. "Fantasies of the Autobiographical Self: Thomas Bernhard, Raymond Federman, Samuel Beckett." *Journal of Beckett Studies* 11-12 (1989): 91-107.

Hunkeler, Thomas. "The Role of the Dead Man in the Game of Writing: Beckett and Foucault." *Beckett and Philosophy*. Richard Lane, ed. New York: Palgrave, 2002, 68-79.

Huyssen, Andreas. *After the Great Divide: Modernism, Mass Culture, Postmodernism*. Bloomington: Indiana University Press, 1986.

Ilhyung, Park. "Beckett's Autobiographical Drama, Allography or Thanatography: Not I and That Time." *Journal of Modern British and American Drama* 17:2 (Aug 2004): 49-73.

Jauss, Hans Robert. *Toward an Aesthetic of Reception*. Timothy Bahti, trans. Minneapolis: University of Minnesota Press, 1982.

Kant, Immanuel. *Critique of Judgment*. New York: Hackette Publishing, 1987.

Kaufmann, Walter. "Translator's Introduction." *The Gay Science*. Walter Kaufmann, trans. New York: Random House, 1974.

Kawin, Bruce. *Telling it Again and Again: Repetition in Literature and Film*. Denver: University Press of Colorado, 1972.

Kelley, Paul B. "Correspondence with the Void: Negativity and Narrativity in Sartre's *La Nausée* and Samuel Beckett's *Malone meurt*." *Dalhousie French Studies* 59 (2002): 76-82.

Kenner, Hugh. *Samuel Beckett: A Critical Study*. New York: Grove Press, 1962.

Kierkegaard, Søren. *Fear and Trembling and Repetition*. Howard V. and Edna H. Hong, eds. and trans. Princeton: Princeton University Press, 1983.

Knowlson, James. *Damned to Fame: The Life of Samuel Beckett*. London: Bloomsbury Publishing, 1996.

Koller, Hermann. *Die Mimesis in der Antike: Nachahmung, Darstellung, Ausdruck*. Dissertationes Bernenses, Ser. 1,5. Bern, 1954.

Koppers, Wilhelm. *Die Bhil in Zentralindien*. Horn-Wien: Verlag Ferdinand Berger, 1948.

Kristeva, Julia. "Freud and Love: Treatment and its Discontents." *Tales of Love (Histoires d'amour)*. Leon S. Roudiez, trans. New York: Columbia University Press, 1983, 238-271.

————. "Postmodernism?" *Bucknell Review* 25 (1980): 136-141.

Lecercle, Jean-Jacques. "'Speaking Is Dirty, Writing Is Clean': The Rules of Dialogue." *Comparative Criticism: An Annual Journal* 2RU (CCAJ) 20 (1998) : 17-32.

Lévi-Strauss, Claude. *Le cru et le cuit*. Paris: Plon, 1965.

————. *The Raw and the Cooked*. John and Doreen Weightman, trans. New York: Harper and Row, 1969.

Levy, Shimon. *Samuel Beckett's Self Referential Drama: The Three I's.* New York: St. Martin's Press, 1990.

Lewis, Philip E. "The Measure of Translation Effects." *Difference in Translation.* Joseph F. Gramm, ed. Ithaca: Cornell University Press, 1985, 31–62.

Lukács, Georg. *The Meaning of Contemporary Realism.* John and Necke Mander, trans. London: Merlin Press, 1963.

Lyotard, Jean-François. *La Condition Postmoderne.* Paris: Editions de Minuit, 1979.

————. *Lectures d'enfance.* Paris: Galilée, 1991.

Mallarmé, Stéphane. "Mimique." *Œuvres complètes.* Henri Mondor and G. Jean-Aubry, eds. Paris: Gallimard, 1945, 310–11.

Mayberry, Bob. *Theatre of Discord: Dissonance in Beckett, Albee, and Pinter.* Rutherford: Fairleigh Dickinson University Press, 1989.

McCarthy, Gerry. "Emptying the Theater: On Directing the Plays of Samuel Beckett." *Directing Beckett.* Oppenheim, Lois, ed. Ann Arbor: University of Michigan Press, 1994, 250–267.

Melberg, Arne. *Theories of Mimesis.* Cambridge: Cambridge University Press, 1995.

Mercier, Vivian. "The Uneventful Event." *Irish Times,* 18 February, 1956.

Merleau-Ponty. *Phénoménologie de la perception.* Paris: Gallimard, 1945.

Nietzsche, Friedrich. "The Convalescent." *Thus Spoke Zarathustra. The Collected Works of Friedrich Nietzsche.* Oscar Levy, ed. London: Foulis Press, 1909 – 13, 269–271.

————. *The Gay Science.* Walter Kaufmann, trans. New York: Random House, 1974.

————. *Fragments posthumes (Printemps 1884-Automne 1884),* Colli/Montinari, eds., Jean Launay, trans. (OPC 10) Paris: Gallimard, 1982.

————. *Fragments posthumes (Automne 1885-Automne 1887)* Colli/Montinari, eds., Jean Launay, trans. (OPC 12). Paris: Gallimard, 1978.

————. *The Will to Power.* W. Kaufmann and R.J Hollingdale, trans. New York: Random House, 1968.

Norris, Christopher. *Deconstruction: Theory and Practice.* New York: Methuen, 1982.

Olney, James. *Memory & Narrative: The Weave of Life-writing.* Chicago: University of Chicago Press, 1998.

Oppenheim, Lois, ed. *Directing Beckett.* Ann Arbor: University of Michigan Press, 1994.

Perloff, Marjorie. "Between Verse and Prose: Beckett and the New Poetry." *Critical Inquiry,* Chicago, IL. 9:2 (December 1982): 415–433.

Plato. *Cratylus/Plato.* Dorothea Frede, trans. Indianapolis: Hackett Publishing Co., 1993.

————. *Philebus/Plato.* C.D.C. Reeve, trans. Indianapolis: Hackett Publishing Co., 1998.

————. *The Republic of Plato.* Allan Bloom, trans. New York: Basic Books, 1968.

Rabinowitz, Rubin. *Before Reading: Narrative Conventions and the Politics of Interpretation.* Ithaca: Cornell University Press, 1987.

————. *The Development of Samuel Beckett's Fiction.* Urbana: University of Illinois Press, 1984.

————. *Innovation in Samuel Beckett's Fiction.* Chicago: University of Illinois Press, 1992.

————. "Samuel Beckett: Revisionist Translator." *Review,* Charlottesville, VA, 13 (1991): 273–281.

Riera, Gabriel, ed. *Alain Badiou: Philosophy and its Conditions*. Albany: State University of New York Press, 2005.

Riffaterre, Michael. *Semiotics of Poetry*. Bloomington: Indiana University Press, 1978.

Robbe-Grillet, Alain. *Snapshots and Towards A New Novel*. London: Calder and Boyars, 1965.

Robinson, Michael. *The Long Sonata of the Dead: A Study of Samuel Beckett*. New York: Grove Press, 1969.

Ronell, Avital. "Why I Write Such Good Translator's Notes." *Glyph: Textual Studies*, Baltimore, MD, 7 (1980): 176-201.

Rorty, Richard. "Philosophy as a Kind of Writing: An Essay on Derrida." *Consequences of Pragmatism*. Minneapolis: University of Minnesota Press, 1982, 90-109.

Rousseau, Jean-Jacques. *Confessions*. Paris: Imprimerie nationale éditions, 1995.

———. *Du contrat social ou principes du droit politique*. Paris: Garnier, 1962.

———. *The Social Contract and Other Later Political Writings*. Victor Gourevitch, trans. Cambridge: Cambridge University Press, 1997.

Rudnick, Hans H. "Joyless Laughter: Sophocles - Hesse - Beckett." *Enjoyment: from Laughter to Delight in Philosophy, Literature, the Fine Arts, and Aesthetics*. Tymieniecka, Anna-Teresa ed. Boston: Kluwer Academic, 1998, 257-265.

Sartre, Jean-Paul. *Qu'est-ce que la littérature*. Paris: Gallimard, 1948: Gallimard, Idées, 1972.

Schenker, Israel. "Moody Man of Letters." *New York Times*, May 6, 1956, part two, 3.

Sollers, Philippe. *La Guerre du goût*. Paris: Gallimard, 1996.

———. *Théorie d'ensemble*. Paris: Seuil, 1968.

Sörbom, Göran. *Mimesis and Art: Studies in the Origin and Early Development of an Aesthetic Vocabulary*. Bonniers: Scandinavian University Books, 1966.

Starobinski, Jean. *Jean-Jacques Rousseau: Transparency and Obstruction*. Arthur Goldhammer, trans. Chicago: University of Chicago Press, 1988.

St. John Butler, Lance. *Samuel Beckett and the Meaning of Being*. London: MacMillan Press, 1984.

Suchman, Susan. *Samuel Beckett, Eugene Ionesco, and Julio Cortázar: A Study of the Absurd in Modern Drama and Narrative*. Dissertation Abstracts International, 1978.

Suleiman, Susan and Crosman, Inge. *The Reader in the Text: Essays on Audience and Interpretation*. Princeton: Princeton University Press, 1980.

Tassi, Marguerite. "Shakespeare and Beckett Revisited: A Phenomenology of Theater." in *Comparative Drama* Vol. 31, iss. 2 (Summer 1997): 246-276.

Tew, Phillip. "Philosophical Adjacency: Beckett's Prose Fragments via Jürgen Habermas." *Beckett and Philosophy*. Richard Lane, ed. New York: Palgrave, 2002, 140-153.

Tompkins, Jane, ed. *Reader-Response Criticism: From Formalism to Post-Structuralism*. Baltimore: The Johns Hopkins University Press, 1980.

Trezise, Thomas. *Into the Breach: Samuel Beckett and the Ends of Literature*. Princeton: Princeton University Press, 1990.

Uhlmann, Anthony. *Beckett and Poststructuralism*. Cambridge: Cambridge University Press, 1999.

Ulrika, Maude. "The Body of Memory: Beckett and Merleau-Ponty." Lane, Richard, ed. *Beckett and Philosophy*. New York : Palgrave, 2002, 108-122.

Vattimo, Gianni. *The End of Modernity*. Jon R. Snyder, trans. Cambridge: Polity, 1988.

Velissariou, Aspasia. "Not I: An Aborted Autobiography." *Journal of Dramatic Theory and Criticism* 8:1 (Fall 1993): 45–59.

Watt, Ian. *The Rise of the Novel: Studies in Defoe, Richardson, and Fielding.* Harmondsworth: Penguin Books, 1963.

Worthen, William. "Beckett's Actor," *Modern Drama* 26:4 (December 1983): 415–424.

‡ Index

A

Abbott, H. Porter, 113, 141, 162, 167
absence, xxi, 44, 58, 63, 95, 101–105,
    107–108, 128, 136, 141
Adorno, Theodor, xvii, xviii, 26, 53, 58,
    142, 153, 155, 167, 169, 171
Alvarez, A., 49, 152, 167
anamnesis, 7
Anaximander, 4, 8
aporia, 71, 86–87
Archytas of Tarentum, 4
Aristotle, vii, xxi, 11, 16–17, 146, 167
    Poetics, 16, 146, 167
Artaud, Antonin, 97, 101–102, 160–161,
    167
Attridge, Derek, 26–27, 39, 63, 149–150,
    155, 167, 170
Auerbach, Erich, xxi

B

Bacon, Francis, 56, 144, 154, 167
Badiou, Alain, 53, 153, 174
Barker, Ronald, 54, 153, 155, 167
Barthes, Roland, xviii, xix, 26, 61, 125,
    127, 141–143, 155, 167
Baudrillard, Jean, 134–137, 164, 167
Beckett, Samuel,
    Act Without Words, 45, 60, 109
    Cendres, 88, 109

Company, 44, 46, 52, 55, 76–77, 89,
    118, 121–122, 127, 152–154, 157–
    158, 163, 168
"Dante...Bruno. Vico...Joyce," 126

La dernière bande, 49
Dream of Fair to Middling Women, 47,
    168
Echo's Bones, and Other Precipitates, 49
Embers, xiv, 115
Endgame, xiv, 44, 45, 58, 97, 100, 109,
    139, 142, 152–153, 155, 160–161, 167,
    169
Film, 43, 109, 139, 149, 153, 160, 162,
    167, 172
Footfalls, 99, 115, 161, 168–169
Happy Days, 44–45, 99, 101, 109–110,
    115, 161, 168
Ill Seen Ill Said, 50–52, 152, 154, 158,
    163, 168
Krapp's Last Tape, 100, 110, 112, 162,
    168
The Lost Ones, 46
Malone Dies, 31–33, 44, 46, 56–57, 67,
    69, 73, 81–82, 90, 115, 117, 123–
    126, 149, 151, 154, 157, 167–169
Malone meurt, xiv, 88, 90, 153, 157–
    158, 163, 168, 172
Mercier and Camier, 44, 46, 89, 92, 150,
    151, 168, 169
Molloy, xiv, 1, 29, 31–33, 39, 42, 44,
    46–47, 57, 67–69, 72–73, 79–82, 88,
    90–91, 104–105, 118–119, 143, 147,
    149, 156–159, 167–168
Nacht und Träume, 109

Not I, 44–45, 115–116, 121–122, 142, 151, 163, 168, 172, 175

Ping, 88–89

Premier amour, 89, 159, 168

Quad, 109, 149, 168, 170

Rough for Radio I, 43

Rough for Radio II, 43

Rough for Theatre I, 43

Rough for Theatre II, 43

That Time, 44, 151, 172

The Unnamable, xiv, 31, 33, 44, 54, 57, 61, 63, 67, 69–71, 73, 79, 81, 83, 95, 115–116, 118–121, 124–125, 127–128, 133, 142, 149, 152–154, 157, 167–168

Waiting for Godot, xvi, xviii–xix, 26, 31, 44–45, 54, 60, 90, 95, 98–101, 109, 141–143, 149, 151, 153, 155, 159–162, 167–169, 171–172

Whoroscope, 57, 152, 155, 168

Begam, Richard, xvii, 47, 71, 141, 143, 152, 157, 162, 168

Samuel Beckett and the End of Modernity, 47, 141, 152, 157, 168

beginning, xiii–xiv, xx, 1, 2, 5–6, 20, 26, 28, 31–34, 39, 45, 62, 66–68, 80–84, 93, 101, 104, 123, 130, 132–133, 137, 143, 147, 152, 159, 161, 164

Benjamin, Walter, xxi, 17, 18, 92, 146, 159, 168

"The Work of Art in the Age of Mechanical Reproduction," 17

Berkeley, George, 53, 90, 97, 153, 167, 169

Blanchot, Maurice, 32, 61–63, 78, 117, 124, 127, 141, 155, 162–163, 169

"Où maintenant, qui maintenant," 61

The Book to Come, 117, 162–163, 169

Blau, Herbert, 97, 101, 160–161, 169

Blin, Roger, 99, 161

Borges, Jorge Luis, 2, 135

Brater, Enoch, 95, 97, 101, 151, 159, 161, 169, 171

Butor, Michel, xix

C

Celan, Paul, 86

Clurman, Harold, 54, 60, 153–155, 169

cogito, 57, 98, 113–114, 160, 162

Cohn, Ruby, 53, 95, 100, 139–140, 149, 156, 159, 161–162, 164, 168–169

Condillac, Etienne Bonnot de, 103

Connor, Steven, 75, 89, 96, 101, 139–140, 143, 145, 157–159, 162, 169

copy, xiii, xx, 13–14, 16–19, 23–24, 80, 83–85, 137, 139

Critchley, Simon, 55–56, 58, 63, 143, 154–155, 169

D

Danto, Arthur, 130–134, 136–137, 164, 170

After the End of Art, 131, 164, 170

Encounters and Reflections, 131

"The End of Art," 131, 164

The State of the Art, 131

Dasein, 98, 101

de Man, Paul, 34, 114, 125

Dearlove, J.E., 42, 46, 58, 60–61, 143, 150, 152, 170

"Weaving Penelope's Tapestry," 46

Deleuze, Gilles, xv, xx–xxiii, 2–3, 5, 10–12, 18–19, 27, 29, 30, 34–35, 58, 65, 69, 74–75, 78, 93, 102, 106–107, 113–114, 116, 118, 122–123, 125, 128–130,

132, 135, 139, 145, 148-150, 153,
155-159, 162-163, 168, 170
Difference and Repetition, xxii, 11, 34, 69,
74, 114, 145, 150, 155-157, 159,
162-163, 170
Différence et Répétition, 11, 157
"L'épuisé," 27, 29
Derrida, Jacques, xv, xvii, xx-xxiii, 1-3, 5-
6, 10, 14, 18-19, 20-28, 30-32, 35-41,
43, 45, 55-56, 58, 63, 65-66, 69, 73,
79, 84-87, 91, 93, 98, 101-108, 112-
113, 125, 127, 129-130, 132, 135-36,
147-151, 153-162, 167, 170, 174
"La carte postale," 35
"La différance," 107
"La double séance," 22
"The Double Session," 35, 148
"From/Of the Supplement to the
Source," 103, 162
Glas, 56, 79, 154, 170
"The Law of Genre," 37, 39-40, 150,
155, 156, 170
Marges de la philosophie, 28, 148, 156,
158, 162, 170
Margins of Philosophy, xxii, 148, 149,
158, 162, 170
Of Grammatology, 65, 103, 113, 156,
159, 160, 161, 162, 170
"Shibboleth," 86, 158
"La structure, le signe et le jeu dans le
discours des sciences humaines," 21,
170
"Tympan," 28, 35, 79, 127, 170
"Ulysses Gramophone," 86, 158
Descartes, René, xv, 57, 68, 87, 103, 114-
116, 132, 164, 171
Cartesian, 55, 57, 68, 113

Discours de la méthode, 57, 68, 87, 164,
171
Descombes, Vincent, 18, 20, 25, 34, 74,
78-79, 102, 107, 145-148, 150, 158,
161, 171
Le même et l'autre, 18, 78, 146-148, 150,
158, 161, 171
Modern French Philosophy, 34, 147-148,
161, 171
Diogenes, 6
Duckworth, Colin, 54, 60, 109, 153-155,
159, 171
Duthuit, Georges, 69, 155-156, 158, 168

E

Eliade, Mircea,
The Myth of the Eternal Return, 4, 143,
145, 171
Empedocles, 4, 8
endings, xiv, xix, xxii, 3, 29, 31-32, 34-35,
48
existentialism, xvi, xix, 56-57

F

Fitch, Brian, 89-90, 159, 171
Foucault, Michel, xviii-xix, 26, 53, 74,
142, 147, 153, 157, 171-172
Freud, Sigmund, 2, 18, 75, 139, 142, 147,
171-172
Frye, Northrop, 51-53, 139, 152-153, 171
Furman, Nelly, 58-59, 155, 171

G

Genesis, 5, 66, 83-84, 156, 158
Genette, Gérard, xxii, 40-41, 48

genre, xiv, xx, xxii, 2, 35–46, 48, 53, 59,
    60–61, 91, 150–151, 156
God, 15, 66, 83–84, 104–105, 115, 136,
    143, 151, 167
Gontarski, S.E., 76, 122, 141, 153, 158,
    160, 168–169, 171
Great Year, 4, 5
Greenberg, Clement, xvii, 132, 164
Guatarri, Félix, 79

H

Habermas, Jürgen, xvi, xxii, 35–37, 41, 48,
    53, 150, 153, 171, 174
    "Excursus on Leveling the Genre-
        distinction Between Philosophy and
        Literature," 35
Haerdter, Michael, 96, 160, 171
Harvey, Lawrence, 49, 54, 152–154, 162,
    172
Hedberg, Johannes, 49–50, 152, 172
Hegel, Georg Wilhelm Friedrich, xiii– xv,
    11, 18, 53, 79, 129–131, 133, 144, 148,
    153, 172
Heidegger, Martin, 18, 28, 53, 117, 144,
    153, 162, 167
    l'être-pour-la-mort, 117
Heine, Heinrich, 8, 144
Heraclitus, 4, 53
Hill, Leslie, 73, 88, 91, 141, 143, 151,
    157–159, 167, 172
    Beckett's Fiction, 141, 152
Hölderlin, Friedrich, 8
humanism, xvi, 54, 56
Husserl, Edmund, 18, 144
Huyssen, Andreas, xvi–xviii, 141–142, 172

I

imitation, xx, 13–17, 23, 49, 51, 131, 140,
    145–146, 164

J

Jauss, Hans Robert, 42, 150, 172
Joyce, James, 2, 34, 126, 133, 164, 168

K

Kant, Immanuel, 53, 56, 114, 132, 149,
    172
Kawin, Bruce, 95, 139–140, 159–160,
    162, 172
Kenner, Hugh, 97, 154, 162, 172
Kierkegaard, Søren, xxi-xxii, 2, 5–6, 11–
    12, 18, 139, 144, 170, 172
Knowlson, James, 49, 152, 172
Kristeva, Julia, xvii–xviii, 26, 142, 143, 172

L

Lacan, Jacques, 117, 125
Lecercle, Jean-Jacques, 79, 158, 172
Leibniz, Gottfried Wilhelm, 11, 56, 103,
    155
Levinas, Emmanuel, 53, 148, 153
Lévi-Strauss, Claude, xix, 2, 22, 172–173
Levy, Shimon, 63, 95, 144, 155, 159, 173
Lewis, Philip E., 85, 158, 173
Lukács, Georg, xviii, 26, 142, 173
Lyotard, Jean-François, xvi-xix, 26, 34,
    141–142, 173

M

Malebranche, Nicolas, 103
Mallarmé, Stéphane, 22–25, 35, 79, 148,
    173

Marx, Karl, 18, 147, 171

Mauriac, François, 49

McGreevy, Thomas, 88

Mercier, Vivian, 45, 99, 100, 161, 173

Merleau-Ponty, Maurice, 53, 78, 144, 153, 173-174

Meschonnic, Henri, 90

metaphysics, 18, 20, 24-25, 28, 30, 66, 97-98, 104, 135, 161

mimesis, xxi, 3, 13-18, 22-24, 30, 132, 134, 146

modernism, xvi-xix 6-8, 18, 29, 41, 48, 53, 61, 78, 101, 131-133, 141, 154, 164

N

Nietzsche, Friedrich, xxi, 2, 5, 8-12, 18, 74, 144-145, 147, 170-173

O

Olson, Gary A., xix

original, xiii-xiv, xx, xxii, 5, 13-20, 23-24, 56, 74, 78, 80, 83-93, 102-106, 108-109, 136-137, 139, 141, 146

Other, xvii, 18, 66, 114, 117-118, 124, 146, 148, 152, 168, 174

P

Parnet, Claire, 106, 158

Perloff, Marjorie, 47, 50-53, 58, 143, 152, 173

Plato, xv-xvi, xxi, 4, 7, 13-18, 22-23, 25, 35-36, 53, 79, 83, 103, 109, 144, 146, 173

Cratylus, 13-16, 83, 146, 173

Philebus, 23

Symposium, 109

The Republic, 13-16, 83, 146, 173

postmodernism, xvi, xvii, xviii, xix, 113, 140-143, 172

poststructuralism, xiv-xix, xxi-xxiii, 142

presence, xx, xxii-xxiii, 2, 17, 19, 29, 41, 44, 60, 92, 95, 96-103, 107-110, 112-115, 121, 128, 146, 159, 161-162

Pythagoras, 4, 140

R

Rabinowitz, Rubin, 47, 89, 139-140, 149-150, 152, 159, 167, 173

Reader Response Criticism, 42, 150

recollection, 7, 147

repetition, xiii-xv, xx-xxiii, 2-3, 5-8, 10-13, 17-20, 23, 30, 36, 38, 51, 71, 73-75, 83, 85, 93, 99-101, 129-131, 135, 137, 139-140, 145-148

repetition and difference, xiv-xv, xx-xxi, xxiii, 1-3, 6, 8, 10-12, 19, 20, 22, 25, 28, 30, 38, 45, 49, 69, 74-75, 79, 82, 85, 88, 101, 107, 110-111, 114, 127, 129, 130, 134-135, 139-140, 145-148

Riffaterre, Michael, 42, 150, 151, 174

Robbe-Grillet, Alain, xix, 34, 97-98, 100, 160, 174

Ronell, Avital, 91, 158-159, 174

Ronse, Henri, 66, 155

Rorty, Richard, 36, 150, 174

Rousseau, Jean-Jacques, 95, 97, 103, 105-106, 108, 113-114, 159-162, 174

Russell, Bertrand, 39

S

Same, xiv, 4-5, 11, 13, 18-19, 30, 40, 42, 74, 139, 147-148

Sartre, Jean-Paul, xxii, 48, 53, 152-153, 171-172, 174

Saussure, Ferdinand de, 2, 25, 104

Schneider, Alan, 99, 160

Schopenhauer, Arthur, 53, 153, 167

Seaver, Richard, 88, 90

sign, 14, 63, 84, 104, 105, 107, 108, 136

simulacrum, 118, 134-135

Sollers, Philippe, xviii, 26, 142, 143, 174

Sophocles, 53, 153, 174

speech, xxiii, 21, 26, 29, 45, 51, 53, 60, 71, 83, 99, 102-103, 105-110, 112-113, 128, 161

Spinoza, Baruch, 53, 56, 153

St. Augustine, xxi, 5, 143

Starobinski, Jean, 113-114, 162, 174

subject, xxiii, 5-6, 11, 13-14, 21, 23, 26, 32, 34, 39-40, 43-44, 47, 52, 56-59, 62, 67-68, 71, 80, 84, 112-129, 131, 133, 154, 163

the self, xiv, xxii, xxiii, 4, 7, 9, 12, 25, 28, 30, 54, 57-59, 62, 66, 71, 74, 81-82, 87, 98, 101, 111, 113-115, 117-118, 123-125, 131, 133, 159, 162, 164

supplement, 14, 83-84, 92-93, 104-105

T

Theater of Cruelty, 97, 160-161, 170

Theatre of the absurd, 44

Tompkins, 42, 150, 174

Tower of Babel, 30, 83

translation, xxiii, 84-92, 144-147, 149, 159, 160

Trezise, Thomas, xvi, 54, 143, 154, 174

U

unthinkable, xxii, 22, 30, 66, 123, 128

V

Vattimo, Giannai, xvii, 141, 174

W

Watt, Ian, 46, 57, 68, 81, 88, 140-141, 151, 156, 169, 175

Weber, Samuel, 8

Whitelaw, Billy, 115

writing, xv-xvi, xviii-xix, xxii-xxiii, 11, 26-27, 35-36, 41, 44, 46, 49-50, 53, 57, 59-61, 63, 65-69, 72-74, 78-80, 83, 87, 90, 92, 95-96, 103-110, 112-113, 117, 124-130, 140-143, 147, 150-151, 173

Z

Zenon, 4

STUDIES IN LITERARY CRITICISM & THEORY

Hans Rudnick, General Editor

The focus of this series is on studies of all literary genres that elucidate and interpret works of art in the context of criticism and theory. Theory and criticism are held to provide the hermeneutically most rewarding access to specific authors, works, and issues under consideration. Studies of a comparative nature with special reference to issues of literary history, criticism, and postmodern theory are the distinctive features of this monograph series. Emphasis is on subjects that may set trends, generate discussion, expand horizons beyond present perspectives, and/or redefine previously held notions about "major" and "minor" authors and their achievements within or outside the canon. Approaches may center on works, authors, or abstract notions of criticism and/or theory, including issues of a comparative nature concerning world literature.

For additional information about this series or for the submission of manuscripts, please contact:

> Peter Lang Publishing
> Acquisitions Department
> P.O. Box 1246
> Bel Air, Maryland 21014-1246

To order other books in this series, please contact our Customer Service Department:

> 800-770-LANG (within the U.S.)
> (212) 647-7706 (outside the U.S.)
> (212) 647-7707 FAX

or browse online by series at:

> www.peterlang.com

Notes

It could have been him. He had the same forehead
the same backhead the same short

hair, the same blonde hair, the

same laptop, the same fingers,

the same fingers and fingernails

It could have been him

Write a chapter called:

1. repetition and desire

2. repetition and endings

3. repetition and death — Fran
                                  Hea
                                  (af